BEYOND THE CALL OF DUTY
A Biography of Whitland's Dr Penn

ROGER G. K. PENN

Beyond the Call of Duty

A BIOGRAPHY OF WHITLAND'S DR PENN

Gomer

Published in 2012 by Gomer Press,
Llandysul, Ceredigion SA44 4JL.

ISBN 978-1-84851-571-0

Printed and bound in Wales at
Gomer Press, Llandysul, Ceredigion

This book is dedicated to
Mrs 'Peggy' Penn,
my mother.

Without her,
Dr Penn would not have been the same person.

Contents

Thanks and Acknowledgements

WHEN MY FATHER's medical career came to an end, I was one of a number of people to suggest that he should write a book about his life experiences. He was, most certainly, an unsung writer, proud of his turn of phrase, easy style and descriptive flow, and he did have rather a lot to share with readers. I urged him to find a room in Hillside where he could surround himself with notes, files, paper-cuttings and the vast array of memorabilia that he had collected, to piece together an account of his fascinating life story.

Sadly, this never happened and it is for this reason that I have stepped in on his behalf. Not quite knowing where to begin, given the volume of information at my disposal, I felt that the best idea was to slip a portion of his life events into an historical account of his former surgery, which resulted in the book, *Dolycwrt – the Days of a Country Doctor's Surgery*. This made my task more manageable, although it still left me with a lot of information to share.

In a sense my father was one of those people who had already prepared his own story by leaving a remarkable written record of his life from early childhood onwards. When we consider his particular journey, he was an amazing person throughout. Likewise, he has continued to assist me in the course of compiling *his own biography* – remarkable – just as he still helps and inspires many of us today.

It is my pleasure to thank everybody who has supported me in the completion of this work, from the first contributor to the last, as well as the staff at Gomer and the Welsh Books

Council. Likewise, I am pleased to acknowledge the wealth of information found in newspapers, past and present, that helped me with my research: *The Cardiff Times and South Wales Weekly News, The Glamorgan Gazette, The Neath Guardian, The Carmarthen Journal, The Western Telegraph, The Weekly Observer, The Cardigan and Tivy-side Advertiser, The Western Mail, The Daily Telegraph, The Times* and *The Daily Express.*

Viewing the above mentioned publications has meant visiting libraries in Bridgend, Cardiff, Carmarthen and Neath, and I wish to offer to each in turn my gratitude, as well as to the staff of Pembrokeshire Records Office in Haverfordwest.

Once again, I am especially indebted to Dylan Williams at Gomer, who has worked closely with me throughout this project.

And now, I sincerely hope you enjoy the story.

ROGER PENN
Dolycwrt Cottage
August 2012

Foreword

My FIRST PARISH was Llanfallteg, and I was privileged to serve in that part of the world where I met some remarkable people, amongst whom Dr George Penn was a dear friend.

We often met on our respective rounds and engaged in some very interesting conversations. I would see his A35 driving around the country lanes of the Taf valley and we frequently paused for a chat.

He was the best sort of medical practitioner of the 'Old School' that I was privileged to know.

THE RIGHT REVEREND J. WYN EVANS
Bishop of St Davids
April 2012

Stanley and Beatrice Penn

G EORGE KEMPTON PENN was born on Tuesday May
17th 1927 in the busy seaport city of Cardiff. He was
the second son of Jennet Beatrice Penn, a well-respected
nurse who was regularly seen attending to the patients of
her private practice in the city centre. Beatrice had spent the
days leading to this celebrated event in a small, comfortable
nursing home in Newport Road. George's arrival provided
every good reason for family celebrations – the news being
shared with others in a few simple words that appeared in the
births section of the *Cardiff Times and South Wales Weekly
News*:

> Penn – on May 17th at Stoneborough Nursing Home,
> Newport Road, to the wife of Stanley Kempton Penn,
> a son.

The proud father of George was now thirty-four years of
age and in the prime of his life. Captain Stanley Kempton
Penn, born on July 12th 1892 at his parents' long established
residence, Holmdale, 214 Newport Road, Cardiff was a
successful merchant naval officer who had already sailed
the world's wide oceans for nineteen years. In his early life
he developed an appetite for a challenging seafaring career,
having regularly followed his father, George Williams Penn,

an engineer, down to the city's Bute Docks. Indeed, his father was superintendent in charge of the Lloyds Proving House, which included supervising a large number of workers as well as testing chain cables, anchors and other shipping materials for which he earned the reputation of a much sought-after expert. George had married Mary Ann Kempton, a spinster living in Pontypridd whose family originated from London, in 1881. Stanley was one of their four children, two boys and two girls.

Stanley knew only too well that the spirit of enterprise associated with daring, hazardous days at sea came with inherent risks and real dangers. Cargoes were known to get lost; vessels were mercilessly lashed in wild storms; sailors disappeared overboard; men fell prey to sickness; heated disagreements arose on board, and even mutiny was known to rear its ugly head. But Stanley had courage and, intent upon climbing the career ladder and aspiring to become a sea officer, he acknowledged the weight and demands of such responsibilities. Besides having command over the vessel and serious amounts of cargo in the vaults, he presided over people's lives, well-being, health, safety and morale. Naturally, for a young officer, all of these presented an extraordinary challenge.

Stanley was a tall, slim, smart man, with strong good-looking features. Resolute and determined, his thoughtful expression and quiet contemplative manner indicated a deeper, well-founded intelligence. He was well read and educated, possessed of good communication skills, both spoken and written. In his many photographs he always appears smart, usually dressed in double-breasted jackets, sometimes with a trilby hat, and nearly always with a cigarette in his hands, but never in his mouth. In a letter to a shipping company in Auckland, New Zealand, some four years before

Whitland's future Dr Penn was born, he described himself as follows:

> I am thirty years of age, and I am physically fit in every respect. During my career I have risen from the position of third in command to Chief Officer. I have sailed in this latter capacity for the last six years, and I have served on numerous vessels trading between various parts of the world. I have acquired a complete knowledge of navigation, and I have considerable experience of taking charge of ships.
>
> I am intimately acquainted with all harbour, dock and river work, including the loading and unloading of cargoes, thoroughly understanding all the incidental routines and documentation connected therewith; I am also accustomed to controlling men, and I have obtained my First Mate's and Master's Certificates.

More importantly, senior officers presiding over Stanley at sea recognised his qualities. During the earlier years of the Great War, when he was rising through the ranks, he served on board a number of merchant shipping vessels, earning praise for his professional character and capabilities from each of the masters in charge. The following words relate to his period of service aboard S.S. *Blackheath*, the ship Stanley served on before completing his examinations:

> I have always found him to be strictly sober, most trustworthy and a first class officer in every respect . . .

Being away from Cardiff for lengthy periods, Stanley fully appreciated returning home to his family and friends. On one such occasion when he was unwell, he was introduced to a smart, dark-haired nurse named Jennet Beatrice Howell, who cared for him in the course of her practice work in the city.

Her professional skills and conscientious manner opened many doors in Cardiff, usually leading into the grand houses of elderly, wealthy, private patients. Beatrice had every reason to be proud of her achievements and her education at Clifton and Gloucester, and it was from this initial meeting that marriage followed in later years.

Beatrice's father, George Howell (born George Howells, before his daughters shortened the name), was raised in the Rhymney valley, the son of an intelligent blacksmith-teacher who married Sarah Jones. George Howell's father sadly died at a young age, prompting him to step up to the plate. Soon taking to the road in search of his own way in life, he settled in Abergarw farm, Brynmenyn, having by now met and married Jennet Morgan, who became Beatrice's mother. Over the years, he advanced from being a carpenter to a manager at Bryncethin's brickworks, whilst also constructing six delightful stone-built houses in the village of Brynmenyn. During George and Jennet's first twenty-three-years of marriage they lived and raised their family on the farm premises, before moving to one of his new residences across the road from the farm, named Abergarw House.

This meant that Jennet's brother, Jenkin, remained on the farm, attending to the animals throughout his remaining life. Beatrice was fond of her Uncle Jenkin, a well-loved character who she often helped as a child. Indeed, Uncle Jenkin relied on her when he ventured outside into the dark cold winter nights to attend to newly born calves in the manger. This was long before electricity lit up Brynmenyn, and it was Beatrice's job to light the way. 'Coda'r golau yn uchel,' he would shout in his native tongue ('Hold the lantern high').

Beatrice was one of six girls, all of whom enjoyed helping out on the farm. They grew to love the animals and a few of the girls saw no danger in jumping onto the back of a wild pony – some even riding motorbikes when they became available. Sometimes such courage can lead to risk and danger; sometimes to disaster, too. This is what occurred on Tuesday December 19th 1911, when Beatrice's eldest sister, Sarah Jane Howell, was drowned whilst attempting to save a child who had fallen into the Llynfi river near her home. Sarah Jane was an assistant-teacher at the time and is remembered to this day with great affection in Brynmenyn and the village primary school, particularly as the young scholar, Bertie Gubbins, survived.

As a schoolgirl, Beatrice was sent to boarding school at Clifton for a privileged education. In a large central town house, she settled well alongside a handful of other girls of similar age. There, in the strict, but friendly, atmosphere of tall ceilings and warm coal fires, she was encouraged to aim high. Clifton was a delight, with the wide acres of Clifton Downs a short walk from her school accommodation. This is where Beatrice loved to take in the fresh air, whilst striding across the broad green expanse on most weekends. When she wondered what the future might hold for her, it is unlikely that Whitland, a busy railway town in West Wales, ever entered her mind. This is where her future son, George, was to practise medicine for forty-two years, and where Beatrice would spend hours weeding onions on her knees at his family home, Hillside.

Gloucester Royal Infirmary welcomed Beatrice, the student nurse, into its once iconic building in Southgate Street. This happy hunting ground – well-placed for the Forest of Dean, Worcester and the Cotswolds – had much to offer a girl from the countryside. But in the stately and sober surroundings of her strict wards, where the bed linen was crisp and white, and cleanliness was sacrosanct, she was taught the finer arts of nursing. Happily posing for a photograph with colleagues –

which she posted to her parents – she looked both professional and proud in her white hat and uniform frock, draped fully to her feet. 'What do you think of my new ward?' she asked proudly on the reverse, 'Hope you like it . . . My love Beatrice.'

The birth of Beatrice's first child, Neville Howell Kempton Penn, in November 1921, marked the start of a happy family life which saw Stanley, still sailing the high seas, seeking a shore appointment nearer to home. But with high and rising unemployment, this did not prove easy, and his days at sea were far from over. But having now acquired 58 Canada Road, a traditional terraced house of modest dimensions in the fashionable area of Cathays, Stanley's home life was, at least, beginning to take shape. George's arrival six years later completed the family picture and with his proud grandparents holding high hopes for him, no one ever imagined George would become a railway-loving country doctor.

Sadness Befalls the Family

FROM THOSE EARLY beginnings, the young George Penn was a happy smiling little boy with an agenda and purposefulness of his own. From the moment he first clasped a small colourful beaker in his hands, it was always half full, never half empty, and, by the time he had finished with it, the same vessel was overfull, spilling down the sides. Little did he know in those tender years as a baby that he regularly visited Abergarw House, the home of Beatrice's parents, with his mother and brother, Neville – and his father also, when home from sea. And little did he realise that Brynmenyn was soon destined to be his home.

Jumping aboard the steam train, the Penn family pulled out of Cardiff Station on the way to Bridgend, amidst a groundswell of activity as people rushed around looking for their carriages. It is there that they jumped aboard a local train, which passed through Tondu, an important railway junction employing gangs of men just as Whitland Station once did. Only a mile away, Brynmenyn was the next stop and they disembarked near the present-day Fox and Hounds, once a busy hotel where Coal Board officials stayed overnight when inspecting mines in the Garw and Ogmore valleys. Thereafter, it was no more than a short stroll to Abergarw House, where Beatrice's parents, George and Jennet, and her sisters awaited their arrival.

The young family also made the much shorter journey from their home in Canada Road to Newport Road, where Stanley's father, also George, of course, witnessed their arrival from the front room window. He was affectionately known as Grandpa Penn now – although, sadly, there was no Grandma; she had died years earlier. But George Penn senior was happy to continue living in the same house, Holmdale, where his personal memories were strong. Situated on the outskirts of Cardiff, beyond the long straight stretch from the city centre, this fine residence was passed by traffic on the way to Newport, mainly horse and carts, carriages and bicycles, but, by the early 1930s, also cars and buses, too, exciting George Penn, the distinguished engineer.

Holmdale is a tall and commanding house and was the scene of happy family life, where Stanley was born – and, no doubt, Clifford, Gladys and Gwennie, too. Today, Holmdale stands near the pavement, having probably surrendered much of its front garden to road improvements, but in those former years the family enjoyed the light and space of its large double bay windows, sitting one upon the other, whilst the rear south-facing garden provided a warm place for the children to play on sunny afternoons in summer.

It is from the narrow pathway of this residence that George Penn, the engineer, set off daily for Bute Docks. Beginning in early 1870 and ending in late 1920, he served a remarkable full fifty-years at the Lloyds Proving House. When he retired as superintendent, a dinner was held in his honour at the Carlton Hotel, Cardiff, on January 17th 1921, food being served at 7.30 p.m. 'sharp.' An outstanding souvenir programme of the evening describes the event. The work's choir led the singing, with songs such as 'The Grey North Sea' and 'Because I was Shy'. In addition, a soloist performed to the tune of 'Land of My Fathers'. There was a presentation and speech, whereby George Penn was the recipient of a toast to 'The Retiring Superintendent', as well as being the proposer of a toast to 'The New Superintendent'. Inside the programme, bearing an inscribed photograph, was a brief *résumé* of his career:

> When he took charge, the Proving House contained one testing machine, one eight-horse-power engine working one set of pumps – and the personnel was four men. Today it consists of one testing machine of 350 tons, two of 250 tons, and one of 50 tons – and forty-five men. The whole of the alterations and additions have been carried out under his supervision.
>
> In addition to the testing of chain cables and anchors, he introduced the testing of samples of iron, steel, concrete, wood, and other material, also steel wire ropes for colliery purposes and ships' use.
>
> In passing, we might state that Mr Penn has been a ready adviser – as much at home in explaining the testing of English cables to a Japanese, as smoothing the difficulties of foreign cables to Spanish, American and, in short, all nationalities of Inspectors who have visited him from time to time.
>
> We shall never know the necessary part the Proving House played in the Great War; obviously, that is shrouded in mystery.

To his son, Stanley, this gentleman was a kind and sincere friend. They corresponded regularly during long days apart, as was expected when telephones were few and far between. In December 1917, when Stanley was at home studying, he wrote enclosing birth certificates that he had obtained from the official registry at Somerset House, London. As he ended the letter, he demonstrated his usual attention to detail, emphasising a legitimate technical irregularity that clearly interested him:

You will notice that they spelt 'Accountant' on the certifi-
cate as 'Accomptant' in 1847 . . . Sincerely trusting that you
are keeping fit, in health and strength for your Exam . . .
Fondest love from all . . . Your affectionate Father.

As regards his grandson – young George was the apple
of his eye. They played together on the lounge floor, when
Whitland's future doctor was crawling around. It is likely that
he envisaged young George being another fine sea captain
though he could not possibly have realised how much his
grandson would later resemble him. They both had kind
faces full and fine, similar foreheads and an identical lack
of hair – the one difference being that Grandpa Penn wore
a beard. They were, no doubt, proud of each other and it is
a pity that Grandpa Penn never saw young George being
photographed among some thirty graduates years later,
qualifying as a doctor. That day his grandson was seated in
the middle of the front row, a handsome young man draped
in robes as president of the students of his year. What a day
that might have been for Grandpa Penn – but, of course, he
had long since departed, his obituary in the *Western Mail &*
South Wales News on March 21st 1931 paying respect to his
peaceful passing, at home, in Holmdale.

A year later, when Grandpa Penn's loss was still keenly
felt, his son, Stanley, whilst still at sea, could not arrive home
quickly enough to be with his growing family. For Beatrice
and Neville, he was their inspiration and they desperately
awaited his return – whilst George, aged four, was expected
to acknowledge his father's presence in a more meaningful
manner for the first time. Every one was looking forward to a
happy reunion when disaster struck.

As Beatrice boarded her train to Hartlepool to meet his
ship, she was approached by shocked shipping representatives

at Cardiff station with awful news. Amidst bewilderment and disbelief, tears and a broken heart, she tried to comprehend that Stanley was not returning with the vessel, the British steamer S.S. *Umberleigh,* from South America. He was seen falling overboard about twenty miles from the English coast, and, after an extensive search, he could not be found. Detailed investigations and inquests followed, but Stanley was reported lost at sea.

A New Beginning in Brynmenyn

IN THIS WRETCHED hour of her life, Beatrice needed to be strong, allowing two of nature's most natural instincts, survival and protection, to take over. Nursing had prepared her for good times as well as bad and, of course, she took delight in seeing the injured returning to health and strength. And so it was with Beatrice, whose terrific personal powers of will, supported by her devoted family, drove her ever onwards, tackling the circumstances she now faced: no Stanley, the torture of the unknown truth and two innocent, fatherless, little boys.

Although the tears continued to flow she did not lose sight of her tasks. As mother, guardian and bread-winner, she set about her duties with such a sense of purpose that nothing got in her way. This meant a return to nursing, not difficult in Cardiff, where her credentials were already proven. But it also meant parting from young George, who relocated to Brynmenyn – where Bryn Haf, a house built by his grandfather, just down the road from Abergarw Farm, now became home. There, his aunty Margot, sister to Beatrice, cared for him, whilst her parents and sisters gave their added support. For George, who had never consciously known his father, this was the start of his own journey in life.

Taking his place at Brynmenyn School, sitting on sturdy wooden chairs behind an inkwell desk, George Penn started to make friends with like-minded little boys from the close working-class environment of this mining community. Whilst Brynmenyn Colliery had long ago been closed after a short lifespan, there were long-established mining works around the farms and open hills, as well as quarries and local brickworks. These hotbeds of industry provided work for the men, as they had done for years.

Brynmenyn, like so many other small villages, was linked to the country's extensive network of steam railways. Indeed, its station boasted the two busy platforms of another important junction point, where the in-coming passenger carriages and freight wagons were directed up the nearby valleys. It is probably in this setting that George first took a liking to trains, gathering and storing vital ammunition for his later railway campaigns, when line closures began to decimate the countryside.

In this close-knit community, there is no doubt that memories of, and respect for, Brynmenyn's local heroine, Sarah Jane Howell, cushioned her nephew, young George, when he arrived at the school. Following her tragic drowning in 1911, Sarah Jane's memory had been kept very much alive by the school and young George was, no doubt, constantly reminded about this incident as he grew older. Margot, who was also a teacher at this same school, kept the press cuttings, including a detailed description of the funeral that took place just a few days before Christmas that year.

But life moved on for Sarah Jane's brokenhearted parents, George Howell and his wife, Jennet. They lived through the Great War and beyond, sharing the delights of the early days of grandson, George, in the little school in the early 1930s. They wandered down the road to see him happily playing with the children on the front school yard just in front of Brynmenyn Common, but, sadly, their days were coming to an end: George dying in 1933, and then Jennet three years later in 1936.

It is from this moment that young George grew in feet and

inches, in more ways than one. He and Neville were the only young men left in a family mostly of women, and, although Neville was older, he, too, needed George's protection, being one of nature's more gentle boys. This is the time when George started to step up a gear. 'By Jove,' as he used to say in those days, he needed to, as he was soon to experience a significant change.

Beatrice always held close to her heart the treasured memories of her happy schooling in Clifton and was now looking to provide a similar education for George and Neville, somewhere to give them a head start in life. Still busily attending to the sick and needy in Cardiff, Beatrice was now rubbing shoulders with people of considerable influence, many born into aristocracy with good intentions and kind hearts. On the subject of her sons' education, she welcomed their thoughts and help. In time, Neville was located to a school for boys of seafaring fathers, whilst George's future was considered.

By now the Royal Masonic School for Boys was firmly established in Bushey, Hertfordshire, having advanced from its early beginnings and premises at North London's Wood Green. Comprised of an older Senior School and a relatively recent, and totally separate, new Junior School, this is where the sons of freemasons were given a boarding school education under the guidance of ambitious teachers and within the confines of a strict and disciplined regime. Funded by the Freemason's Charity, together with generous sponsorship, subscriptions and donations, this was now an outstanding establishment. From its earliest days, and even before its beginning, there had been no lack of interest in the Masonic movement from members of the Royal family, as the school's name suggests. Way back in 1814, the Duke of Kent gave his support, as did the Duke of Sussex, for almost thirty years. By 1863 Queen Victoria, approaching the halfway mark of her long reign, was established as a patron, carrying this proud Royal relationship into more modern days.

Because of Beatrice's contacts in Cardiff and the fact that George's father, Stanley, and possibly Grandpa Penn too, once belonged to a freemason's lodge, George's placement at Bushey was secured. And, regardless of well-intentioned opposition from her sisters who questioned George's early removal from the family nest, Beatrice, doing her level-best for her son, was not swayed. George, still only eight years of age and perfectly content in Brynmenyn, was plucked and dropped into another world. Now a completely different future lay ahead of him in Bushey.

PART II

THE ROYAL MASONIC SCHOOL FOR BOYS

A Brave Fight – and a First Round Victory

THERE WAS A TREMENDOUS sense of achievement when the new school opened its doors in 1903 having safely completed the move across London.[1] This was an impressive establishment, consisting of a series of tall, red-brick buildings, with separate chapel, dining room, and gymnasium, all shaped in proud early-day design – interspersed, yet connected, by cloisters, alleyways, archways and big open quadrangles. Entering through the wrought-iron gate entrance, there was a long driveway leading to the famous clock tower. It stood tall and proud, way above its neighbouring structures, perhaps serving to remind young scholars to aim high.

Years of prosperity led to a new purpose-built Junior School being opened in 1929 catering for 400 boys. This entirely separate complex consisted of a series of large, parallel 'houses' aligned one alongside each other in a uniform pattern. George soon found that each house accommodated fifty boys and there were two dormitories in each house, with a strict 'lights out' policy enforced by the resident housemaster. There were washing, clothing and locker room facilities, and a common area for reading or writing or playing games. The boys awoke in the morning before assembling in school uniform to walk in an orderly 'crocodile' manner to breakfast.

1   A. L. Parks and E. A. Riches, *A History of the Royal Masonic School for Boys, Vol 1: 1798-1938* (White Crescent Press, 1975).

This took place in a large dining hall where long tables and benches were laid open for meals. Assembly featured before long days of schoolwork and study began.

Beatrice was aware that sports lessons had pride of place in the week's programme of events, as well as walks, projects and other activities to break routines. There was a gymnasium and outdoor swimming pool, and hockey, football and cricket were played, whilst the running tracks were put to good use in the summer term. *A History of the Royal Masonic School for Boys*, written by two former teachers, claims that the school's cricket field was prepared by the groundsman of Surrey's county ground, the Oval. Certainly nothing was spared when assembling first class facilities for the boys to enjoy. In this same book – whose author, Edward Riches, sometimes wrote to George in later life – we learn that the school stood in acres of delightful open countryside, with trees and meadowland. It is also claimed that . . .

> everything has been carried out on a really magnificent scale, and there can be no doubt that the school is now one of the finest scholastic establishments in England and one of which all should be proud.

This was all encouraging, but young boys such as George were also entering into a harsh world, beginning with a 'Dartmoor crop' of their long and curly locks:

> After farewell scenes, which were often painful and sometimes even harrowing, the parents departed, leaving the staff to begin the hard task of teaching their charges to 'stand on their own two feet' . . . Discipline was strict; punishment was severe, and most often summary and corporal. The headmaster, of course, used the cane – frequently for reasons which seem trivial.

In this same book, Messrs Parks and Riches outlined the views of some critics who questioned the school practice of moving young boys away from home comforts into an all-male environment:

> There was no woman to whom a child could turn for a kind word, a little sympathy, or word of encouragement. There was no mellowing influence to leaven the hard bread. There was no one to intercede . . . affection in its mildest sense, or even the ability just occasionally to turn a blind eye, was wholly lacking.

Accompanied by his mother and, no doubt, one of his aunties, Margot, Mattie or Katie, George entered the fray in optimistic spirits – but, by the time his family were leaving Paddington Station on their return, reality had sunk in. At the tender age of eight, miles away from his friends and family, the fun-loving George might as well have been stranded on a desert island; emotionally, it was enough to break his heart. If there was one consolation – and he looked hard for this – it was that the other boys in his year were suffering just as badly, the scale of the huge buildings, long corridors, and big dormitories, adding to the hardship and pain. Besides a friendly and reliable postal service in the school, collecting and receiving letters, there was no meaningful contact with the outside world: even worse, there was no escape.

In these early days, George tried everything to smooth his rocky passage. *The Boys Own Paper* was a favourite read, offering a little courage and hope, whenever he got hold of a copy. But in all he saw and heard at the school, he perceived 'misery'. He tried hard not to show it, and succeeded too, but inside his world was falling apart. When he climbed into bed in the big dormitory full of boys, he thought about the warmth of his little bedroom in Bryn Haf, looking onto the small green meadow of the Ogmore river with a glimpse of Abergarw farm up the road. When he awoke and assembled his clothing, he imagined Aunty Margot handing him a fresh towel for his bath. At breakfast in the crowded, noisy, echoing dining hall, he thought of the peaceful bowl of porridge he enjoyed before going to Brynmenyn School. And when he sat in the classroom full of unfamiliar faces, he visualised the happy children of his former class, reaching for coats and satchels, and going home.

But anxious to fulfil the expectations of his family, he turned and soldiered on. In lessons he made a good impact: in English, Arithmetic, History, Geography and Scripture, his ratings were good; in Handwriting, Drawing and Physical Drills, he was considered fair and, in Handicraft and Singing, poor. Overall, his report was in the 'Quite good – can do better' bracket. There were no problems with conduct and he was ranked 6th out of 25 boys. As Christmas announced the end of term, and freedom, he had won the first round. When he was collected at the school by his family, he walked tall. Now George was going home to enjoy time with his real friends, and especially best-pal, Gwilym Rees.

Gwilym and George had been friends since meeting at Brynmenyn School and Gwilym lived with his parents only eighty yards away from Bryn Haf. His father was a well-known railway man in the area, who progressed from being a ticket boy to more senior posts in various locations in South Wales, before ending his fifty year career as station master at Tondu. Gwilym remembers his father and George 'talking trains,' and George's Aunty Mattie calling to check train times. George got on well with most people, but the kind and quiet-natured Gwilym was the sort of person that George felt most comfortable with. Gwilym recalls their time together:

In those days, Brynmenyn was a pretty place, and there was a railway crossing in the middle of the road, which was manually operated. Nearby, stood the Fox and Hounds pub – we called it the Foxes – and, as soon as George saw it from the train, he knew he was home. Of course, Brynmenyn was a small station, although usually busy; and its station master lived, more or less, by the platform. It was well kept and decorated: platforms being clear for people to walk, with potted plants around the place.

I don't remember George saying a lot about Bushey. He was more interested in what was happening in Brynmenyn. George was very fond of taking a walk up the old road out of the village. It was like a narrow lane leading to Llangeinor but, along the way, we could turn through the woods and park, down to the Ogmore river. George's brother, Neville, came with us. And, when the weather was fine, we sat around and talked.

George was quite a serious boy, but with a mild sense of humour. He thought a lot about the welfare of people. It was probably a little later on, but we used to talk about the North American Indians and the Australian Aborigines. I noticed his caring ways from an early age. I knew he'd make a good doctor; there were signs of a considerate bedside manner from the beginning.

Occasionally, George and I went to the old farm, Abergarw, where George's family farmed for generations. On one occasion we arrived at harvest time. The dog, Rover, was running around everywhere and, in his excitement, he bit George that day. We often teased George about Rover biting his backside. We also used to make dens, and one of these was in the back garden of Bryn Haf, where there was a little tree. Only a few doors up the road, George's Aunty Katie was living in Abergarw House. This was a really nice place. It had big rooms and bay windows; we used to enjoy playing there.

When the school terms ended, George couldn't get back to Brynmenyn quick enough. If the weather was fine, we'd walk all the way up Llangeinor Mountain. It was a steep two-mile climb and we enjoyed the views from there. Blackmill was down in the valley across the hills. And, on a clear day, we looked straight-ahead towards the coast. It was great fun during fine weather and, for George, it was very much a favourite place.

'Top of the Class' —
To Cardiff Royal Infirmary

JANUARY'S RAW WINTER weather had set in by the time George returned to Bushey School. Christmas at home had been a time of warmth and fun, but he now faced a cold and miserable world. After the open hearth of his Aunty Margot's cosy living room, where the blazing coal fire warmed every fibre of his body, he now experienced the common room's chilling emptiness, lacking atmosphere, natural comforts and any hint of homeliness. School made him feel small and insignificant, and he was continually accompanied by a sense of hopelessness. As he reflected upon the recent Christmas carols at Brynmenyn's Betharan Chapel, these words made him doubly sad:

> In the deep mid-winter, frosty wind made moan,
> Earth stood hard as iron, water like a stone . . .

> If I were a wise man, I would do my part,
> Yet, what I can, I give him: give . . . my heart

It is said that many of life's great achievers emerge from hardship and misery at an early age. It is in those tight corners that they nurtured strength through adversity to lead them on to greater success. 'What does not destroy you completely, will only make you stronger,' were the words of advice offered by Terry Venables, England's former football manager, to his senior players – and how true. For George these words also resembled, in outline, the size and shape of his personal motto. Besides his own plight, he had noticed his brother, Neville, returning home from naval boarding school totally disillusioned and of broken spirit.

It was time for the same dogged determination of his mother to emerge. Now immersing himself in work, and whatever play he could find, he enacted a few words from the same Christmas carol. George would always *give his heart*; now his personal will *stood hard as iron,* too. In lessons, sports, games, chapel, bible-reading, letter writing, all, he stepped up the pace. This is what his mother had hoped for from the beginning; he was not going to disappoint her now. With a touch of defiance he was even outwitting the bully-boys who lurked cowardly in the same cold school corridors. Indeed, it was a case of 'Try and catch me if you can!' Michael Davies, originally from Barry, but today living in Tavistock, has memories of George arriving at Bushey:

I remember George as a new boy because I was in the same 'house' as him – although, by then, I must have been nearly ready for the Senior School. I know how George felt because I had the same experience myself; it was one of loneliness and homesickness – although he seemed to settle well. He soon had a few contemporaries that he got on with and I also spent more time with George than other boys of his age. We used to chat now and again because of the Welsh connection. He used to enjoy talking about home life whenever he had the chance; he liked to chat.

In the Junior School we had an outdoor swimming pool and it was open for the summer months, which began early in May. You lost your breath when you went into the water and I remember the house master teaching people to swim, with some kind of support round their upper bodies, attached to a long rod held by the master at the poolside.

For me to get to Bushey, I caught a train from Cardiff to Paddington, and then a taxi to Queens Park Underground Station. Then the train took me all the way. Occasionally, I met other boys, such as George, on the train. But there wasn't a great deal of conversation – not when we were going back to school!

At the end of Easter term 1937, George Penn was top of his class of twenty-six boys. The housemaster reported, 'He has worked splendidly throughout the term.' The headmaster added, 'An excellent term's work,' and even the music teacher had to admit that George's singing was not as bad as once suggested, now, being described as 'fair.'

With the country steeling itself for an impending war, George read about a certain Winston Churchill and was inspired by a genuine respect for the great man. George needed his inspiration; when it appeared that his fortunes were on the rise, he was struck down by a serious heart complaint. As all his lessons were immediately put on hold and sport became taboo, he was taken to Bushey Hospital, before returning to the school infirmary, where, amidst great uncertainty, he was closely observed. His illness troubled the doctors, who decided to send George home to recuperate with specialist supervision. It was a worrying time and these precautionary measures were the start of a long period of absence from school.

But all was not complete darkness. In his days at Bushey Hospital, George met a kind gentleman, named Fred Gillett. Fred and his wife, Joyce, who lived in Bushey, injected much-needed light into George's world. Fred teased George like a favourite uncle might have done, and they exchanged letters often. For whatever reason, but most likely because it was the name given to certain items of soldiers' belt-ware in memory of Sir Samuel James Browne V.C., George called him 'Sam Browne'. In 1940, aged thirteen, when World War II took a grip on life across Britain and Europe, and when children such as those in Hertfordshire were evacuated to the countryside to avoid the threat of German bombs, George prepared two letters for Fred. The first was sent from the school infirmary and the second from 177 Albany Road, Cardiff, then his home:

Dear Sam (Mr Gillett),
Gee, I say I'm sorry for not having written this week.

You'll be pleased to hear I'm going home on Thursday. My mother is coming up on Wednesday, staying the night in Rudolph Road. And I am going to taxi to Paddington, catching the 11.55 back home to Cardiff where I shall be met by my uncle. We shall then proceed to Brynmenyn, near Bridgend.

Oh yes, I was talking to Mrs Ashby yesterday. I will not attempt to explain it all. I couldn't get a word in edgeways. 'My son is chief gardener. Yes *thoy all* do it voluntary you know. My brother-in-law's son is *chief hofficer* – and the shoes *hoint they horful?*'

So long . . .
Yours sincerely
George Penn

Dear Sam Browne,
Well, as you will see from the above address, I am in Cardiff. I am home for a few days and I am supposed to be seeing a heart specialist here.

Well I should have gone back to school on Tuesday, but evidently I am not up to the mark. I don't know what the shape of affairs with me is exactly. One specialist says that I won't properly get my heart back ever, and somebody else says I'll be OK. But I don't care what anybody says, I think I'll be OK after a bit.

We had a sharp air raid on Cardiff last Tuesday night, and we were up for three hours under the stairs. I hear that the damage was quite bad. I don't think Cardiff was the actual objective. I think they thought, 'We'll drop our bombs here and bolt!' That is only my opinion. In the paper it just says, 'South Wales Coastal Town Sharply Raided.'

Look here, you'd better join the army and you might scare the enemy a bit! It's about time something happened.

Well I must be saying goodbye for now.

Yours sincerely

P.S. How's Ole Gillett today? (not so much of the 'Ole Gillett' neither!)

Today, Fred's daughter, Susan Proctor, lives in Cambridgeshire. She also knew George well, although, as she explains, she was not aware of the letters:

My father was working for the fire service at the time but he was admitted to the Bushey Heath Hospital where George was in the next bed. When they started talking, they became friendly. George was naturally interested in people, and information; he absorbed all that my father was telling him.

With the country being at war, my father was able to explain to George what was happening. He told him stories and, no doubt, Winston Churchill's name entered into their conversations.

George was really friendly and both my parents grew fond of him. They were living in Bourne Hall Road, Bushey, at the time and my mother used to take a few goodies to him whenever she went to the hospital.

When George got better, he often called round. My mum

and dad were always pleased to see him, and this was the start of a fond friendship that continued.

There was great excitement to see the cheerful George back in town, although news of his heart condition was disturbing. Within a short time he was admitted into Cardiff Royal Infirmary in Newport Road. He was on home territory now; he had been born just up the road at Number 171, and his father had been born on the opposite side at Number 214, Holmdale, Grandpa Penn's former house. On the day he entered this famous medical establishment, George arrived without his other great inspiration at the time, the *Holy Bible*. This meant that his mother had to go back to the house to fetch it. George's family took every opportunity to visit him, one member being his younger cousin Janet, daughter of Aunty Katie, who was now living in Abergarw House:

> Everybody loved George. He was kind to everybody. When he was a little boy in Brynmenyn School, he was forever nursing me. I was a baby then and I often appeared in family photographs in George's arms.
>
> Throughout his life, which was extremely difficult at times, he simply smiled his way through his troubles. In Cardiff Royal Infirmary, he was just the same. When my parents visited him in the warm summer months, he was in bed outside on the veranda. Being a child, I wasn't allowed into the hospital, so I would look up and wave to him. And when no one was looking, he threw his sweets down to me.
>
> At this stage, George was seriously considering taking Holy Orders. He didn't go far without his Bible, and he harboured these thoughts for a long time. Back in Brynmenyn, the family always put a drink out for the doctor when he called. George noted this – thinking doctors were onto a good thing. He was always going to be either a vicar or a doctor.

When George, Gwilym and Neville walked up the 'old road' to Llangeinor Church, I often joined them. It is a lovely place to go, peaceful, with just a church, a pub and a farm. On the way we often had a picnic, or roasted some potatoes over a little fire.

After George was discharged from hospital, he was thrilled to return to Bryn Haf. Aunties Margot and Mattie, like my mother, Katie, and George's mother, Beatrice, were the sixth generation born at Abergarw farm. They had been six girls, but Sarah Jane and Marjorie died at a young age. George had plenty of female attention, and he was also a big friend of Mack, our little dog. So it was understandable that he was never in a hurry to go back to Bushey.

Some Deep Thoughts –
before Cycling into the Sunset

GEORGE'S ENFORCED absence from school hindered his studies, but he was welcomed back to Bushey with genuine warmth and sympathy. At the end of December term 1940, his house master stated, 'He was working well before his illness came upon him.' The following term, ranked eighteenth in the class, the headmaster was equally gracious, 'I consider this an excellent report in view of his long illness and absence. It shows grit and determination.' These comments were encouraging; more importantly, they signalled that George was back.

There is no doubt whatsoever that Bushey School fired the imagination of the boys when it came to leadership, and credit for this is rightfully deserved. Besides direct involvement in the school's cadet corps, which saw parades and marches taking place around the premises and summer camps, many of George's written assignments focussed on heroism and life's great leaders. When aged fourteen, now well settled into the greater comforts of the Senior School, he wrote an essay on heroic British people. He mentioned Captain Scott's Antarctic Expedition, and David Livingstone's penetration into unknown Africa, stating that 'Livingstone's personal safety, from death, plague, arrow, spear or bullet, seemed to matter little to this great man.' In summarising, George made a statement that typified his philosophy for life, found in one of his school exercise books:

If there was not something to battle against, something to strive for, and something to be sacrificed, life would be valueless. We shall have lost the vital point of life – namely to leave the world a little better than it was upon our entry.

'We shall pass this way but once' . . . is an extract from a well-known poem. It implies that we must do everything possible as we journey to help others and improve the road.

At times, we have to plod forward doggedly, battling against the overwhelming difficulties ahead. In this battle, life needs heroes – to succeed.

As regards English poetry and literature, George completed many assignments designed to make him appreciate the subjects' masters, and their legacy. He referred to the uncontrollable conscience of Macbeth after Banquo's murder, and described John Milton's compassion and motives in the sonnet describing his blindness. Then, highlighting writers and religious leaders of the Middle Ages, he stated, 'Through Shakespeare we have the practice or body of Medieval Britain, and through Dante, the faith and soul of medieval times.' And, describing the deep sentiments of William Wordsworth, a lover of nature and Tintern Abbey, George wrote:

> Our birth is but a sleep and a forgetting. We originate, says the poet, from heaven. As infants, heaven still has its celestial influence over us. In our growing up, Earth's influence pervades, and the celestial vision fades into the light of common day.
>
> As tenants of Earth's habitation, we have a good landlady. Earth supplies us with such an abundance of good things and we even forget the glories of heaven, which we once apparently knew.
>
> Oh child! Little do you realise that you possess knowledge of life and heaven that men are toiling hard to find.

Inspired by such words, George in 1943, aged fifteen, had tasted a little adventure of his own, having cycled through mid-Wales. The early stages of this tour were captured in a small notebook – until torrential rain caused him to put it away. Here are his memoirs:

I took a train to Blaenafon, where I met Ladbrooke. We had tea together, and then started for Crickhowell at 4.50 p.m. He escorted me over the mountain and pointed out the Crickhowell Road. The wind was just terrific. I arrived at Crickhowell, a pretty village through which runs the River Usk.

With the Sugar Loaf Mountain nearby, I passed through Tretower, challenged by miles and miles of 'uphill' towards Talgarth. With contrary wind and intermittent rain, it was hard-going, but I enjoyed a meal on the top of the hill as the sun tried valiantly to break through. Then it was downhill into Talgarth, where I entered my name in the Church visitor's book. I phoned home in the middle of this pretty town. It was now 9 p.m.

I pushed onwards towards Builth Wells as darkness fell upon the face of the earth. At 10.20 p.m., after going through a village or two, without attempting Bed and Breakfast, I asked a farmer if he had a warm spot where I could spend the night. 'Sure, I'll put you up in an outhouse with some straw,' said Mr Pryce, whose farm was two miles out of Builth. I had a jug of tea before retiring and I drank it with sandwiches. Then on this superbly moonlit night, I made my bed in some straw. It was chilly, but I dug deep down and this, somewhat, alleviated matters.

I got up at 7.10, took a stroll up the mountain, saw three rabbits and came down and had breakfast with tea provided. Cycling onwards, I arrived in Builth at 10.10

a.m. and I recollected its appearance from my 1941 stay
at nearby 'Llanwrtyd.' At a wayside stall, I drank three
glasses of milk and two glasses of lemonade. I arrived in
Llandrindod Wells at midday. I put my bicycle in Norton's
Garage and went to the park. I drank a glass of magnesia
water and paid to go inside the pavilion to hear a concert
and have a snack. I took a stroll then to the lake. It was
beginning to rain.

I pushed-off for Newtown, arriving at Crossgates where
I called at the Builder's Arms for a meal: . . . Two legs of
chicken, spuds, peas, broad beans, apple sauce and thick
gravy . . . Rich rice pudding and black currents . . . Coffee,
biscuits and home-made cheese: cost of meal – 3 shillings!

I was not half way to Newtown before the rain had
become intensified, to such an extent that I was drenched
through and could no longer tolerate it . . .

Even though George didn't complete his notes, he reached his
destination, Wallasey, alongside the Mersey river, where he
visited his brother, Neville. Soon afterwards, he was planning
his next major cycling expedition, all the way home from a
holiday camp near Taunton, where he had a summer job.
Here we have his commentary, a weekend in the company of
the young George Penn, aged 16 years, entitled:

A Trip from Durston Harvesting Camp to Cardiff,
on Saturday & Sunday August 4th and 5th 1943.

On the Saturday before breaking up, I purchased a Raleigh
Sports model complete with dynamo, 3-speed, pump, bags
and goodness-knows-what for £14. The owner was a Mr
Smith of Kingswood; he wanted £15, but I raked up the
necessary £14 and bought it just as somebody was in the
act of offering a higher price.

Anyway, at camp in Durston, I decided to cycle home for the Bank Holiday because:

a) I owed Riches [his house master] £10 for the cycle and wanted to economise

b) I wanted to test the cycle, and

c) I also wanted the experience – so I set out at 2.30 p.m. on Saturday.

George briefly outlined the route – via Durston, North Petherton, Huntspill, Bristol, Sharpness, Lydney, Chepstow and Newport to Cardiff.

I was finding my cycle well, justifying my £14 spent on it and, for the first twenty miles in the flat countryside I was just churning my way along, with little or no effort and much smoothness and celerity. Later, however, the route became hilly: there being several hills of a mile or more in length to either wearily overcome in ascent under the fierce summer sun, or to soar down at 40 miles-per-hour or more.

One rather amusing item was the crest of a hill near Bristol which was, in actuality, an aerodrome. Along the road were signs 'Keep Moving' and 'Beware of Low Flying Aeroplanes,' which I thought was very amusing – because what the Dickens they expected us to do about the flight of their aircraft, I just don't know?

Bristol eventually came into view, rather like viewing Cardiff from Tumble-down-Dick, but on a far greater scale. After a long descent, before I had time to appreciate the fact, I was right in Bristol. I arrived at 6.25 p.m. and my intention was to be directed to Aust and, thereby, catch a ferry boat over to Beachley, getting home the same evening. Unfortunately, these intentions were never to be realised for the last ferry boat was at 7 o'clock, and it was now 6.45 p.m. with 9 miles to go. It was hopeless; I gave up the idea and attended to the needs of the time.

George explained that he purchased 'three meat pies and 6d worth of chips with a fish', eating all but two of the pies which he saved for later. In the meantime, he was enjoying Bristol, fascinated by the Clifton Suspension Bridge 'that appeared as an extremely long plank over a vast gulf.' But darkness began to descend and he became concerned:

> Here I was, past Aust ferry, 31 miles from Gloucester and possessing the knowledge that if I didn't get over the other side of the River Severn that night, I should not be home the following day before dinner time. Even this, however, wouldn't have mattered, but an indescribable determination bade me 'get over' this very night whatever happened.

George called at a public house for 'a pint and a couple of cigarettes,' where he was told that there was a G.W.R. railway bridge nearby crossing the Severn between Sharpness and Lydney. Now, cycling into the dark night, he set off in search of it:

> 'Where's the bridge?' I asked.
>
> 'You can't get to the bridge – it's out of bounds,' was the reply. 'And anyway, there are no trains; it is impossible and, I say Mister, there aren't any places that can put you up for the night, either. We're all booked up.'
>
> This was disheartening, but I asked a railway man, coming home, for help. He very decently told me of a slim chance at Sharpness, so onwards I pushed to Sharpness. There was no life about the station so I hid my bike and went to the nearest station-box. I told my story as pathetically as I could to the two occupants and waited for the decision of the evening's fate.'

'Well,' said one, 'There is a goods train at twelve midnight going over the other side, but then it depends on whether the guard would let you in, and it would be unusual if he did. Could he walk it, they questioned one to the other.

'Yes,' I interposed, 'Quite easily I could walk it; I have a good light.'

'Well in that case, don't turn it on, because if someone comes along and you are seen pushing a bicycle over – questions will be asked.'

If I had to go over with no light, I knew it would be difficult; it was a dark night with no moon.

Nevertheless, George was determined to get across this wide stretch of water:

> I decided to chance it, since there were other men down along the line who could receive me at different points and give further directions. I was set going by one of the occupants of the signal box and eventually heard a voice beaming out of the darkness giving me encouragement (of which I needed plenty) and further directions to get onto the actual bridge.

But this was no ordinary walk in the dark:

> There were several planks or sleepers about a foot high traversing the width of the bridge at the beginning and intermittently all the way along, over which I had to continually lift my bike. This became arduous work, especially as the railway bridge was one-and-a-quarter miles across. I had eighteen inches between the rail track and the side of the bridge – and just a few wires to stop me falling in! It was a very nerve-racking business.

Not surprisingly, the experience was also rather eerie:

My steps on the iron seemed to make a thunderous din in the blackness, while below (far below), I could just make out the Severn. And all I could see of the bridge either way was the first half of the next arch looming up in the darkness. When I thought I had come to the end of the bridge, I would see another arc sleepily in front of me, until after many such disillusions, I reached the end and approached the signal box some distance the other side.

At this point George heard a welcome voice from another signalman confirming that he had arrived at the other side and was directed to the town of Lydney:

By Jove, was I thankful. But the realisation of how intensely sleepy I had become, swiftly dawned upon me. And all I wanted was to find a place to sleep.

George had just traversed the Severn Railway Bridge, known as the 'White Elephant'. This structure was completed in 1879 and for many years served as a back-up for the later Severn Railway Tunnel. During its fascinating history – which saw coal supplies being taken away from the Forest of Dean, and Spitfires flying beneath its tall structures during World War II – it is doubtful that it ever again experienced the journey of one young man and his bicycle. Many years later, in 1960, when George Penn, the doctor, was purchasing his fine residence, Hillside, two petroleum vessels struck the bridge's uprights in foggy conditions, causing it to be completely demolished in later years.

Bowing out of Bushey in Style

IN THE LAST year at Bushey, it is understandable that the Royal Masonic School saw a very different George Penn. The days of insecurity that once haunted him as a junior boy had long gone. The cycling expeditions had hardened his resolve, giving him a sense of achievement, whilst shaping his confidence, too. Now, looking forward to playing the part of well-to-do Sir Henry Martin, in the school comedy *It Pays to Advertise*,[2] and with his mind made up on pursuing a medical career, he was beginning to relax his guard a little too much.

As Christmas 1944 approached, George was a prefect in his final year. This was good news for the boys of his house; equally it was the cause of some sleepless nights for his house master. George could never be an outright rebel – he was too polite and respectful for this – but he campaigned for what he felt was right, and he bent the rules a little too. Yes, he took heed of that classic wartime movie *Reach for the Sky*, when a legless Douglas Bader took charge of his new platoon and declared to a startled messenger-boy delivering circulars and files for him to read: 'Rules are made for the observance of fools and the guidance of wise men'.

Although George did not have quite such a carefree outlook on life as this, it was still obvious that one day soon he would stray across the line. It happened in the early days of November 1944 when, in just one evening, he took it upon himself to rewrite most of the school rules. Of course,

2   *The Old Masonians' Gazette*, June 2012.

his conduct fell under immediate scrutiny, and it was soon time for him to face the music, yet allowances were already being made for this outspoken young man. The letter that he received from his house master came with the discipline of a headmaster, the humanity of a father and the sincerity of a friend. It was the perfect combination and, strangely, many years after it was written, it offers the perfect tribute to Whitland's Dr Penn:

Dear Penn,

I am severely annoyed with the events of last night.

Some time ago I made a report on you that you were inclined to be too individualistic, and last night was a case in point. I could quite appreciate the fact that you wanted to give Pilling a happy send off, but I cannot approve of your methods.

In the early evening you gravely offended Mr Blake by inviting Alexander, of E- House, to play our hymn without a word of warning, and you are well aware that Mr Blake always plays the hymn when on duty. This was tactless to say the least.

Then I was allowed to know of the proposed celebrations only because two little boys required official leave on Wednesday afternoon. This I could have understood and lived down.

However, I cannot approve of the fact that you apparently withdrew all the prefects from House duty and allowed the unfortunate remainder of the House to fend for themselves. In consequence, Mr Blake had to ring the bell at three minutes to nine and order the juniors to go to bed, and this they did apparently without supervision.

But I regard as your greatest misdemeanour the fact that you apparently took it upon yourself to give certain juniors permission to stay up to join in the fun. In consequence, I was greatly shocked at the appearance of one of them in my room at twenty five minutes past nine – when he should have been in bed – making an entirely unlawful request for a broom!

The letter then spelt out in no uncertain terms the gravity of his actions in a school known for strict discipline. 'No prefect has a right to allow any boy to remain up when it is bedtime,' were the words, followed by a clear warning not to repeat such behaviour. But then the author's human touch emerged – not unlike Captain Mainwaring's ways in the famous *Dad's Army* series – decency shining through his words, at a time when George had again disappeared to enjoy himself:

> I had intended to speak to you personally this evening but, on my return to the House, I was merely greeted with a message that you had gone out to a dance. As I feel that this is a matter that ought not to be left dragging on, I am writing this letter since I imagine I shall have gone to bed before you return.
>
> I treasure you too highly, Penn, to wish to quarrel with you unreasonably, but there are some things you know which go beyond the bourn. I can assure you that there are no ill feelings on my part, and I trust that there are none on yours. I shall be glad to hear from you.
>
> Yours sincerely

When all was said and done, Bushey School had pointed George in the right direction. He emerged as an outright leader, a young man capable of influencing people and making a difference. Of course, he felt indebted to his tutors for this whilst also acknowledging that his mother's great gamble had paid off. In later years he took delight in attending the School

Open Day, when he walked around the green playing fields and through the impressive buildings reflecting upon past times.

And, so it was when, after having completed his final examinations, he took time to look back, venting his feelings in characteristic verse and rhyme. In reality he was searching for words to describe his release from captivity, now that his wings had been given freedom to fly once again. Beyond all doubt, his school experiences had been no picnic, and this explains why his words at the time appear to be unusually harsh. However, time was to prove his undeniable respect for a school that had taken him from a junior boy to an impressionable young man. Here are his words, entitled 'Closing Chapter':

Zest, promise and friendship I thought I'd hallow,
And yet was I blindly making them shallow.
This folly cannot forever last
Time must come when chances are past.
Life cannot last forever –
Deaths last failure it must sever.
Yes – chapters good and bad must close.
This one, I regret it ever arose!
Let the future now my mind enrapture,
For I leave behind this closing chapter.

G. K Penn, July 19th 1945

PART III

CARDIFF MEDICAL SCHOOL

Bar Duties and
Studies at the Wyndham Hotel

A S FATE WOULD HAVE IT, the deep roots of early medical
schooling in George's birth place were set in a landmark
building in Newport Road just a few doors away from Grandpa
Penn's house.[3] This was once the famous 'Glamorganshire
and Monmouthshire Infirmary and Dispensary,' an iconic
institution that served the sick people of the district, before
later becoming known as the 'Old College'. It is there that
learned and energetic scholars of medicine arrived in proud
Victorian costumes to grapple with Anatomy, Physiology[4]
and all traditional teachings of the day. Indeed, it is also at
this old infirmary that Cardiff Medical Society was formed
earlier in 1870.

At a time when Cardiff was rising as a seaport, and
its population was expanding, the functions of this early
infirmary were moved to a nearby complex housing 180
beds. As a place of magnificent stately splendour, it is little
wonder that Cardiff's new infirmary was later awarded Royal
credentials: generally known as Cardiff Royal Infirmary,

3   John Surtees and Alan Trevor Jones, *The Medical Teaching Centre Cardiff*
(University of Wales Press, 1971).
4   *Welsh National School of Medicine*, Golden Jubilee Appeal booklet
1931–1981.

whilst also being called King Edward VII Hospital for a period. It stood tall and commanding, once looking out onto terraced gardens, lawns, steps, bushes and trees with its stand-out dome commanding centre stage.

With students of medicine clearly wanting to work in tandem with this new medical centre of excellence, the Cardiff Medical Society and all like-minded people with medical advancements in mind, pushed hard for Cardiff to be recognised as an approved medical school. This happened on July 1st 1931 when the Welsh National School of Medicine was founded, setting the scene for George's return to within a few doors of his place of birth, ready to hunt through myriads of medical theories and practices for a coveted M.B. B.Ch. (Wales) degree. Setting up a den in his top floor study at Cardiff's Wyndham Hotel, Cowbridge Road – where his mother, Beatrice, having taken a break from nursing, was now established as proprietress alongside Neville, her rock of support – George immersed himself in books. And there were many of these, most being full-bodied, rather chunky, often frightening-looking medical manuals.

It was in this cosy bird's-nest of a retreat, looking down onto one of Cardiff's busiest streets, that George paced around, head bowed in thought, cigarette in hand, encouraging and cajoling himself to grasp the meaning of medicine's many rather difficult-looking words. It was here also that he sat behind his cluttered desk, sketching in fine detail volumes of medical drawings and illustrations – waste paper bins spilling onto the mat, and the wall clock ticking quietly into another day. Yes, happily getting to grips with his next major challenge, George was forging into the distance, whilst jotting one or two additions into his little notebook:

Oh to be a doctor, to treat people's woes!
For me, no office-boy's, or teacher's, dreary task.
To take a place in this great world, God knows;
To be a doctor – this is all I care to ask.

When George's mother, Beatrice, was offered the tenancy of the Wyndham Hotel by a relative, she needed no second invitation. Beatrice could go the distance with most people. Her farming background had given her strength which, steeled by Stanley's tragic disappearance, had also given her a resilient inner core. In taking over the Wyndham Hotel, she was embarking upon a huge challenge but, for Beatrice, it was a challenge to overcome. It also provided George and Neville with a stable home base in the middle of Cardiff; a stability vital for George's future studies. There was no question, however, that in the midst of rebuilding a post-war Cardiff, Beatrice and her family would have their work cut out at the 'Wyndham'. Meanwhile, her private nursing was put on hold.

Cricket and rugby were hugely important to the city during these days, as Cardiff Rugby Club stalwarts like Billy Cleaver, Jack Matthews and Bleddyn Williams were hailed as the next British Lions. There was certainly no shortage of activity at Cardiff Arms Park, especially as the greyhound races were also flourishing – and, not far away at Ninian Park, things were just the same. At this stage in Cardiff City's famous footballing history, the proud club was attracting huge crowds. Over fifty thousand spectators were present at the Easter 'derby' with close rivals Bristol City in 1947, and five thousand more packed into the ground for the Tottenham Hotspur match a year later. Positioned midway between these two sporting arenas, the Wyndham saw it all. This was no quiet backwater; its position could not be bettered. And Beatrice embraced the challenge.

In the great majority of cases, the busy social evenings at the Wyndham were nights of fun. Beatrice teased and charmed many of her regulars, and there was always cheerful banter in the midst of general merriment. However, it is understandable that Beatrice, like all busy landladies, had moments when she found herself up against some troublesome characters, the worse for drink and looking for trouble. In such circumstances she unashamedly – and who could blame her – saw them out of the main door in sometimes unceremonious manner. Occasionally, however, and only occasionally, she was beaten: forced to play her last card. This was George, puffing away at his cigarettes on the top floor, in a world of medicine and not wishing to harm a flea.

On one of these crunch occasions, George was called into action because a strapping character had refused to leave and was determined to cause a scene. As a slim George came down the stairs and slipped quietly into the bar – having been built-up to be one of the beefiest bouncers in town – he tactfully suggested that there might be merit in asking a friendly policemen to the scene. But Beatrice would not hear of such a thing.

As she now pushed and shoved the man to the door, half closing it behind him, he turned defiantly to face her, stopping the door from closing with the bulk of his size twelve boots. At this point Beatrice turned to George, and blasted out a few short, sharp words that he never forgot.

'Well George,' she said, 'it's a case of one bully against another!'

Then facing the man she yelled,

'Gettt Ooowwwttt!' and gave his exposed shin the biggest kick of its entire life.

Yes, Beatrice could handle her clients; her will and determination knew no bounds; traits inherited by George.

Around this time, Gwilym from Brynmenyn, was also a student in Cardiff, studying Physics and Chemistry for external university exams. Gwilym had experienced the war years just down the road from Abergarw House. He remembers soldiers around the village as Bridgend played a vital part in the war operations due to its famous munitions factory and underground storage base. Throughout those years, Gwilym kept George up to date with stories from the home front, as George dealt with his own battles at Bushey. Now, years later, they occasionally met in Cardiff.

I was living in student digs then. I used to see George around the place. Our paths often crossed; then we caught-up on the news.

The Wyndham was a really busy pub, situated on the corner junction of two roads. There was an awful lot of activity outside, and close by was the old St David's Hospital. One of the roads led into Cardiff from Leckwith, so people passed the Wyndham front door all day long. George's mother was busy organising the bars and the staff, and so was Neville. And there were many beer barrels to move around in those days.

I can remember a pleasant warm atmosphere in the Wyndham; it was welcoming and friendly. There were a few different bars and people used to come and go. Some attended meetings in the private rooms; others enjoyed playing dominos and darts in front of the open fires. There was a piano in one of the rooms, and this is where George's mother arranged entertainment for winter nights. My impression was that George's mother had a big task on her hands, but that she was more than equal to it.

And I remember having a meal there once. I had been invited round and we all sat upstairs where the family lived.

Mrs Penn was kind, but extremely ambitious for George. She looked forward to him finishing in medical school, excited and overjoyed at the thought of him becoming a doctor.

A 'Doctor's Diary'. . .
and 'My Glorious Hitchhike to Blackpool'

WHENEVER GEORGE had the time, he took delight in writing his thoughts, memoirs and experiences into notebooks. He was a compulsive writer, always scribbling away, making notes, or filling a postcard and dropping it into a red box for a friend or relative. Even in retirement, he was the same: updating diaries and drafting letters with characteristic transparency and easy style. No doubt, this was another gift from Bushey School, at a time when there was no television and few available telephones. It is amusing that some of George's little books appeared too small to be of any significance – yet, surprisingly, they were packed full of stories, often his best.

One such book provides a glimpse of his life in the summer of 1946, when, free from 'med' studies for a few months, he was enjoying a summer break whilst saving for a trip to Blackpool. Each day, after breakfast, he rushed off to catch the works wagon taking casual helpers to the surrounding farms. There, they picked potatoes, pruned bushes, planted shrubs, trimmed hedges or did some weeding. Leckwith Avenue and Culverhouse Cross were the main pick-up points and, if he missed the vehicle, he would race off to the next stopping-point where he could jump aboard. Heavy rain often put an end to such work and in these circumstances, George would return to the Wyndham to run errands for his mother and brother, whilst usually finding time for some pleasure or fun.

He would then return to his little notebooks:

Thursday August 15th
I rushed to the Prince of Wales to see Diana Churchill's performance in *Soldiers' Wives*. All booked out, but I had a ticket given back – damned lucky. During the performance a woman tried to push herself onto me – but she was far too 'quite so' a type, and got on my toot with affectations worn into false naturalness.

Friday August 16th
Played tennis with Lewis on the grass courts of Llandaff Fields – before Howell Jones and I entered into a bit of a drunken orgy in the latter part of the evening, in which a considerable part of my earnings went.

Saturday August 17th
I hope to augment my meagre earnings (about £2 per week) by backing 'White Jacket' in the St Ledger. One can't lose on this; it is bound to get a place – but who knows.

The next working day was described as 'important' because George managed to catch the works lorry, but this meant weeding recently planted fir trees. 'For monotony and heart break, this job takes the biscuit', he wrote. Later he met his friends:

I found Dan, Burt and Charles, in the bar. So I took them into the darts room and we had a party, which was a great success. I thoroughly enjoyed it, although I got a little boozed, maybe.

Gwilym, his friend from Brynmenyn, was not far away either:

I met Gwilym looking forlornly over the bridge at the cricket ground in the afternoon. He'd come up to watch the match, but Glamorgan had won before he arrived. Anyway, I invited Gwil along to Penarth with us in the car for a picnic, and had a grand talk.

Whenever he could, George went in search of the sea, but upon returning home he was expected to help his mother:

Saturday August 24th
Arrived at Pier Head at 9.30 and got a skiff out to the main vessel. It reminded me of *The Scorcher*, on which I had been out with the fleet, in its smallness and compactness. When, eventually, we did make Weston, all we did was to relinquish our charge and came right back home. Later, I was summoned to the bar by mother, when enjoying my drink in a packed dining room. Eventually I conceded, and spent the rest of the evening in beer-pulling occupation.

Sunday August 25th
We went to Lavernock Point for the day and we had a marvellous picnic. I then went down the beach and had a really beautiful bathe in the approaching-dusk evening sea: nobody else about. Atmosphere nippy, but water itself quite warm; even mother and Janet paddled.

Now, having saved enough money, George was planning to set-off for Blackpool, but the lorry that was scheduled to help him start his journey failed to arrive. But this was only a small setback. Soon he was filling a travelling bag with his requirements for the next few days, and had every intention of enjoying his 'glorious hitchhike to Blackpool.'

I left home with a case, a parcel and my raincoat loaded up with food. I caught two trams to take me to Newport Road and I was just passing the depot when I saw Dan, the land-worker at Sherman's. I was talking to him when a lorry pulled up. I saw a hitchhiker boarding it, so with hasty farewells to Dan, I boarded it also, all set for Newport. It was a brick transport lorry, and dust was flying around like fun, so I just nestled within my raincoat the whole way. The bloke couldn't understand it, but I gave him five Woodbine for his decency.

We two hitchhikers joined forces now to alleviate the vile monotony of getting a lift. We started in a trudge out of Newport, trying continually, but with no luck. Getting thoroughly fed up, we cribbed and caught a bus to Chepstow Road, nearly outside Newport – but since we didn't pay, this must be considered a lift!

There we walked two miles, got really down in the mouth, and then picked up a lorry for three miles to New Inn. At least this was a more salient point for our sport and, after a twenty-minute wait, a lorry turned up with the delightful information that it could take us within eight miles of Gloucester. Now, of course, hitchhiking wasn't as bad as concluded five minutes ago. We arrived after picking up 'another gentleman of the road.' This new addition was a veteran; he never spent money on transport, and had been up to Scotland and goodness knows where by this method.

When George arrived in Gloucester, he felt 'the pangs of hunger':

After a long walk, I sat down by the roadside to eat some sandwiches, hailing each transport in the course of passing. Eventually I cared little whether I was picked-up or not. I had no faith in my thumbing, performing the rite as a matter of course. Only one thing interested me now: getting a lot to eat and I began to satisfy my interest with a will.

This meant that he was not ready when a car offered him a lift.

He didn't object to the continuation of my meal and here was started the basis of an interesting ride. Firstly, he gave me a piece of advice – not to thumb when a vehicle was just passing. This didn't give a driver enough time to pull-up unless with detrimental effect to the tyres. Then he questioned me about the nature of hitchhiking today, and my success in it – being rather struck by the idea of going to Blackpool.

The driver was also enthusiastic to hear that George was a medical student and congratulated him on attaining his 1st M.B.

He told me he imagined I would do soaringly well and reach something like King's Physician. He said I had it in me and he liked my temperament. He was a Freemason and was interested in my school, and me going in for medicine against all obviously correct advice. He thought it was excellent show that I had 'confounded the critics.' We whistled through Tewkesbury and were so engrossed in our discussion that he nipped a stationary car and dented the mud guard. However, we didn't worry much about this, and I left him as he thanked me for the company.

Now it was time for some cooked food:

Is there any wonder that I flew to the nearest restaurant for a hearty meal? I despatched a post card to mother and got a five-mile lift to Kidderminster. Then a lorry driver picked me up, advising me to chuck my Shrewsbury idea, and go his way. So we went through Wolverhampton, where he showed me the football ground, the hippodrome, and the dance hall. He gave me a jolly fine lift and deposited me just before Cannock. By now, I had given all my fags away.

A car then took George as far as a pub called the Eagle's Head:

By now it was getting dark and I half thought of spending the night here, but I didn't see the logic of hitchhiking, and then forking out a lot for bed and breakfast. So I pressed on, while darkness rapidly overtook me.

Now it seemed impossible to catch a lift and anxiety crept in:

I asked a sozzled farmer on his way home for a haystack, but no-go. He advised me to push on to a Bed and Breakfast place just a bit further on. I did this, but not to a Bed and Breakfast place – there weren't any! Another farmer stared goggle-eyed at the mention of a barn to sleep in, until the farming world around here was represented by a slow rhythm of shaking heads.

But George reached another pub, which looked hopeful:

In the end I arrived at the Bell Arms (or something like that – I've forgotten being behind with this diary as usual), but nothing doing. I had a drink and tried on the opposite road at the lady's recommendation, but the good lady there, although she always had a bed for wayfarers, had just given it to her aunt – too bad! Again I asked the pub lady if I could have so much as a shelter – it was raining – but no.

But, at last, there was a breakthrough:

I hailed cars and lorries, until an eight-wheel diesel pulled up and offered me his cabin to sleep. So I nestled down in this enormous thing, top speed twenty miles-per-hour, making enough of a row to evoke the Gods. It was quite an experience, and I felt oddly triumphant, confident, and in out-of-the-rain, with a trusty Yorkshireman at his responsible post. His cold tea helped to down my sandwiches for me, and my sandwiches his cold tea for him.

George explained that the driver was delivering a by-product of coal tar to a chemical works near Llangollen:

How sorry I was, I remember, when we pulled into this wretched works at 1.30 a.m. I'd just found a comfortable posture and dozed with ease. Although the driver was jocund, it all seemed highly dramatic. The factory was deadly quiet, deserted except for the watchman who helped us unload in the chilly night air. The whole thing seemed to be unreal and eerie.

We went to a derelict room to have a cigarette and chat – and what a chat. The driver explained the economics of lorry fleets, mentioning he did London to Glasgow runs aged sixteen having to put in extra loads at cheaper prices to make it pay. He then spoke of the war from which he was demobbed six months ago.

His work was to drive lorries and tanks from the front line, whose owners had been killed, or whose vehicles needed repairing. He outlined the effects of war on different people: how he saw men in nervous shivers before action, and others going stark mad. It wasn't so much the fear of instantaneous death; it was the fear of serious injury, whilst being conscious and alive to everything.

Now indoors and away from the rain, George explored the possibilities of staying in the works for a few hours' sleep:

One of the night keepers in the boiler house led me up flights of transparent (perforated iron) stairs, which was quite an awe-inspiring sensation among enormous pipes, high up a loft, with the floor far beneath, through the transparent stairways and floors.

He led me to a corner of reasonable temperature, where there was dust, dirt, a few planks – and probably rats. So two planks laid across a couple of buckets formed my bed; my case . . . my pillows; and my raincoat . . . my blanket: this at 2.30 a.m.!

Three hours later, I was awakened because (the bloke said) most workers arrived at six o'clock, and I wasn't supposed to be there. When I stepped out into Llangollen it was without my A.A. map book, which proved a nuisance. At this unearthly hour the early-risers gazed at me with peculiar interest, knowing I was a stranger (and what a time to arrive!). Anyway, I caught the bus towards Wrexham for 7d, walking the three remaining miles, where I purchased a filling breakfast for about 6d and cups of tea for 1d each.

At this point, George offered his services to a local farmer – and had a bit of a shock:

Pushing on to Gresford village, I found a farm – but no-go. He was a decent chap, however, and, thinking I was a tramp, said 'Just a minute,' and dived into the house with 'Here's something for your breakfast' – two eggs, which I accepted, greatly touched, staggered and enormously amused! I thought this was more than sufficient compensation!

When he returned to the road, eventually there was the chance of a lift:

After about three miles, I suppose I looked down and out, because a chap on the opposite side of the road just started yelling the offer of a lift, which I accepted.

He had a son in the Army and another in the Navy. He himself couldn't stand the sea, due to a horrible sea sickness caused by his smashed ear-drum. He was in the immediate neighbourhood of a grenade explosion in the Great War and it is a marvel that he was not killed outright.

This gentleman took George to Tranmere and, after a lengthy walk, he reached the home of his friend, Harold:

A young girl, aged twenty five, answered the door; this was Mary, Harold's cousin. It shows what I must have looked like: the first thing that she suggested was a wash and shave, which, of course, I wanted desperately. As it happened, she remembered me from the other time I called when Neville was in Liverpool.

I was going to spend the day in New Brighton, but Mary vetoed this and made me accompany her friend, Valerie, for dinner. We had a glorious chat altogether, which only took respite when Eddie, her husband, came back from work. Mary and I grew to understand one and other very much. She was my type, adventurous, impetuous, irritable and (here perhaps she differs) possesses a very level head. We spent all afternoon talking about Harold, who was working in a tough engineering place, which was getting him down.

George was excited to be reunited with his old school friend from Bushey:

Harold eventually arrived through the back door, really amazed to see me. That evening we crossed to Liverpool, and the thrill I had in stepping about the old ferry boat again in the busy Mersey, was terrific. We went to the Trocadera and saw *Somewhere in the Night*, with John Hodiak, which was pretty good, following which we took a walk to see night life in Liverpool.

We walked down Lime Street and I honestly found it

difficult to believe what I saw. The short road was lined with women. It was all the more difficult to appreciate because there was plenty of street lighting and one could plainly see them. And it struck me that they looked much the same as any other girls, wore fashionable clothes of today – pleated skirts (which I like) and looked ordinary and smart. Yet even as we walked along, two girls just, seemingly naturally, stepped out and joined pace with us – until they perceived we were no customers of theirs. I noticed one chap: by his eyes he looked very drunk that evening, standing fiery-eyed, waiting for somebody's first move.

George went on to say that Harold took him through Liverpool's Bond Street, and then to the bombed alleyways. It was a ghastly experience, especially as Liverpool had been so badly hit during the war. George was then on the point of explaining that Harold had often wanted, but never managed, to make this same little trip into the damaged parts of the city, when his note book ran out of pages! Regrettably, there are no more details of his 'Glorious hitchhike to Blackpool.'

This is how George was throughout his life. There was always a goal to aim for: always some bright light shining in the distance, firing his imagination, driving him on. It is certain that he arrived in Blackpool, where he was photographed bathing beneath its famous tower – a landmark ever since the mayor of Blackpool, hotelier John Bickerstaffe, returned home from a holiday in Paris in the late 1800s, wanting to give Blackpool its own 'Eiffel Tower.' As for the young hitchhiker, he arrived safely back in Cardiff, having no doubt encountered a few more thrills and spills along the way.

A little 'Rugger' and lots of
Variety for the 'Meds' President

GEORGE PENN NEVER admitted to being a total rugby enthusiast, although he genuinely appreciated the game. Its social importance to a country whose small towns and villages nearly all ran a team cannot be over-emphasised. In the mud and rain of winter months, 'rugger' (as he called it) provided an opportunity to slip away from the reference books and relieve the tension of long hours of lectures and study. Rugby also gave the Welsh population home-grown heroes to admire, people who at the height of their international prowess walked on water. It was around this time, the late 1940s, that George rubbed shoulders with Bleddyn Williams, the 'prince' of Welsh centres, under the grand pillared porchway of Cardiff's Angel Hotel. Bleddyn was now scaling the great heights of his playing career, soon to tour Australia and New Zealand with the British Lions. He interested George, who was blissfully unaware of his own impending flight to far-away Nigeria, for his National Service.

Well down the rugby pecking order was Cardiff Medical School's second team, for which George acted as secretary. The team provided good old-fashioned social rugby at its best: lots of fun and not too demanding. There was no coach, and it was George who arranged the occasional run-outs whenever he could assemble the boys together. This was one of his proud functions, along with the more important task of finding somewhere suitable for the players to share sandwiches and jugs of ale once the final whistle had been blown.

As for the game itself, George found it something of a slog. If he had been given a wider berth in the backs, with plenty of time to regain his breath, he might have enjoyed running around in the open spaces. But he was a forward: jumping in the lineouts, pushing hard in the scrums, and getting bumped-about in the loose-play as he chased around the field. George was glad when it was all over, happy to return to the bar – often the Wyndham for home matches – where the drinks led to a sing song, and the sing song to more drinks.

Most matches were local with many being staged in the nearby hills and valleys of Glamorgan. One day, George was 'off-colour', taking a bottle of stout from the Wyndham cellar to invigorate him at half time. In a varied fixture list his team sometimes travelled further and he had fond memories of visiting Llandovery College, playing on the old field alongside the traditional college buildings.

Mostly, George's team performed on park pitches and lesser grounds, sometimes with poor markings, no flag posts, and last-minute referees. Understandably, it was something of a shock when he appeared one day at Bristol's famous Memorial Ground, drafted into the first team to cover for a missing regular. The memory of that day never left him – not for the pride of appearing at this first-class venue with tall stands and enclosures (although all empty that day) but for the extra running, at a faster clip.

The fun side of rugby in medical school enriched George's days of study and brought him in contact with some great characters and close friends. One or two of the boys, such as David Boyns, George's second row partner, and Colin Evans, later his best man, teamed up with George in the summer of 1948 for a cycling tour of the youth hostels of Wales. Then, the following September, another group of boys accompanied him on a more adventurous tour of the west coast of Scotland. Although there are no diary entries referring to this occasion, George took time to explain on the reverse of some small photographs exactly what they were doing:

Wednesday 21st . . .	bathing in Loch Lomond
– ditto –	walking at Rest and be Thankful
Thursday 22nd	cruising on board a ferry to Connel
Friday 23rd	admiring the scenery at Kyleakin, Isle of Skye
Saturday 24th . . .	taking-in the sea breeze near Mallaig.

During the summer months, George also made a point of returning to Brynmenyn where he stayed with his Aunty Margot in Bryn Haf, still home for him, where life effectively started and his heart undoubtedly still lay. This is where he escaped, totally, from lectures, infirmary wards and the hurly-burly of life, visiting Janet, his cousin, and her parents, George's Uncle David and Aunty Katie, at Abergarw House. This property was, of course, the fine work of grandfather, George Howell, as was the row of three terraced houses next door and a small terrace-of-two a short walk down the road. It is little wonder that George Penn clung so tightly to Brynmenyn, where his family's creations still stand in distinguished alignment today.

For the carefree medic, a trip to Brynmenyn meant another challenging walk up the old mountain road to Llangeinor, which started from the back garden of Abergarw House. This narrow winding lane – cut into the hills for the horse and carts of old – extends through wide open moorland, emerging onto the high and holy ground of St Cein's Church. Standing alongside is the Llangeinor Arms where George had many a swift drink in his younger days.

This hidden highway was where George pondered life's trials and tribulations and also derived the strength and inspiration to overcome them. He was not alone; as far back as July 27th 1897, a reporter for *The Glamorgan Gazette* had this to say about the famous incline:

> It is Prince of the hills of Glamorgan, and once
> you get to his breezy crest, all is well with you.

George's cousin, Janet, explained that during his medical school days, George loved to go out on Sunday evenings, often arriving on the doorstep of Abergarw House.

> He was fond of our house: a show piece property in its heyday. He enjoyed the peaceful drawing room with its piano, and also the dining room where we had meals around the large oak table. He never returned to Brynmenyn without escaping up the old road; it was that special to him.
>
> In the summer months, George drove up with his mother and Neville. Sometimes, he arrived with his college friends too – knowing that there was always food in Abergarw. In the summer months, he liked to go down to the sea. The Cold Knap at Barry was one of his favourite places, as well as Rest Bay, Porthcawl. He always enjoyed having a bathe and, for George, the rougher the sea the better.
>
> During these days of study, he was settled in the Wyndham with Beatrice and Neville. I often went along to see them, and I remember the doctors from the nearby St Davids Hospital regularly occupying the main lounge.
>
> When George attended his interview for medical school, two candidates stood out, and he was one of these. This news got back to Beatrice from a friend on the selection board. When he was asked why he wanted to be a doctor, George admitted that he had, at one time, wanted to go in for Holy Orders. 'But I have an ambitious mother', he smiled. No

doubt, at that point, the interviewers appreciated the depth of his sincerity in serving others. He certainly impressed everyone that day.

Once he was accepted, he worked around the clock. Having left Bushey with London qualifications in Art, he had to do more Physics and Chemistry, with a Wolsey Hall correspondence course. But he soon caught up and was always going to pass; he was not going to let his mother down.

Janet was familiar with the Cardiff Medical Social Club at Howard's Gardens where George made time to meet his colleagues. This was a pleasant old house where, upstairs, many students had their 'digs'. It was therefore an ideal base for quiet drinks during the week days, and not-so-quiet dances on Saturday nights. By the time George entered his final year, he visited the 'med-club' as President of the Cardiff Medical Students Association, an honour that took him to functions across the country. One of these was the National Conference of the British Medical Students, held at Liverpool Town Hall, at the invitation of the Lord Mayor and Lady Mayoress on Tuesday September 12th 1950. Then, three days later, came the dinner at this same venue. George was not required to make a speech on this occasion, although, in later life, he was often asked to say a few words in public. Here is an extract from an address he later made, describing the time his studies ended:

> I qualified as a doctor, much to my surprise and joy, in the summer of 1951, and I did six-month jobs in General Surgery, Midwifery and General Medicine – in Llandough Hospital Cardiff, Neath General Hospital and Port Talbot Hospital.
>
> My first job was that of House Surgeon to Mr Douglas Foster, a General Surgeon at Llandough. This was a

beautiful hospital, and I had a job which I was proud of. The chest surgery was fascinating although the lung operations would take three hours – and I thought Mr Foster was wonderful.

Mr Foster usually called me 'George' except when he wasn't happy about things; then I would be 'Penn'. So, when he started calling me 'Penn' I could be in for a stormy time for a while. But I almost worshipped him, so I could not be too upset.

One day he asked me how much I was enjoying the job, and I told him that I was happy, but that I thought I ought to be having experience of actual surgery. I said I didn't want to do anything ambitious, such as an appendix operation, but a few lumps and lipomas would be fine, and he agreed with my request.

About that time, a gentleman came in for a stomach operation, which had previously been planned, and I noticed a big lump the size of a chicken's egg on the side of his head. 'Here's my chance,' I thought, and I suggested to the patient that he have the lump removed, which he agreed to. I told Mr Foster who said, 'Yes, you could do that while I see to his stomach.' Well, we started at the same time; I tackled the sebaceous cyst while Mr Foster started the stomach operation.

Mr Foster finished the major operation before I had really started my minor operation – and, saying, "Get a move on," he marched down the corridor to the Surgeon's Room. However, he kept coming back to ask how much longer I would be. I wasn't getting anywhere; I couldn't find the actual cyst, and there was just blood, so I couldn't see what was what. I asked Mr Foster if he could help me, but he said, "No." I had started it and I must finish it. Every time I heard the squelch-squelch sound of his surgeon's wellingtons coming closer, my heart sank to my boots, and with the theatre sister taking the 'micky' out of me by suggesting a blood transfusion, it just wasn't my day.

However the result was fully satisfactory and the patient was grateful to me for the improvement in the appearance of his head – and I hope the stomach got on equally well, too!

Mr Foster continued to give the ambitious George Penn every encouragement, and it was during these early days of his career in Llandough that he discovered an enjoyment for minor operations that never diminished. Meanwhile, away from medicine, he had also grown fond of his trusted motorbike, as Janet again explains:

When George was in Llandough Hospital, I was in college in Barry and he used to take me out every Wednesday on his motor bike. One day, we went round the Vale of Glamorgan and we were late getting back. I was a boarder at the college, which was strict. I was dying a slow death, knowing I was in for a row.

Then to make matters worse, George insisted on pulling up right outside the principal's window. Of course, when it came to visitors, the college grounds were sacred, out of bounds for most – but he didn't care about this; George was returning me to the door. But, later that evening, I was sent for by the Principal:

'What was I thinking about? . . . a young man . . . returning on a motorbike . . . riding pillion passenger . . . what was I doing?' asked my mistress, Miss Evans.

'He's not my young man,' I replied. 'He's my cousin.'

'And what does this cousin do?'

'He's a doctor,' I replied – and that was the end of the story.

This, no doubt, amused George, who was now taking up a placement at Neath General Hospital, undertaking midwifery, gynecology, as well as being medical superintendent. George Penn was never happier than when learning alongside the senior doctors of his younger days, and this period was challenging and rewarding in equal amounts. As ever, he was anxious to start well and to make a good impression: filling, and usually over-filling, his day with work. Whilst enjoying the friendly atmosphere of Neath General Hospital, he also made an impression at the reception desk, where a certain young lady was keeping an eye on his every move.

PART IV

PEGGY

'Dr Penn –
You're wanted at Reception, please!'

NEATH IN THE EARLY 1950s was a busy market town. Just a cursory glance at the outside porticos of the beautiful bank buildings, or a peep inside their hallways and lobbies, suggested that here was a town conducting large volumes of business. Priding itself on catering for the growing needs of an increasing population, Neath was also George Penn's type of place, one that honours tradition, refusing to forget the past. It was also the home of a popular twenty-two year old local girl who lived half a mile away from the town centre in a row of terraced houses, known as Leonard Street.

This was Margaret May Evans, affectionately known to all as Peggy. She had a twin sister called Glenys, and two brothers, Noel and Gwyn. Her mother, Margaret Olwen Evans (née James), came from Ferndale, in the Rhondda, while her father, David, was born in Bethlehem, near Llandeilo. David and Margaret started married life in Neath after David opened an ironmonger's shop in Stockhams Corner, on the outskirts of the town, just a few doors away from the aromas of home-made bread at Stockhams Bakery.

After an early education in the schools of Neath and district, Peggy left to help her mother, now sadly widowed, to run the shop. This was not an easy task because it was an old-style ironmongery, selling everything from the smallest nut-and-bolt to heavy fireplaces. Regular stock-takes, alone, took time: Peggy ticking-back items, painstakingly, to the inventories, in between manning the big wooden counter where the family conducted a steady trade. Peggy gave invaluable help to her mother until brothers Noel and Gwyn, in turn, took over her duties, allowing Peggy to join the staff of Neath General Hospital. This was a proud medical establishment that had served gallantly in the traumas of World War II.

One of Peggy's duties whilst working alongside the ladies at reception desk was to pass on information to the doctors. Her soft but efficient voice was heard in the narrow corridors of the hospital on the loudspeaker system, prompting doctors to call and collect their messages. Naturally, the newly qualified doctor from Cardiff was on her radar; and it was there that Peggy said just a few simple words to introduce herself, 'Dr Penn – you're wanted at reception, please.'

Dr Penn did not have many free hours, and work often spilt into his private time, but this was normal for an ambitious doctor. However, he made time for Peggy and the relationship developed simply and naturally, the bigger decisions coming without delay. Dr Penn knew that he soon had a period of National Service to prepare for, which could take him overseas. So he went about his courting days with the commitment, endeavour and reliability that he was noted for throughout his life.

Neath offered so much at this time. Television had not quite arrived, so the three cinemas, the Empire, Windsor and Gnoll Hall, competed with each other in providing the best movie action on the big screens. In those days, cinemas were more self-sufficient than today – arranging their own dances and running their own cafés and restaurants – so that going to the cinema for the evening had greater appeal. Likewise,

Neath's Gwyn Hall, another fine building with striking archways and presence, was known for miles around as a musical theatre of distinction.

Both Dr Penn and Peggy loved music. Peggy had taken piano lessons from an early age and now had quite a collection of certificates. As for George, he expressed a liking for the classical variety, even in his schooldays at Bushey, where the names of Mozart, Stanford, Elgar, Rachmaninov and Tchaikovsky featured amongst favourites in another of his little books. Wherever they planned to go – and their interests were wide and varied – Peggy, peeping through the curtains of her front bedroom window, was always thrilled to see her future husband arriving on his motorbike. She was fond of their faithful friend, which carried them safely through courting days and on towards future happiness.

Peggy's meticulous wedding preparations kept her busy in the months and weeks leading up to the 'Big Day', Thursday April 23rd 1953. Having drawn up a long list of things to do she set upon these tasks quietly, until everything had fallen neatly into place. Of course, the wedding day could not come quick enough – arriving amidst great anticipation and excitement when crowds of family, visitors and friends descended upon the small terraced house with gifts and cards. On the eve of the wedding, Peggy performed her last job, decorating the chapel with flowers. Then she returned home knowing that Maes-yr-Haf looked a blaze of fresh colour, ready for the occasion.

Dr Penn was ready too, looking spick-and-span with top-hat-and-tails as he sat in the front pew with best man, Dr Colin Evans, a close friend from medical school. As a railway enthusiast Dr Penn was at home in Maes-yr-Haf which stood alongside the east-bound platform where passengers departed for Cardiff and beyond.

There could be no better place for the reception than Neath's Castle Hotel, a two-minute walk away in the next street. This charming 17th century building, a former coaching inn, offered a warm and inviting welcome for guests who entered its double doors that day. Dr Penn and Peggy, stepping onto the shining polished wooden block floor at reception, felt the sense of history associated with this fine old building. Besides being a meeting place for the trustees of the Neath Turnpike Trust in the days of toll gates, and a stopping point for the London-bound Royal Mail coach, it is understood that Lord Nelson was a frequent visitor, accompanied by Lady Hamilton when his vessel was anchored off Milford Haven. Rugby enthusiasts, however, remembered the Castle Hotel for a very different reason: hosting a meeting to form the Welsh Rugby Union on March 12th 1881, an event that changed the social history of the entire country.

For Dr Penn and Peggy, the Castle Hotel provided a glance at the past as they set off into the future. That afternoon drinks were served in the high-ceilinged lounge, where wooden panels and small lights still adorn the walls, whilst pelmets and full-length curtains shaded the large windows. Doctors Penn and Evans coordinated a happy reception in an atmosphere full of good humour and bonhomie. That day, Dr Penn's cousin, Janet, and her parents travelled with others from Brynmenyn on the train:

> It was a friendly service and I can see them all there now. I remember the reception being nearby, and there were some medics, and some of George's rugby pals, and one or two 'blue' jokes – but it was all really pleasant and we had a comfortable room to ourselves. My mother was very fond of Peggy's mother, Margaret, and I remember her being impressed with the way the wedding day had gone.

Of course, Dr Penn had some choice words to say on his big day, whilst proposing a toast to bridesmaid, Glenys, who he first met with Peggy at London's Charing Cross railway station. Glenys recalls:

> It was a really happy occasion. Peggy had been excited for months, busily counting the days. She planned it well; her hard work paid dividends. We all had a lovely time.
>
> That day I had to leave early to return to Kent, where I was teaching. George and Peggy came to see me catching the train. They were on the platform, waving me goodbye. But, I think *I* should have been waving *them* goodbye!
>
> George hired a car from the local garage in Neath. Soon they were heading for the Llanina Arms, Llanarth, later exploring New Quay, Aberaeron and Aberystwyth.

In customary manner, Dr Penn never left a party in full swing, waiting for the guests to make their way home before heading north with Peggy. Together they made people happy on their journey through life: always considerate, always kind to everyone, with a generosity that knew no bounds. That day a local journalist captured the story which appeared in the next edition of the *Neath Guardian*:

> There was a charming wedding at Maes-yr-Haf chapel, Neath on Thursday of last week, when the Reverend E. B. Powell married Dr G. K. Penn, son of Mrs J. B. Penn of the Wyndham Hotel, Cowbridge Road, Cardiff, and the late Captain S. K. Penn – to Miss M. M. Peggy Evans, the twin daughter of Mrs M. O. Evans, Leonard Street, Neath, and the late Mr David Evans.
>
> The bride, who was given away by her brother, Mr D. Gwyn Evans, was attired in a figured nylon gown and carried a bouquet of pink rosebuds.

In concluding, the article mentioned the reception and the honeymoon on the Cardiganshire coast. Then it described Peggy's navy going-away outfit, with matching accessories in light shades of blue.

PART V

THE ROYAL ARMY MEDICAL CORPS

A Posting to West Africa for Captain Penn

D R PENN'S DAYS at Neath General Hospital came to an end when he volunteered to fill a vacant house physician's post at neighbouring Port Talbot Hospital. He worked for two senior consultant-physicians, Dr Howell and Dr Dyson, whilst also assisting a gynecologist-specialist and a chest surgeon. But this was not all: he also became the out-of-hours anaesthetist for Dr Kim Sabir, an inspirational Indian doctor, resident in the hospital. Dr Sabir taught him how to give anaesthetics while working together on minor operations and casualty work. For the young Dr George Penn, this was an immensely fulfilling period of work, in a 'happy family' atmosphere. He enjoyed getting to know the Port Talbot general practitioners, often joining them for a drink after work, as he later said in a speech to Royal British Legion members:

> Then I was called into the Royal Army Medical Corps, in Crookham, near Aldershot. We had a period of introduction, including a lot of square-bashing etc, but I have to say that I wasn't one of the army's brightest or best recruits!
>
> Although I wasn't all that thrilled about the Army, it gradually cast its spell on me and I remember one evening being quite thrilled and impressed to be present at an evening of boxing which was attended by the 'top brass', as well as the wonderful band, of The Royal Army Medical Corps.

But I was worried about being sent to an early end somewhere, and the two places of dread at the time were Korea and Malaya. However, we were reassuringly told that we could apply for any of the areas being served, and I took heart from this, having just got married, and my three choices were: firstly, the United Kingdom; secondly, Germany; and thirdly, the Middle East.

When they had decided where they were sending all of us young doctors, their decisions were listed on the notice board, and I saw: G. K. Penn, West Africa! I didn't really know where West Africa was – but, I soon found out.

For Dr Penn and Peggy, this was a heart-wrenching moment in their early married lives. Initially, Peggy intended joining her husband in West Africa, but regulations got in the way, so the idea was forgotten, meaning an eighteen-month parting. But they adjusted well and began writing to each other in earnest, virtually every day. Endearing themselves to the positive elements of their new circumstances, this was an excellent opportunity for Dr Penn to practise medicine in a different world, full of challenges. For Peggy, this period extended her enjoyment at home in Leonard Street, whilst marking the countdown to her married life. It allowed her time to absorb all that had happened and to look forward and prepare for the future. Immersing herself in work, home duties, helping in the shop and quietly enjoying Neath – Peggy's joy came in the form of seeing the postman or woman dropping another blue-square envelope through the letter box. Every one of these treasured little packages had travelled six thousand miles and, as they started to mount up into big piles, her husband drew nearer.

Dr Penn's expedition to Nigeria, in early June 1953 saw him and colleagues flying over the Sahara Desert on route to Kano in northern Nigeria, before proceeding south to Lagos on the coast to meet up with doctors of the military hospital. For two weeks, this is where they integrated with colleagues, learning about medicine and everyday life in their new surroundings. The first lesson was to prepare thoroughly for bedtime, with special light-weight close-fitting clothes and boots, as well as a mosquito net to cover the bed. In the dark of night, mosquitoes were most active: their deadly bite carrying malaria. They had to adjust to this, as well as to tropical conditions generally. Here are Dr Penn's words, taken from a speech to members of the Royal British Legion:

> The climate was warm, wet and humid, and everyone perspired profusely. Our uniform comprised of boots, a hat like the hat worn by the soldiers in Burma, and a military sort of shirt-jacket and shorts. Everyone's forehead was perspiring and the tunics visibly wet under the armpits with perspiration.
>
> After two weeks in Lagos we were flown to Accra in Ghana, known as the Gold Coast then. But now all flying was done with West African Airways, a civilian organisation. I was impressed at the way that African women nonchalantly got on and off aircraft with the same ease and acceptance as they got on and off their 'Mammy Wagons', which were effectively lorries, packed with people, bouncing over the rough tracks of West Africa.
>
> Accra was pleasant, although very, very warm. The sea had wonderful breakers and we went surf riding almost every day. We also accompanied the doctors in their work, both in the hospital and in the outlying district.
>
> Our arrival was the excuse for a party and I was quite frightened when I realised that fellow officers were trying to get myself and other new arrivals drunk with whisky

– and they at least half succeeded. During the drinking session, an Irish doctor, who was also a vet, went chasing a lethal snake – a huge thing, the length of a room – with an axe; and managed to cut its head off. I really felt uneasy, as if the place was eerie – and I wasn't sorry to be flown back to Lagos, where the doctors were more composed and sensible.

Soon Dr George Penn was bound on a West African Airways flight to Kaduna in the centre of Nigeria. For a few days he worked in the local military hospital before travelling on a two-day train journey south-east to Enugu. This was a permanent post for fifteen months as Regimental Medical Officer to the Second Battalion of the Nigerian Regiment. There he saw to the medical needs of officers, sergeants and regimental sergeant majors – and the many Muslims amongst them who had as many as four wives and many children.

The Africans were delightful people and they were just bursting with rhythm. In fact, most of them carried drums – a bit like an hour-glass in shape with a narrow middle point and attached to a sling so that they could carry the drum around with them. Whenever they had a spare minute they beat out a rhythm and often danced to the beat.

I was once invited to the wedding of a nice civilian African doctor but for reasons beyond my control – or we'll say that anyway! – I was late, but I thought that I would still go to see them coming out of the church. As I approached the church there were a lot of people outside and I moved up quietly to join them. There was a line of about six African women waiting patiently while, seemingly, chewing a little stick, and I could see their somewhat large bottoms moving from side to side slowly and gracefully to the accompaniment of quiet humming and small foot movements. I was quite enthralled. Rather than fretting about waiting, their amazing sense of rhythm, music and dancing kept them happy.

The African women used to carry enormous amounts of shopping and food on the top of their heads. On their backs would be a little child from any age from birth to about four years. As far as I recall, there was no such thing as a cot death, and I have reflected a lot about this and I have come to the conclusion that a cot death may often be caused by leaving a baby on its own for perhaps slightly too long – causing the baby to feel isolated and to give up and die. I have sent this theory of mine to medical journals, but to my disappointment they weren't at all impressed and didn't publish my essay.

Dr Penn was fascinated to learn that if a man had more than one wife, they all seemed to get on well in each other's company:

> But, of course, this depended a lot on how the man managed his household! I think that the man needed a lot of tact and psychology. I remember one occasion when I was being driven in a Land-Rover around different camps I asked the African driver, 'Tell me driver, how many wives 'do you catch?'
>
> 'Master, I "catch" two wives,' he replied.
>
> 'You're a lucky bloke,' I said. 'I only catch one wife.'
>
> Then he replied, 'Master, not so lucky – plenty wives, plenty palaver!'

Due to the climate, little work was done in the afternoons:

> We used to get up at about 6.15 a.m. and be at work by 7 a.m. I had, what we might call, a big surgery of African soldiers followed by wives and children – seeing perhaps

forty or so people, but I had the help of the African medical orderlies, and it was all well organised. I even had a ward and a little laboratory in the medical centre and a trained laboratory attendant who was an expert at looking at blood slides down the microscope, and he could tell me if a person had malaria, or anaemia, or other blood disorders and he would also examine urine and stool specimens.

If someone was without any leading symptoms, my laboratory technician would usually provide clues as to what was wrong and I could then give the treatment. Malaria, dysentery – in its different types – anaemia, pneumonia, and a host of tropical diseases, made for an interesting life as a doctor. And of course, I had a fair bit of casualty and stitching work, whilst I also enjoyed doing small operations.

I was fortunate in having the nearby presence and help of Enugu Hospital and I kept in touch with the doctors and was on good terms – which helped me greatly. I remember creating a stir by diagnosing acute appendicitis with our Regimental Sergeant Major, sending him to the civilian hospital in Enugu for his operation.

Eighteen months in Nigeria did not pass without a few funny stories:

When I started, I had a job communicating with the African soldiers. They had their own different language – according to their tribe, but they all had the same Pidgin-English which I got used to, eventually. One day, whilst doing the sick parade, I saw a soldier with tummy ache, and I wanted to know if he had diarrhoea, and when I asked him, he just looked at me blankly. With so many waiting to be seen, the African sergeant, helping me to make progress, said, 'Leave it to me, Sir.' Then he said to the soldier, 'Leester, soldier, the master, he say 'You go Sh**um too much?' . . . And the soldier shook his head!

I learnt a lot from the technician and he was important also in the Freedom from Infection (F.F.I.) Inspection, which was really a venereal disease check. This consisted of seeing about fifteen soldiers per day in a line without their trousers on. There was no such thing as AIDS at the time, and we were interested in finding gonorrhoea or syphilis, both being easily cured with a shot of penicillin.

I learnt that some men went to a brothel down the road. I never actually visited the brothel myself, but I invited the ladies to come and see me – only for examination, of course! Some were in a poor old state with venereal disease, and I injected them with penicillin and they came OK, our V.D. rate quickly dropping.

There was a quaint rule that if a chap had V.D. often, he had to be reported to the senior officer, and this duly happened with one of the soldiers, who was marched into the C.O.'s office with me following behind. And when the C.O. turned to me, I put in a word of defence for the soldier. I explained that soldiers more or less had to go to the brothel, and I had sent for the ladies to treat them – whereupon the officer concerned, who was a rough diamond, but with a soft heart, asked me what sort of state the ladies were in. And I replied, 'In a pretty poor state, Sir' and he turned to the soldier and said, 'I can't understand you chaps. You put your ***** where I wouldn't put my walking stick!' I was quite amused at what he said and I've always remembered it!'

Dr Penn mentioned that he was ever mindful of mosquitoes breeding in the water and this meant making time to inspect the cook house, latrines and the areas alongside the African living quarters – ensuring that puddles of water were displaced or covered with oil. And he also made time for hockey:

> At the end of the morning at about 2 p.m., I'd go up to the Officer's Mess for lunch – and then I'd go to my chalet for a lie down and a sleep, this being the warmest and most humid part of the day. At about 4.30 p.m., I'd get ready for hockey. We had a game almost every day and I played in the Battalion Team, and we used to take it quite seriously. It was a hard game, but I was thankful that we didn't have to play rugby, because the climate was so warm and sticky and the ground so hard.
>
> After hockey, I'd have a cold bath, dress into the 'after dark' attire and then go over to the Officer's Mess for the evening meal and for one or two tankards of lager. The main difference between me and the officers was that I was always on call, and I was frequently called to the Medical Centre for some reason or other, day or night.
>
> Weekends were a bit different. On Saturday evenings we used to go to the European Club in Enugu and have a film show or chat with the civilians there, and have one or two drinks.
>
> On Sunday mornings we went to the Garrison's African Church: quite an experience with the Africans singing and almost dancing to the hymns. Then we were expected to go to the range for shooting practice. There'd be a special curry lunch in the officer's mess to which our civilian friends were invited and in the evening we'd go to the European Church.
>
> Although I was all the time longing to come home, I have to say that my posting to West Africa proved to be a rich and happy experience, for which I was really grateful.

The Road to Dolycwrt – and Good Times with Dr Gibbin

P EGGY COULDN'T WAIT to see Dr Penn's plane safely land-
ing, and joined him at Aldershot for his last two months
in the army. After his long spell in the tropics, Captain Penn
was quickly reintroduced to Britain's winter weather: time
to stock up with coal and logs for the open fire which burnt
brightly into the night at their new military home. Next stop
was Leonard Street, Neath, where his main priority was to
find work. This meant scouring the medical journals and
magazines for suitable appointments and writing to professional bodies for openings. Being familiar with mining in the
Brynmenyn area he enquired at the Labour Department of
the National Coal Board's South Western Division regarding
the position of medical officer, receiving the following reply:

> At present there are no vacancies for Medical Officers
> in this division. However, I would inform you that
> vacancies do occur from time to time in all the divisions
> of the National Coal Board and these are advertised in the
> medical journals and appropriate local press.
>
> I might tell you that consideration has been given to the
> appointment of Area Assistant Medical Officers, which is
> the kind of post that might be suitable for you as a young
> doctor . . .

The letter asked for Dr Penn's particulars, which was encouraging and helpful – although not the perfect welcome home he had hoped for. However, there was soon an opening in West Wales, where due to ill health, Dr Trevor George Davies needed help at his practice in Adpar, Newcastle Emlyn. Dr Davies was a senior doctor who qualified in Cardiff and St Bartholomew's in 1927, the year that Dr Penn was born. He was highly respected in the locality and was formerly a Surgeon Lieutenant in the Royal Navy.

Newcastle Emlyn – on the border between Carmarthenshire and Cardiganshire and within a few miles of Cenarth Falls and the coast – was almost too good to be true. Assisting Dr Davies as a locum suited Dr Penn perfectly. It meant being on call day and night, but the experience was rewarding and the patients, mostly Welsh-speaking, were friendly. Peggy made a comfortable home in a town-centre flat, where they were in easy reach of patients, and after five months they wanted nothing more than to stay in Newcastle Emlyn for good as Dr Penn explains:

> We liked being there so much that it was almost a disappointment seeing the doctor getting better and no longer requiring my services! However, we were equally lucky with me finding a post in General Practice in Whitland.
>
> I heard that Dr Phillip Gibbin was looking for an assistant – so I shot over to apply and was thrilled to get the job.
>
> I was assistant to Dr Gibbin and Dr Gwynne Evans – taking the place of a doctor who had left to be on his own in a single-handed practice.

Dr Penn was highly impressed with Dr Gibbin, a man who had held prestigious medical appointments before arriving in Whitland in the early 1930s to assist the late Dr William David Owen. Likewise, Dr Evans was a really positive influence, a military man who was stationed overseas in the Second World War: also a true character who related well to the country people of this practice. Dr Penn took an immediate liking to Dolycwrt surgery: a traditional stone-built building, with driveway, and a garden that extended down to the river Gronw. He knew that this is where medicine had been practised in the days of the horse and cart, when the first doctor mixed herbal compounds and performed major surgery, sometimes under the dim light of oil lamps.

Of course medicine had moved on in leaps and bounds since then and was ever changing and ever improving. In the local newspaper, the *Carmarthen Journal*, during these same early weeks of September 1955, Dr Penn saw the headline 'Urgent need for Blood Donors.' This report stated that Carmarthen, traditionally well blessed with donors, was now experiencing less interest since a National Transfusion Service had been put in place aided by local centres. Amongst new ideas to attract donors:

> . . . a suggestion was made that appeals from the pulpit should be made in all the places of worship in Carmarthen and district.[5]
>
> Dr Hugh Lewis-Philipps, Llanboidy, who presided, said that during the last war hundreds of lives had been saved in the Western Desert because there was a blood bank out there. 'Lives could be saved in hospitals today with a readily available supply of blood,' he said.

With doctors now working for the National Health Service, Dr Penn was lucky in not having to invoice patients, as his

---

5 *Carmarthen Journal*, September 23rd, 1955

two colleagues had done in earlier years. For a person as naturally kind and generous as Dr Penn, this might have brought problems. Mel Jenkins of Whitland has two stories to share about the new doctor in town:

> When I was young I fell off a horse and had a nasty cut on my face. I needed stitches and I phoned Dolycwrt and Dr Gibbin answered the phone. 'Dere lawr i'r feddygfa,' he said in Welsh. 'Come down to the surgery.' He explained that the 'new doctor' would look after me, because he had been called elsewhere. Dr Penn took me into the old nurses' room and he looked after me well. I do believe that this was the first bit of stitching Dr Penn did in Dolycwrt. And there was certainly no sign of my wound in later weeks.
>
> On another occasion, he came up to Glandŵr to see my parents. Our home was on the side of a hill, so Dr Penn had some narrow roads to travel along that day, then a long walk down the lane. But this didn't worry him; he was enjoying himself, as if he had all the time in the world. When he arrived, he stood at the front door admiring the view. 'Well,' he said, 'this is what heaven must be like: a long journey – but, when you arrive, something special.'

After occupying a few rooms at Dolycwrt as a temporary home, he and Peggy moved into Ivy House, Spring Gardens, at a time when Elizabeth, their eldest daughter, was born. Then, two years later, they moved into a semi-detached house in Bryngwenllian, a modern estate on the outskirts of Whitland, where Dr Penn was probably the first person to use a motor car. He left his mark in other ways too. The late Alan John explained:

> In those days everybody was growing vegetables. It wasn't long after war rations had ended, and Dr Penn was no

different, even planting potatoes in the front of the house. I also know that Dr Penn had steps laid on the gentle rise leading into the back garden – besides being the first to have a telephone in the estate.

Only a couple of doors away, Albert Jenkins, known as Nick, and his wife and family could not help noticing Dr Penn coming and going, also being called out occasionally at night. Their son, Tim, recalls the time:

> I remember Dr Penn going around in his Triumph Herald car. It was very sporty and modern at the time, with a collapsible roof. Dr Penn was setting the trend; we were all very fond of that car. And Dr Penn was fantastic too: always smiling and helpful and considerate to everyone.
>
> At the time, I remember Mrs Hughes, Eric's mother, having a television set, and every Friday night, after school, we all went over to watch Robin Hood, this being the first T.V. to arrive in Bryngwenllian. Then on Sunday afternoon, half of the estate walked down to the Church Hall for Sunday school. We sometimes saw Dr Penn driving past, waving to us, with a toot of his horn as he went by.

In 1958 Dr Evans moved from Dolycwrt to take up a Regional Health Board appointment. He had worked with Dr Gibbin for almost twenty years and his departure heralded the break-up of their successful team. It also created an opportunity for Dr Penn to be made a partner, as his mother so dearly wished and as he now recalls:

> I remember, with a quake, Dr Gibbin meeting my mother, who was a terrific character, and all she was asking was, 'When are you going to make my son a partner – because I'd like you to know that they are calling out loud for him in Cardiff.' I didn't know which way to look or to turn!

This is the moment that Beatrice's wish came true – the two doctors later employing Dr David Bayton for a while, before a former college friend of Dr Penn, Dr John Merrell, joined them. These were thoroughly stimulating days for Dr Penn who learnt greatly from Dr Gibbin, a highly respected physician and also a Fellow of the Royal College of Surgeons. He had nothing but praise for his senior partner, to whom he often referred in later years:

> It was a rich experience being with Dr Gibbin. He was a real country man and a real country doctor. He was thoroughly Welsh – Welsh-speaking and steeped in everything Welsh. He set out to make me believe that Whitland was the best place on earth – and I believe he succeeded!
>
> Dr Gibbin also had an eye for business. He used to tell me not to worry about going thin on top. 'That's worth a thousand pounds a year to you,' he used to say.
>
> I was amazed one day when my daughter, Elizabeth, was ill. Dr Gibbin came to see her and he performed a ventriloquist's act, asking Elizabeth why she had a cat in the bed – to which she replied that she hadn't. Then he made some noises that seemed to indicate that there was a cat there after all.

Doctors Gibbin and Penn had a lot in common and their partnership seemed destined to last. They were often seen together at community events, speaking publicly side by side, sometimes having liaised about their intended speeches. However, December 1959 saw the Dolycwrt practice struck by a bolt from the blue: Dr Gibbin was taken seriously ill and died shortly afterwards. Christmas 1959 was a time of shock and sorrow in Whitland and West Wales, one that few people forgot. And as the senior partner, Dr Penn was left holding the reigns at Dolycwrt.

PART VII

SENIOR PARTNER AT DOLYCWRT

A Thoroughly Modern Man – and a Hobby called 'Hillside'

DESPITE HIS SADNESS, Dr Penn was able to write an obituary for his former partner which was published in the *British Medical Journal* in early 1960. It was a truly outstanding tribute, one highlighting an amazing career and life and demonstrating a deep respect for the late doctor. There would be difficult years ahead, but Dr Penn could respond to the challenge knowing that he had won the confidence of his predecessor as local resident Brian Cook explained:

> As a family we used to see a lot of Dr Gibbin. He was a man of terrific presence and he and his wife, Mamie, used to come along to family weddings and parties. I know for a fact that he was very fond of George Penn – not only because he was a good and hardworking doctor, but because he saw the future of his practice safe in his hands.

Commendations such as this strengthened Dr Penn's roots in Whitland. Just as his father, Captain Penn had lowered his ship's anchors as he came into port, so his son prepared to secure his foothold in Whitland. Dr Penn knew that writing his name onto the deeds of Hillside with Peggy effectively committed him to the town. Beatrice thought they were mad – not for deciding to stay, or for buying a house, but for buying such a large house. Hillside is no ordinary residence but a commanding property with spacious grounds, lawns, outbuildings and, at the time, a four acre field. Maintaining the property would be a full-time hobby in its own right.

In buying Hillside at the age of thirty-three, Dr Penn was thankful for the help and accommodation of Kemes Morris, the popular local Lloyds Bank manager, for a smooth transaction that pleased all parties concerned. The vendor at the time was Ebenezer Evans, known as 'Eben,' who had recently built a bungalow in the corner of Hillside's field. It was reassuring having Eben and his wife as neighbours, as well as Jack Roberts and his young family at Llwyndrissi farm next door up. Dr Penn had taken note of how Dr Gibbin once farmed the fields around his impressive home, Hafodwen – and he, likewise, wanted to try his luck. Jack Roberts helped him along, but Dr Penn's first priority was his medical work.

Now a two-man team, Doctors Penn and Merrell were already hard-pushed when they were hit further by Dr Merrell becoming unwell. Although locums, whenever available, were called for, and a request for a third partner was made to the health authorities, Dr Penn was, at certain times, running the practice alone. But possessed of boundless energy and great determination, he never complained, instead making life easier by investing in a telephone-radio system linking him to Dolycwrt when on his rounds. This was Dr Merrell's good idea, but Dr Penn, now a thoroughly modern man, needed little persuasion – initially moving the equipment to the higher ground of Tavernspite to attract a better signal. Not far away in Glamorgan, members of his ever-supportive family were in full approval, believing that he was setting a trend for country G.P.s. This is what Dr Penn's Auntie Mattie, a school teacher, wrote when, interestingly, Beatrice was enjoying Hillside so much that she couldn't keep away:

Dear George, Peggy and Beatrice (if you are still there),

In today's paper, I see a Swansea doctor is described as a pioneer in Wales for using a radio-telephone in his car. I have written to the manager of the *Western Mail* and said this is not so – as Dr George Kempton Penn, of Whitland has been using one for the past year. I wasn't certain of my facts, so they might want to verify this. You'll be on T.V. next, but I didn't want the Swansea doctor to steal your thunder ...

Ray Vaughan, who lived in Login before settling in Whitland, was equally observant:

I often used to see Dr Penn on his rounds. He had two big masts coming out of his Triumph Herald, one of which handled his walkie-talkie system. Although I wasn't then his patient – everybody knew Dr Penn because he was so helpful.

It was around this time that my son was home from Trinity College. He was feeling not at all well and I happened to believe that Dr Penn was attending a concert in the nearby primary school. He was supporting all the local events, so I guessed he might be there. At the door, I asked a gentleman if Dr Penn could be interrupted. In no time, he came out to have a few words. He was that sort of person; he couldn't do enough for us all.

Back in Dolycwrt, in the summer months of 1962, there was good news about a third doctor joining the practice. This was Dr Malcolm Holding who made his entrance at a time when rail cuts were threatening to chop the Cardi Bach railway into pieces. This was a small passenger and goods service that had run from Whitland to Cardigan for the best part of a century. It was still important for bringing patients from the countryside in the north of the practice to Dolycwrt, and Dr Penn was sickened by the thought of its closure. In every spare moment away from medicine he campaigned to keep the line open – although, after a big battle, he was eventually defeated. Brynmor Thomas, on official duty at Llanglydwen station on Saturday September 8th 1962, when the last passenger train made its way to Whitland, explains:

> I was twenty at the time and I was handling the signals and the crossing gates, making sure that it was safe for the train to pass through. That day the carriages were packed; there were photographers and train-spotters on the platform and people everywhere. It was an historic day. It was also a sad occasion, especially for Dr Penn.
>
> He had been campaigning hard to keep the line open, persuading people to support the railway. He urged patients, everyone, to jump aboard, to use the service, to prove that the railway was needed. He wrote to the local papers, tackled the railway authorities. He knew that we were losing something special, something unique; a part of our heritage was disappearing.

Dr Penn was on this last train, busily taking photographs and gathering cine-camera footage: a beaten force and still smarting about the decision, although his deep sadness was concealed under a cloak of outer calmness. But, when he later read the newspapers, he was saddened even more. This line had been opened towards the end of the last century amidst great excitement, when the stations were decorated with bright floral arrangements. Those early times marked the dawn of a bright new day, the start of an exciting voyage – but now this ending brought the emptiness of community bereavement. Everybody felt the hurt, and the Mayor of Cardigan's words, found amongst Dr Penn's newspaper cuttings, said so much:

There were no banquets, no dinners and no brass bands to mark this closure. Yet, in 1886 the Mayor and Corporation, supported by the volunteer brass band and accompanied by one-hundred tradesmen, proceeded to Cardigan station to greet the first train into the town.

This is indeed a sad occasion for us all. We fought hard to keep the railway, but the battle was lost.

If there was one thing that Dr Penn drew from this defeat, it was the warm feeling of satisfaction in knowing that he had given his all, despite considerable medical demands. But he also realised that there might be a silver lining in this darkest cloud. Just as players of a beaten rugby or football team take comfort from the final whistle, hoping for a rematch – so also did Dr Penn draw relief from the final blast of the steam engine's whistle in Whitland. The rail tracks were staying for a freight service to continue, so there remained a chance that the line could be reopened at a future date.

In the meantime, Dr Penn launched himself into medicine with a vengeance. He gave his time generously in a manner that was winning respect and endearment from all corners of his practice. Despite being a thoroughly modern man, he was a doctor steeped in the traditional and well-founded older values of his profession. In fact, ever since beginning general practice work, he had offered himself to patients as though he was the medicine itself. He had taken heed of an unidentified newspaper article he once read, suggesting that 'doctors' were the 'best drug' available:

Dr Harold Maxwell, of London, says, 'The principle drug which I use is, I like to think, myself. Dr B. Y. Marshall, Bletchingley, Surrey, adds, 'The good old-fashioned bedside manner, given the chance today, would be just as effective and far less costly for the nation.'

'Time with the patient is still the favourite and most needed prescription of any G.P.,' says Dr B. H. Pentney, of London. 'Encouragement, sympathy, listening to the patient, and above-all reassurance are potent therapeutic weapons,' says Dr J. D. E. Knox, of Edinburgh.

If Dr Penn was the medicine – and many patients say he was – he packed punch and strength into his particular pills and potent mixtures. Day after day he put in a long shift before returning home to Hillside for Peggy and his now, three children, Roger, Sarah and Elizabeth. It is there in his spare time and days off that he enjoyed cutting lawns, trimming bushes, attacking brambles and growing vegetables – especially onions, his favourite. They occupied the most fertile bed in Hillside's delightful 'kitchen' garden. And, when the time arrived for harvesting these whoppers, Dr Penn placed them onto large corrugated sheets, before sliding these onto the small pig sty roof to dry in the overhead sun. Of all the garden offerings, onions had the most attention – always.

Since arriving in Whitland, Dr Penn and Peggy had taken every opportunity to drive down to the beach to catch a glimpse of the sea. Amroth was a regular choice, being near to home, but Tenby was the ultimate treat. Of course, being the son of a sea captain meant that Dr Penn valued the bracing sea air blowing through his lungs, and by just strolling along the Esplanade, admiring Caldey Island across the waves, his batteries were recharged. In these new surroundings, the sea invigorated Dr Penn in the same way that the 'Old Road' to Llangeinor had once inspired him so much.

Soon, the weekly family outings to Tenby led to overnight stays and then to extended breaks, weaved delicately into Dr Penn's packed itinerary. Peggy reminds us of one such occasion on the back of a large postcard of Tenby's Castle

Hill, entitled 'Our Tenby Holiday 1962.' Describing their visits to Saundersfoot and Penally, and to the shops where 'we bought Roger a new fawn-coat, George a new hat and Elizabeth a new drawing book', Peggy mentions the family and friends who joined them for their stay. 'George's mother, and Mattie, Margot and their friend, Florence, came to visit us,' she says, and 'Gwyn and Enid [Peggy's brother and wife] met us on the beach.' Then Peggy's mother and sister, Glenys, arrived, before Eddie Evans, the Whitland, chemist called with his wife. There were garden parties to attend, visits to the pictures, people coming, going and staying with regularity – and this was exactly how Dr Penn and Peggy enjoyed life, always amongst people.

Interestingly, that week Dr Penn did some gardening at Hillside, before returning to Tenby for more boat trips and excursions, often aboard vessels such as the *Tenby Enterprise* which went further out to sea. Ever the adventurer, it was now time to have a little boat of his own: *Phyllis*, a small rowing vessel, but powered by a modest, and often ineffective, petrol engine. Dr Penn invited friends to join him at Saundersfoot, where *Phyllis* was moored, for mini excursions up the coastline. Dr Malcolm Holding, who had become a partner at Dolycwrt after Dr Merrell's departure for a new medical appointment, remembers the time:

We liked to meet after work on a calm evening to do some mackerel fishing. We enjoyed going out as far as Monkstone Point, unless we were late setting off, when we didn't go quite so far. Sometimes, there were eight of us in the boat, because George tended to invite so many people along. There was only a small engine and, when it cut-out, there was usually no way of restarting it. Often we'd have to take it in turns to row back to the harbour. All of this was a lot of fun, but it also took up a great deal of time. In the end, George decided to give the boat away because of all his other interests.

Dr Jim Moody of Cardiff, husband of Dr Penn's cousin, Janet, can also remember these days. They used to enjoy travelling to Tenby when on holiday to meet Dr Penn and Peggy. 'I went in George's boat,' explained Jim, 'but we had difficulties. Luckily, we weren't far from the shore, because I seem to remember swimming back!'

Nobody could forget these mini-voyages aboard *Phyllis*, and one occasion also lived on in Dr Penn's memories – when he, Peggy and the family were staying in the Beauchief Guest House, opposite Tenby harbour.

True to form, Dr Penn ventured out to sea one afternoon, however, this time he ventured alone. After a while the engine failed, causing Dr Penn to take to the oars. In all probability, he was a little too far from the shore for comfort, and he tried to claw his way back quietly, the hard way. This was proving to be a challenge for him, which did not escape the notice of a man in charge of a much larger boat nearby.

'Do you want a lift, old boy?' he bellowed out, in Sergeant Major-like fashion.

'No, I think I'll be alright, thank you,' replied Dr Penn.

'Think you'll be alright?' he replied in amazement. 'For heaven's sake, man – take a hold of this rope!'

With both reluctance and part-appreciation, Dr Penn allowed himself the comfort of being pulled back towards Tenby – feeling thankful, and relieved, but highly embarrassed, too. He felt that he had been mildly 'shown-up': something that he tried not to do to others. His pride as a successful army medical captain and senior practitioner in Whitland had been dented. He didn't need to be treated like a schoolboy, thank you. He couldn't wait to give the man his rope back, bid him farewell and hope not to see him again – but he was out of luck.

That night, as Dr Penn ate his evening meal with Peggy, his ears pricked up when he heard a man on the next table talking about his great 'sea rescue' that day. Looking for a sharp exit, Dr Penn discreetly shifted the angle of his chair, so as to give himself the best chance of remaining unidentified – but his heart sank to the floor at the sound of a familiar voice,

'Hold on a minute, it was you . . . wasn't it! You're the fellow in the boat!'

He had been spotted.

PART VIII

COMMUNITY WORK

Rugby's Proud President – and the Start of 'Whitland Week'

SCHOOLING AT BUSHEY had taught the young Dr Penn the meaning of giving respect, particularly to his elders. In those distant days he learnt greatly from conversations with experienced, worldly-wise individuals. This continued throughout medical school to days at Dolycwrt, where Dr Gibbin was another wise counsellor. Now, in the early 1960s, Dr Penn had also grown to respect a doctor who lived and practised medicine at Llanboidy. This was Dr Hugh William Lewis-Philipps, who was to become a big influence, friend and terrific help to Dr Penn for the next fifteen years and more. In truth, the bond went further: Dr Penn never knew his father, and Dr Hugh Philipps (as he was known) had lost his son. To a great extent, this was, most certainly, a father-son relationship.

Dr Hugh Philipps qualified in medicine at Guy's Hospital London in 1926, the same year he competed on the grass tennis courts of Wimbledon. Although not advancing far in the competition this former Captain in the R.A.M.C. was, nevertheless, a talented sportsman who, earlier in his career, was House Surgeon and Casualty Officer at Swansea General Hospital. He resided in the beautiful old mansion of Clyngwynne amongst towering tall trees, steep banks and large lawns, looking down across the gentle rolling hills to Llanboidy's little village a mile away. He lived and breathed medicine, which was his chief passion throughout the course of his long life.

When Dr Penn arrived at Dolycwrt, Dr Hugh Philipps was High Sheriff of Carmarthen,[6] and had raised the local blood donor issues mentioned earlier. He was a shining light for Dr Penn to follow, and their lives overlapped considerably. First and foremost he became a ready, willing and able locum, freeing Dr Penn for the committee meetings and public engagements that were already cluttering his non-medical life. They were also comrades in an active British Legion branch, and their general goals, aspirations and attitudes were similar. Only a few years earlier, Dr Hugh Philipps had been President of Whitland Rugby Club and, upon his retirement from this office, it is not surprising that Dr Penn soon took his place.

Of course, Dr Penn was never an outright rugby man, although he had 'played a bit' as the local boys say modestly. He had taken the bumps and bruises over the years, gladly surrendering the playing days of his life for greater enjoyment in other, less physically demanding community ventures. But Dr Penn acknowledged the importance of rugby to Whitland, recognising the immense lift the local boys gave his adopted town when successful. In his three-year term as President of Whitland Rugby Club, which began in September 1961, he was anxious to lend his weight to the acquisition of a new club house. With a progressive committee and talented, hungry players, the time was right for the club to have its own headquarters – and Caxton House, King Edward Street, fitted the bill.

6   *Carmarthen Journal*, December 24th 1976.

On a dry, but overcast September day in 1963, a strong crowd of committeemen gathered for a photograph outside the new building as Osmond John, District Representative of the Welsh Rugby Union, was given the key to the door. Later that same day, a celebration match took place at Parc Dr Owen, which saw Pembrokeshire beating Whitland by seventeen points to three. Usually, such a result as this would have dampened local spirits, but the town was determined to celebrate, with an evening of entertainment and food. Enjoying the occasion amongst the large crowd was the *Western Telegraph*'s news reporter who explained that the building had been totally refurbished by a willing band of helpers. Here are his words, appearing in the paper's edition of September 5th 1963:

> To face-lift the premises in such an outstanding way must have demanded much time, hard work and skill, and the finished product is a credit to all concerned.

The article stated that the Mary Immaculate School Band from Haverfordwest was in attendance and, as regards the new President:

> Dr Penn spoke of his pride in the honour of being President, and of having the privilege of introducing Mr John. He referred to the spirit and comradeship that existed within the club.

Whitland's Brian Cook, mentioned earlier, was part of this major breakthrough for the 'rugger boys' and explained the part that Dr Penn played:

> George was very much the main leader. He knew that having the premises was right for the Club and he drove the idea forward. If he believed in something passionately,

he was like a tiger. He wouldn't let go – not once he had got his teeth into it. The club house was cosy; there were several rooms and open fires. People gathered there and George loved it as it was. Then the consensus of opinion was to expand it, to make it a bigger more modern place. I don't think George was in favour of this idea.

John Llewellyn agreed:

I was Secretary at the time and I used to write to George about the arrangements for the forthcoming season as soon as the summer came to an end. Of course, he didn't have time to follow all the matches, but he came along to quite a few of them. Sometimes he brought his cine-camera, and he was always cheering the boys on.

I also know that he wasn't happy about some of the renovation work at Caxton House. When he knew that a sledge hammer was used on the old fire places to remove them, he was mad about this. These were nice tiled fire places, old things; he wanted to keep them.

Over the next few years, Dr Penn was thrilled to see Whitland's rising rugby team enjoying continued success, and he attended the high-profile Annual Dinners – often held at the Amroth Arms or the Ivy Bush in Carmarthen – where Carwyn James, the famous British Lions coach of the later 1971 tour, and Terry Davies, of Llanelli, Wales and the British Lions, were among the guest speakers. He often called at Caxton House to join in the fun, as well as visiting this same venue for committee meetings of the Parc Dr Owen 'Festival Week', soon renamed 'Whitland Week'.

The concept of 'Whitland Week' interested Dr Penn greatly: the committee's functions being to raise money for the park's upkeep and then improvement. The family of the late Dr

William David Owen of Dolycwrt had left this vast acreage of prime green grassland in the heart of Whitland in trust to the townspeople. This was an amazing act of generosity in an era associated with great benevolence; and Dr Penn was determined to honour his predecessor's best intentions by bringing special entertainment to the park, whilst also improving facilities by providing swings, roundabouts and such attractions for the children.

From a standing start there was an immense amount of ground to cover for this newly formed committee. Nevertheless, a varied programme was put in place in time for Saturday, August 29th 1964. This was when a 'Six a Side' Knock-out Cricket Competition kicked-off a busy week – and a new era – with a 'Big Day' scheduled for the following Saturday, later known as 'Carnival Day'. In the following autumn, arrangements were made for the next year's entertainment, and, shortly afterwards, Dr Penn became secretary, an office that he held on to for sixteen years until 1981. For a man who worked hard and played hard, the tremendous effort required attracting quality talent and entertainment into the town over succeeding years was his 'play.' He never tired of his efforts: a refreshing experience away from the medical matters that claimed most of his time.

One of the original '1964 Committee' was Fred Merriman of Dursley House, Whitland who, besides running an ironmongers business, sold tractor machinery and petrol at his busy premises in St John Street. 'Freddie' as he was affectionately known, worked hard for the town, but he also found time for the park as Richard, his son, explains:

> To get my father involved in the first place, I think there was a bit of gentle arm-twisting by Dr Penn, probably over a glass of whisky in the Yelverton Hotel on a Saturday

night. Dr Penn was like that; he was usually the leader of the gang. He was persuasive; people couldn't say no to him. As a small committee, they had a lot of fun – and with Dr Penn and my father together, they got up to a bit of mischief, too. When Dad walked out of the door for a Whitland Week meeting, that was the last we saw of him for the day. We said 'Good night,' knowing that he would usually be late returning.

It was never a big committee, but everyone worked hard. Members wanted to provide entertainment for everyone, with lots of variety; events were discussed and planned in great detail. When it came to the actual 'Week', it was a full time effort; there wasn't a minute to spare. In those days, I often went along with my father to help – collecting chairs from the schools, arranging them for a concert, finding volunteers, that sort of thing. After an event, the halls had to be restored to order: cleaned, tidied and made presentable again. There was a lot of running around to do: the 'Week' being the highlight of Whitland's social calendar. Of course, Dr Penn was in the middle of it all; he was the coordinator.

I can remember the carnivals from a young age. There'd be parachute jumps, tug-o-war, miniature railways, children's bands, marquees and a number of other attractions. We'd also have pony rides, ice cream vans, various stalls and fancy-dress competitions. The President of the 'Week' opened the event, and the carnival queens and attendants were always the centre of attraction. Later in the evening we had firework displays, and barbecues. Then the Carnival Dance took off, and we'd hear music blasting away, late into the night.

It was not long before a little more 'gentle arm-twisting' saw

Dr Penn's colleague, Dr Malcolm Holding, getting involved:

> George really carried the torch for Parc Dr Owen – and I
> remember when he made me a partner, he suggested that
> I give a donation to the park funds. 'You could, if you like,
> make a donation,' he said to me. So the first £100 of my
> pay increase went to George's committee. Later I became
> a trustee, so we both shared the best of intentions for the
> park.

In the Minute Books, Dr Penn's hurried notes capture every
detail of the committee's on-going plans. In readiness for
carnival day, dignitaries from neighbouring towns were
invited to judge competitions; local groups were persuaded
not to compete or clash with events; and traders were invited
to set up stalls. Cooperation and help came from all corners of
the community, as an overall sense of unity and togetherness
prevailed. Seeing everybody gelling as one – working for,
and enjoying, the Week – pleased Dr Penn, who knew that
everything else would fall into place. Here is a typical minute
from one of the earlier meetings that he attended:

TUG-O-WAR ACROSS THE RIVER

Mr Wills reported that Mr Rhodri Thomas had been
approached about organising this [event] and seemed
quite prepared to do so. Several suggestions were put
forward – that there be a container of beer as a first prize;
that every person competing be guaranteed a pint of beer,
and that possible teams might be: the Rugby Club, Angling
Club, Young Farmers Club, and the Dairies, Farmers, and
Railways.

Another early committee member was Les Evans, who has
fond memories of the Jalopy Races, staged at Trevaughan
Meadows, being himself one of the brave men to take part:

I remember being as nervous as anything. The adrenalin was flowing around inside me. The noise was terrific, because we didn't have exhaust boxes, and the fumes were heavy, too. Crowds of local people came along, and Dr Penn brought boys down from Cardigan, Lampeter, Llansteffan and Llanybri. He seemed to have contacts everywhere; he knew how to draw the crowds. A lot of the spectators came for the spills. I was lucky; I only had one upside-down-job, and I came away from it unhurt.

After a few years, we had Motor Bikes and Side-Cars as well as Jalopies, and I remember Dr Penn inviting competitors from Blaenwaun. One day, a member of the gang didn't have anyone to join him in the sidecar.

'Would you mind getting in with me?' I was asked.

'I don't mind, if you go easily,' I replied.

Go easily, my word; there was none of that. At every bend I was hanging out of the side, stopping us both from tipping over. It frightened me stiff; that was not a nice experience.

Les added his personal weight to a committee whose steady progress brought one success after another. Having laid the foundation for the 'Week', with local events like concerts, film shows, and cricket and rugby matches, the committee soon began to attract crowds to Whitland for a feast of more selective entertainment. Wrestling, Mohican displays, Skydivers all featured – whilst the Dagenham Girl Pipers, the London Irish Girls Band, and the Moody Blues thrilled audiences. As for celebrities, Richard Burton, Harry Secombe and Sir Francis Chichester all received invitations from Dr Penn, whilst *Coronation Street*'s Bernard Youens and Jean Alexander (Stan and Hilda Ogden), Julie Goodyear (Bet Lynch) and Pat Phoenix (Elsie Tanner) thrilled the crowd by making the journey. This was undoubtedly the beginning of a special era in the town and, throughout, Dr Penn would be a major driving force.

A Visit to Blenheim Palace –
and a spot of Farming

IN JANUARY 1965, an event took place which saddened the world at large, whilst helping to shape the future of a certain young doctor in West Wales. The death of Sir Winston Churchill – a visitor to Whitland[7] during the Blitz of 1941 – added a touch more steel and courage to the often outspoken, but sometimes still shy, Dr George Penn. From this sad moment onwards, Dr Penn undertook an internal metamorphosis of a kind which caused him to batten down the hatches, harden his resolve and stand bolt-upright for his country as, on a far greater world stage, Mr Churchill himself had done. At home in Hillside, Dr Penn digested every word of the national newspapers covering this ground-breaking news – part of a slow process of absorption and digestion that added the missing ingredient to his already strong make-up – 'Menace!'

This was a time when Fleet Street and its global contemporaries went to town on the finer details of Sir Winston's life and deeds with the most amazing glowing tributes. In our own *Western Mail*, the headlines for Monday January 25th 1965 read 'A Time of Shared Grief – World Mourns Sir Winston'. Later, in this same extraordinary week, reminders of his amazing legacy surfaced in every conceivable column – the *Daily Telegraph* reporting that world leaders had arrived

7   Roger G. K. Penn, *Dolycwrt – The Days of a Country Doctor's Surgery* (Gomer, 2011) p. 108.

for the funeral. It is not known whether Dr Penn travelled to London to see his hero lying-in-state in Westminster Hall – although this is highly likely – but if he happened to be in surgery or visiting patients on funeral day, his thoughts were not far away from the extraordinary scenes that gripped the eyes and ears of the world.

It was during Dr Penn's days of sickness at Bushey that Winston Churchill first came to the attention of young George Penn. Seeing the leader hardening British resolve in the face of greatly superior military manpower and might was enthralling. And it surpassed the benefits of the most special brand of balsam that the proud medical profession had ever, or could ever, produce. For Dr Penn, it was as simple as that.

Not far away in Cardiff, his mother felt just the same:

Dear George,

Since having a telephone, I seem to have gone-off letter writing – but now I am going to write.

No doubt, you heard the news at 9 a.m. yesterday, as I did, and it made me quite sad, as I felt I had lost such a wonderful leader. My mind went back to the war days when there was a huge air raid on Cardiff, and I had to walk from Albany Road for night duty because there were no buses or taxis out. As I walked along Cathedral Road with only male wardens to be seen, they kept saying, 'Take care, madam.' It was such a gorgeous night, with the moon out, and I kept thinking, Who am I to waste a bomb on? If Mr Churchill can stick it – surely, I can, too.

Then again, he came to Cardiff to see the war damage, and passed the Wyndham while I was there. We were closed in the afternoon, so I went out to see him. I rushed to the car and told the police, 'I want to touch him.' He was my hero, and now he is dead. I have followed his illness every day. Yesterday, I had the BBC television on all day, to have every scrap of news about him. I hope Elizabeth and Roger saw Harrow School Boys in their chapel, which I thought was splendid, especially when they sung *All Through the Night.*

Wonderful tributes were paid in his memory last night and I felt proud that he was an English gentleman. I am awfully glad that Neville took me to Blenheim Palace, and we saw his bed, etc. It is a wonderful place and well worth a visit.

A former Lord Mayor of Cardiff, who presented Sir Winston with the Freedom of the City, was on the wireless today saying that it is his proudest memory. He is the person who has brought me home and taken me to work a couple of times since my illness, being old friends of Mrs Mathias and living opposite now.

Beatrice ended the letter offering her support, as she always did:

Well George, I hope things with you are looking rosy, and that everything is alright. Don't forget, that if I can help or advise you in any way – I am only delighted to do so. Nobody knows your business except yourself. So you must have time and peace and quiet to work things out. I have no special news . . .

Following Beatrice's advice Dr Penn took Peggy and their young family to Blenheim Palace on a day's outing. He walked peacefully around the impressive buildings and the expansive green gardens in a contemplative manner, as though lost in a world of his own. And why not for, Blenheim Palace is, after all, a national treasure, but there was something else on Dr Penn's mind that day, over which he had little control.

This entire experience crystallised the subtle, yet quite obvious, transformation in Dr Penn's soul. By the time he returned to Whitland, it was as if a little piece of Mr Churchill had been injected into his system – rather like a blood transfusion, causing a touch of the great man to run through his veins. All of this was pretty serious. He had already given officials of British Railways a tough time; Heaven spare them from now on!

Back at his own country treasure of Hillside in Whitland, Dr Penn had ambitious farming plans, including the purchase of livestock. For the moment, however, the only animal on the property was a rather excitable sheepdog called Peter, who took great delight in chasing Jack Roberts' herd of cattle around their field. Before too long, however, Peter had cattle of his own to contend with, as Howie Roberts, Jack's son, explains:

When Dr Penn and his family moved to Hillside, my father rented his field for a few years. When it started to get a bit rough, he thought that it had better be ploughed – so we arranged for Tommy Lloyd, a local contractor from Henllan Amgoed, to do the job. Then Dai Skyrme sowed the seeds with one of the hand-held sewing machines.

When the grass came, Dr Penn decided to buy some store cattle of his own. Then he bought some heifers and wanted to bull them. Of course, he ended up with three or four suckler cows; then the fun started.

Looking back, we had some terrific moments with the cattle, but one of the funniest stories that I can remember goes back to the time when one of Dr Penn's calves wasn't well. The vet had called, and because there was a warm Rayburn in the kitchen at Hillside, Dr Penn felt that the animal would benefit from being brought inside for a good warm. When he came home that night, he gave the calf a couple of raw eggs and made it comfortable. Then he closed the kitchen door tightly and went to bed.

But, in the middle of the night, he and Peggy heard a noise downstairs. And when he went to see what was happening, the calf was walking around with the kitchen table on its back. It had clearly fallen asleep, and when it stood up, it lifted the table as it stretched. Then, as it moved around, it was banging into other furniture. Dr Penn was terribly amused about this; as for me, I was in fits of laughter.

Howie's wife, Heulwen, added:

When George started to tell a story, he was so lovely. Everybody pricked up their ears; we all knew there was some excitement and humour to follow. He gave the community a wonderful service as a doctor, too. He was one in a million. I remember one Christmas day, I wasn't well at all. He came down and he was with us for ages. Peggy phoned to say that dinner was ready in Hillside, but he wouldn't go back until I was better.

Then Howie recalled another story:

I can remember the time he was thinking of taking his bullock down to the Whitland Fat Stock Show. In those days you had to lead the animals by the halter. It was a requirement, so that judges could put their hand on them. Dr Penn knew this, so he had been busy practising. We were all having breakfast one morning – my father, Dai Skyrme and Heulwen – when there was a knock on the door. It was Dr Penn with his bullock, led by a long piece of rope, with the end tied around Dr Penn's waist. We were thrilled to see that he was getting the hang of it all, but

I remember my father urging him not to have the rope round his middle, just in case the animal ran off.

When the time of the show arrived, Dr Penn was ready. He had groomed his bullock which was in fine shape. I happened to be going to Whitland when I saw him leading the animal down the road. By the time I passed him he was alongside Wenallt [opposite the old Grammar school entrance]. He had stopped to talk to somebody; the bullock was standing by his side!

In the *Carmarthen Journal* for Friday December 23rd 1966, the results of that year's Christmas Fat Stock Show were announced. There had been 49 cattle exhibited, and the entry from Hillside had done well:

Dr Penn, Hillside, Whitland exhibited a good Hereford cross steer to become reserve champion of the show.

Again, Howie explained:

We had some fun in the Yelverton that night. Dr Penn was chuffed to bits. He only had half a dozen animals – yet he was beating farmers who had a hundred-and-fifty.

Then a couple of years later, he was President of the Show, and presented the prize to my father. We still have the photo – a real treasure – of them both standing in the Yelverton's courtyard, alongside the animal and with a crowd of Whitland farmers in the background.

PART IX

THE CAMPAIGNING YEARS

The Tide Turns at Tenby
as Railway Line Lives on

As EVENTS TRANSPIRED, there was no opportunity for the Cardi Bach line to reopen with a passenger service. To the contrary, the line closed altogether – the freight run coming to an abrupt end in May 1963, some nine months after the famous last passenger journey. This was another blow to Dr Penn, who no longer saw even the heavy wagon loads of timber, coal, milk churns, even cattle, being pulled through the winding Taf valley of his practice area. He knew that if he was going to get the line used again – perhaps as a tourist attraction – he had to act quickly. It would be a mighty challenge, and he was losing momentum; being so heavily involved in practice work, and with a young family and other interests, he really had little time, or capacity. But he hoped that his day would come. The track bed was intact, the ballast was set, and, given the old saying about new fires being lit on old hearths, there was room for optimism.

But this time Dr Penn had missed the boat. Whilst heading into the countryside on his visits only a few months later, he noticed a large crane in the lower section of the Taf valley. When he pulled up to see what was happening, he saw to his horror that the lines were already being lifted. Worse still, the land was sold, not in one strip but in many sections. Like the steam that once poured forth from the engines, now his dream had also vanished into thin air.

The late Peter Wills, who worked with Dr Penn on many committees, once told me:

> George was always your man when it came to riding the river. You could rely on him in every respect. He was also a pioneer; he liked to take the lead – sometimes stepping back when things got going, but usually to take on another project.
>
> I remember George telling me that his greatest regret in life was failing to save the Cardi Bach line.

Only a few years later, in 1966, Dr Penn was shocked by another railway announcement. Lightening had struck twice in the same place, but now with far greater severity. Unlike the Cardi Bach, which was a small country branch line, the Pembroke and Tenby Line (known as the P & T Line) was a bigger concern altogether; yet, it, too, was facing the axe during an era of rail closures now associated with Dr Beeching.

In a railway brochure entitled *The P & T Line*, compiled by Dr Penn and his committee in later years, local author, John Morris, also a railway worker and historian, provides an account of the line's early beginnings and history from the arrival of a mainline railway in the county midway through the nineteenth century:

> The South Wales Railway came to Pembrokeshire in the early 1850s. It was intended to establish a harbour at Fishguard and to lay branches to Neyland and Pembroke Dock. However, the potato famine in Ireland forced the company to revise its intentions and the plans for a branch to Pembroke Dock were dropped.

The people of South Pembrokeshire were naturally incensed by being left without a railway, and so they formed their own company . . . The necessary Act of Parliament was duly passed on July 21st 1859, authorising the construction of the line between Pembroke Dock and Tenby . . . The line was opened on July 30th 1863, with the usual celebrations.

John explained that, within a year, a further act was passed for a much needed extension from Tenby to Whitland – a line that has since carried hundreds of thousands of holiday-makers and tourists to Tenby's golden sands, as well as to the stunning scenery, coves, beaches, villages, countryside and general attractions of this idyllic part of Wales. 'Fashionable Tenby'[8] had been appreciated throughout the ages, and Pembroke and Pembroke Dock were also long-established towns with vibrant economies of their own. But now the line was being sent to oblivion on the grounds of unprofitability – seemingly without a care for the social impact this might have in the area.

To put it mildly, Dr Penn was stunned; he thought the railway authorities had simply – well, gone off the rails. Whilst he acknowledged that a failing business could not be subsidised forever, he knew that the line's performance could be improved. With its undeniable potential for tourism, freight and rural development, the line's closure would be a sad step back. Dr Penn was not prepared to envisage the consequences; instead he was going to act, and to act quickly.

If Dr Penn had been given the chance, he would have brought a brick or two back from Blenheim, for the influence of the great man, Sir Winston, was already rubbing off on him. Dr Penn was himself at war now – with the railway authorities. He had already lost the Doctor's Train (the Cardi

8   *Fair and Fashionable Tenby*, (Tenby Museum, 1987).

Bach), taking patients to Dolycwrt from the countryside, and here was further territory under threat, the rail route to Tenby and Pembroke Dock. The time for niceties was over – at least until the voice of the people had been heard, and these senseless rail closures had been arrested. This was no vain fight for glory. Dr Penn had no place for that sort of thing: romance – yes; vanity – no. But now he had to act quickly. Whether he realised it or not he was, in essence, following the great man's lead in standing up to powerful forces threatening to alter the course of everyday life.

In the words of his mother, Beatrice, Dr Penn was now becoming 'a big noise with the railways'. But, equally, he was the first to admit that he was following the courageous stand of others in fighting to keep the P & T line open. These stalwarts were mentioned by Dr Penn in his retirement party speech in later years. Here is a small extract:

> Perhaps it was this feeling for Whitland which made me unwilling and indignant towards the plans to get rid of most, or all, of our railways – I couldn't get over the cheek of it. We saw the much loved Cardi Bach being closed and lifted under our eyes and, little by little, our railway service and railway personnel were whittled down. We saw the destruction of St Clears station and Neyland and the closure of goods depots – and it seemed that our railways were being lined up for the chop. And all we could do was to watch this terrible destruction taking place. I took heed of a defiant stand being taken by the Mayor of Tenby, Alderman Ivor Crockford and Tenby's Town Clerk, Mr Wyn Samuel.

Dr Penn started banging the drums by distributing little leaflets and flyers. He left them here, there and everywhere: simple messages, easy on the eye, but also packed with 'menace' and directed to the heart of the matter. Dr Penn was not used to conflict, but neither would he shy away from it – not given the circumstances. He was a busy man; there was no time for beating about the bush. This is how one of his publications read:

> Are the Railway Boards going Crazy?
> Do your bit to defeat their crazy idea
> of stopping rail services to
> South Pembrokeshire
> Come to the Public Meeting
> Whitland Grammar School
> Thursday, October 5th

Three weeks after this event, on Friday, 28th October 1966, another highly charged meeting was held at Whitland Grammar School when 152 people gathered in the Assembly Hall.[9] Councillor H. G. James of Whitland took the chair, coordinating some powerful deliveries from the likes of Alderman Ivor Crockford, Lord Gordon Parry, Jack Sheppard and others. These men had done their homework: facts were at their finger tips. Mr Eddie Gough, from Milford Haven, for instance, explained that by closing the line some 6,500 lorry-loads would take to the already busy roads, meaning 13,000 trips to the depot and back. Meanwhile, Mr W. D. Williams, of Crymych, explained the serious loss to his community in the north of the county since the Cardi Bach had ended:

> He wished that the closure had received far more attention
> at the time. Many people were now very unhappy . . . If the
> railways were going to be further reduced there would need
> to be a tremendous loss of land for building new roads.

---

9 Minutes of the Public Meeting, held on October 28th 1966.

Mr Williams' last statement was another sore point with Dr Penn. He disliked overcrowded roads and could not identify with motorways. Furthermore, he was disturbed by what he later called 'By-pass Mania' and the loss of good agricultural land to facilitate modern roads. He was not wrong. Railways merely demand a narrow corridor for a track bed, allowing them to dissect our countryside in a less harmful manner. They do not create 'concrete jungles' by-passing villages, towns and cities, and as Dr Penn put it perfectly, when dissecting the bones of modern-day transport, 'all the while, the best "by-passes" of all, the railways – are being by-passed!'

As can be expected, there were a number of resolutions to emerge from the meeting, the main one being the need for 'a full public enquiry into the management of British Rail' in the West Wales area. It was recommended that the Ministry of Transport be urged to provide a better road infrastructure before further railway stations and depots were closed, whilst the need for united action from the three counties, Carmarthenshire, Pembrokeshire and Cardiganshire, was recognised. It was also agreed that copies of these resolutions be sent to Mrs Barbara Castle, M.P., the Minister of Transport; Mr Cledwyn Hughes M.P., the Secretary of State for Wales; Mr George Thomas, M.P., the Minister of State for Wales, and to Members of Parliament representing the local constituencies. Dr Penn had some serious work ahead of him and, within a week or two, the postman at Hillside knew that something 'big' was happening. This is when Dr Penn started to receive acknowledgments from personnel in all corners of Westminster and beyond, including the Prime Minister and the Duke of Edinburgh.

In the *Western Telegraph* the following Thursday, 3rd November 1966, there was almost a full-page spread about the meeting in Whitland Grammar School. The headlines

Grandpa Penn on his retirement,
January 17th 1921.

Captain Stanley Kempton Penn,
George's Father.

Nurse Beatrice Penn, George's mother,
at Gloucester Royal Infirmary.

George with Neville, his brother,
and Beatrice.

Preparing to play cricket at Bushey school. George is standing 3rd from the left.

Enjoying the company of Neville and friends at Bryn Haf, Brynmenyn.

The Royal Masonic School for Boys in Bushey, Hertfordshire.

On holiday from Bushey, with Mack, a loyal friend.

A family outing and another visit to the seaside.

The Wyndham Hotel, Cardiff, home to Beatrice, Neville and George during Medical School days.

The 'White Elephant' that George walked across in the Black of night. *Dean Heritage Centre*

What a head of hair! George as a young man with a school friend.

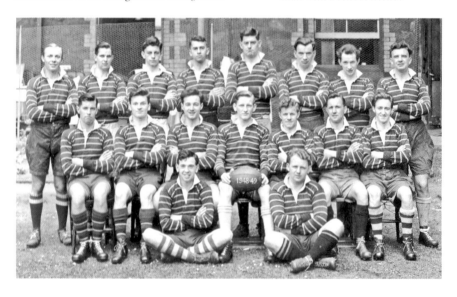

Cardiff Medicals 2ⁿᵈ XV, during the 1948–1949 season. George is sitting alongside the Captain and second-row colleague, David Boyns.

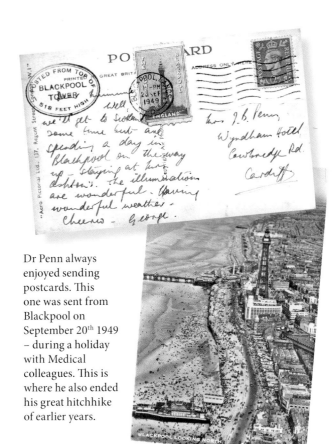

Dr Penn always enjoyed sending postcards. This one was sent from Blackpool on September 20th 1949 – during a holiday with Medical colleagues. This is where he also ended his great hitchhike of earlier years.

The name is Penn, George Penn . . . the debonair medical student at a formal dinner. Not shaken, not stirred . . .

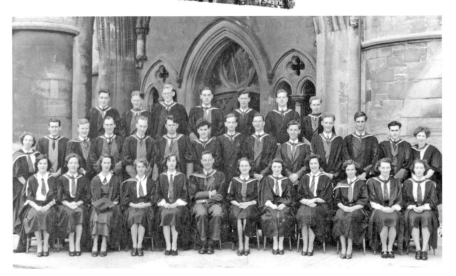

Graduation Day at the Old College, Aberystwyth, 1951.
George is in the centre of the front row – amongst all the ladies.

Dr Penn and Peggy during their courting days, around 1952.

Peggy and George leaving Maes-yr-Haf chapel on their wedding day, April 23rd 1953.

Dr Penn with the military doctors in Nigeria 1953.
His experiences in West Africa made a lasting impression on the young doctor.

Relaxing whilst on military duty.

President of Whitland Rugby Club at
the official opening of its Club House on
September 2nd 1963.
W. D. Evans, St Clears © Alan Evans Photography

Shades of the old road to Llangeinor, as the
Penn family take a stroll

Hillside in the snow of 1963. It is correct to say that this residence was a home, a hobby and a sanctuary for Dr Penn.

Dr Penn, Peggy, Elizabeth, Roger and Sarah, pose for a family photo.
W. D. Evans, St Clears © Alan Evans Photography

With Bryan Thomas and the ladies of Whitland Young Farmers Club. Dr Penn felt that a doctor should be at the heart of a community – and he enjoyed living out his philosophy.

Dr Penn as President of Whitland Fat Stock Show presents neighbour, Jack Roberts of Llwyndrissi, with the Champion's Cup. *Howie Roberts' collection*

The classic friendship of times past. The doctor and the local bank manager – in this case, Kemes Morris – at a dinner in the 1970s.
Squibbs' Studios, Tenby

Dr Penn felt that to lose the railways was to surrender an essential part of everyday life and the legacy of a rich heritage.

The train-loving, campaigning doctor and colleagues embark upon another exciting railway excursion.

Worshipful Master at Teifi (Hall Stone) Lodge, Cardigan with some of his colleagues during his term of office.

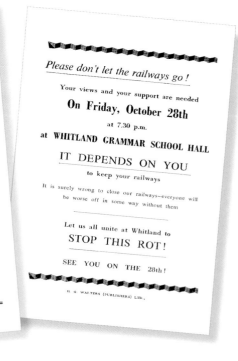

Are the Railways Board going crazy?

Do your bit to defeat their crazy idea of stopping rail services to South Pembrokeshire

Come to the

Public Meeting

Whitland Grammar School
on Thursday, October 5th

Speakers will include :
MR. GWYNFOR EVANS, M.P.
MR. A. KIRKWOOD
ALDERMAN IVOR CROCKFORD
MR. GORDON COLES

Printed by H. G. Walters (Publishers) Ltd., Narberth.

Please don't let the railways go !

Your views and your support are needed

On Friday, October 28th

at 7.30 p.m.

at WHITLAND GRAMMAR SCHOOL HALL

IT DEPENDS ON YOU

to keep your railways

It is surely wrong to close our railways—everyone will be worse off in some way without them

Let us all unite at Whitland to

STOP THIS ROT !

SEE YOU ON THE 28th !

H. G. WALTERS (PUBLISHERS) LTD.,

A couple of examples of Dr Penn's campaign literature over the years.

Glimpses of Whitland Week: being kidnapped ... posing as Pirate Penn ... cycling through St John Street ... winning the sack race ... and being entertained to tea during his presidency.

Photo contributions from W. Rainbow

'When Whitland Week came round, Dr Penn was full of it,' said Eddie Fussell, on the right of the picture.

The cars at Hillside have seen better days – and Dr Penn's former field is now a by-pass.

Eilyr Blethyn, Dolycwrt's caretaker, with Dafydd, her grandson, who today is the green grocer in town.

Proud grandparents with Hywel and Iwan.

Presenting a cheque to Whitland Memorial Hall – as John Llewellyn, a close railway colleague and campaigner looks on.

The surgery front door was always open at Dolycwrt – but here Dr Penn poses with a group of healthy patients and friends.

Happy behind the bar of Waungron Country Mansion Hotel as Mr Ferris, the proprietor, looks on. Recollections of the Wyndham Hotel, perhaps?

Flying the flag for the Royal British Legion, 'a charity which tries to remember those we should remember, and to whom we should be grateful', said Dr Penn.

W. D. Evans, St Clears © Alan Evans Photography

Dr Penn's pride and joy, Dolycwrt, a doctor's surgery for one hundred years. This photograph also appears in *Dolycwrt – The Days of a Country Doctor's Surgery*.

Smiling for the BBC cameras on his last day at Dolycwrt, May 16th 1997. The documentary was known as *The Doctor's Story*, part of a series entitled *Tales of the National Health Service*. The programme went on to win an award and brought Dr Penn's philosophy to a wide audience.

The local school children line up to sing 'Penblwydd Hapus' (Happy Birthday) to Dr Penn on his last day at Dolycwrt, an occasion which – almost – left him lost for words.

'It seems a shame to cut this, Peggy.'
Dolycwrt: the icing on the cake for
Dr Penn's career.

A favourite photo.
W. Rainbow

A lover of all things traditional, Dr Penn at Hillside, with his treasured old cars.

were bold: 'County Protests at Rail Cuts ... Disastrous ... Monstrous ... Appalling ... Ridiculous.' Of course, there is no smoke without fire, and Dolycwrt's senior doctor was fuelling the fire:

> The Secretary, Dr Penn, wanted to see the professional people present. He commented, 'I would like to see all the professional people here and shouting. I am all bound up in my work, and believe it is my duty to come here and rebel against something if it seems all cock-eyed.'
>
> Dr Penn stated the case of a man who had died in a coma, in the back of an ambulance which was held up in a traffic block outside Carmarthen ...
>
> 'They claim they are not interested in human problems,' he continued. 'I am also complaining about the undemocratic way this was done.'

Dr Penn then vented his frustration about the local railway workforce being streamlined or 'pensioned-off', as outsiders – who had no care or feelings for local concerns, and who were 'brainwashed and indoctrinated in the new ideas' – ran the roost. He concluded that there was little 'hope of reasoning' with such people, adding that, 'We must take action; talking gets us nowhere.'

The stage was set for a right-royal-battle which saw members of parliament, councillors, local authorities as well as tradespeople, individuals and societies joining the fray. Three weeks later there was another forum at Carmarthen when Mr R. C. Hilton, a senior representative of British Rail, faced the music and a multitude of questions. Amongst those who took to the stage was Dr Penn, as described by the *Weekly Observer*, Friday, November 18th 1966, under the heading 'Fighting for a Rail Service – Mr Western Region Under Heavy Fire':

There was applause when Dr G. K. Penn, who has been leading the campaign in Whitland . . . rose to speak.

Addressing Mr Hilton, he said, 'Having seen the feeling that exists in West Wales for the retention of the rail services, could you go outside your very narrow brief and consider the social as well as the financial considerations?'

For months, the newspaper columns were almost chockablock with this one issue alone, the P & T line. Dr Penn continued to stoke the fires that spread wildly in Wales and beyond – resulting in some interesting newspaper headlines appearing at this time. These ranged from 'End of Whitland as a Rail Junction' and 'West Wales Farmers Fear Isolation' to 'Women Backing Rail Closure Revolt', 'Bus Service Inadequate' and 'Rail Closure Top Level Talks Demanded'. There was another from a well-known former inhabitant of Whitland, who compared the situation with the Rebecca Riots of the previous century. 'How would daughters of Rebecca deal with rail threats?' he asked in a clever article that conveyed more good arguments, before concluding as follows:

If the Pembroke and Tenby branch closes then the chances of developing an officially recognised development area would be slimmer – and the population will continue to fall. Go to Carmarthen. Play steam. And let's hope the hall for the meeting will be far too small for all of you. Good luck! Yours . . . Gwili Lewis

After a series of meetings in Carmarthen the 'fireworks' were ready to be lit at the De Valance Pavilion in Tenby. The rail chiefs were preparing for battle; so were the railway union representatives, and so was Dr Penn, now forty years of age. Ron Jenkins, Secretary of the Whitland branch of the National Union of Railway workers for twenty-five years, explains:

I invited Gordon Coles, a senior man of the railway union, down, to help Dr Penn. He was lodging next-door-but-one from me, with Tommy Evans and his wife. We all went down to Tenby on the train; we were a big crowd. But I must admit, I feared that we might lose the battle, especially as the railway authorities had made up their mind. But that day, everything went well. There was still a long way to go – but the tide turned at Tenby. There would be a fresh round of talks.

Dr Penn spoke strongly. Once he had something on his mind that was it. He was like a terrier dog and wouldn't let go. Whenever he had time from the doctoring, he was working on this – and it was well worth it in the end.

A reprieve followed – and the P & T line is still in use today! But, around this time, the late 1960s, Dr Penn was not taking any chances: planning a fresh line of attack, firmly believing that this was necessary to protect rural branch railways. On January 30th 1970, at the Queen's Hall in Narberth, he organised the formation of the West Wales Railway Action Committee, taking on the role of Secretary, an office he continued to hold until railway normality had fully resumed some twelve years later. This was a small but spirited group of railway enthusiasts who promoted trains in every way possible. Each year they chartered locomotives to the Royal Welsh Show and the Shrewsbury Flower Show – just as Dr Penn was also doing in a personal capacity! – simply to prove that the Central Wales line was being used. They fought to reopen local stations and linked up with similar action groups in other parts of Wales, ensuring that a united front kept rail closures to a minimum.

In truth, the late 1960s heralded the beginning of a period of sustained and strenuous commitment from Dr

Penn – involving time, effort and sometimes money – to the cause of the railway network in Wales. Certainly, he earned his commendation in Richard Parker's excellent book *The Railways of Pembrokeshire*:

> Credit must go to the West Wales Railway Action Committee, a group determined to keep the railways open. Led by the redoubtable Dr Penn of Whitland, whose remedies were far removed from those of Dr Beeching, but more beneficial to the patient.

A Year in the Life of a Campaigning Doctor

IN THE LATER 1960s, Dr Penn was a well-established member of the Whitland & Llanboidy branch of the Royal British Legion. It is there that he enjoyed the company of Dr Hugh Philipps and fellow members, including Dr Roland Lewis, another general practitioner in Whitland. By 1969, Dr Penn was Vice President and fully proud of his place in the organisation. Here he explains how his 'Legion' years began:

> I never gave the idea of joining the British Legion a thought. However, one day the late Mr Wil Evans, a retired tailor living at the bottom of North Road, asked me why I wasn't a member. I explained to him that I hadn't experienced any real active service and that, in my two years, I had never been in any real danger. But he said that didn't matter and, as long as I had been in the Army, I could join. He asked me for five-bob, and enrolled me there and then.
>
> I've always been pleased that he roped me in – because I have come to realise that the Royal British Legion is first and last a charitable organisation and a grateful one, which tries to remember those we should remember, and to whom we should be grateful – and that can't be bad.

'Loyalty' was, of course, Dr Penn's middle name. Ever since he had finished his studies in Bushey School at the end of World War II, he had wanted to repay the Freemasonry movement which had given him such a privileged start in life. That time arrived when he settled into Hillside in the late 1960s, and he became a member of the Teifi Lodge in Cardigan. Former

Worshipful Master, Jestyn Edwards, of Crymych, explains:

I remember the occasion when George came for an interview. I was on the selection panel that day and I was interested to learn about his school days in Bushey. As soon as he put his name down to join us, he was accepted with open arms.

George and I were big mates in Lodge and we often sat next to each other. Every time we met we had a good chat. When he had the time, he attended our Lodge of Instruction, when we officers had a rehearsal. We used to have coal fires in those days and he was certainly fond of them. He would be there busy stoking the fire, always relaxed, never in a hurry to leave. But, following alterations to the premises, the fires were taken away, replaced by central heating – although nothing really changed with us; we continued to chat well into the night.

One incident that stuck in my mind about George, proves how good a doctor he was. He had travelled up for a meeting in Cardigan and, that night, we were dining afterwards in the Cliff Hotel, Gwbert. We had enjoyed our meal and we were all gathered in the lounge, happily talking away. Then George got up to go, casually mentioning: 'I'm off now Boys.'

'You're going a bit early tonight, George,' a few of us said.

'Yes, I'll tell you why. On the way I came through Efailwen on the cross-country route, and I called with an old lady who was quite frail, and her daughter who was looking after her. I promised that I would pop-in on the way home. So they are expecting me now. I had better go; I'll see you next time.'

It was a long way to travel from Whitland to Cardigan, on the winding roads, but Dr Penn rarely missed a 'Lodge' meeting. He tried to fit these occasions into his visits to the 'Top Country', as he called it – in other words the area north of Llanglydwen, which includes Crymych, Glandŵr, Glogue, Hermon, Llanfyrnach and Tegryn. He was fond of the town of Cardigan and the salty fresh air of Gwbert. Likewise, he enjoyed the social fellowship of members who were his friends.

In truth, Dr Penn's spare minutes were few and far between: busy at Dolycwrt, in Hillside, with the railways, Whitland Week, the 'Legion' and, more recently, as a member of both Whitland Parish Council and the Farmers Union of Wales. Yet, amazingly, he still had plenty of time for everyone – besides, intermittently, keeping a diary. Now, in 1971, when a new decimal currency committed our 'Pounds, Shillings and Pence' to history, and astronauts were driving around on the moon, Dr Penn was writing (what are really) his memoirs. They are certainly not simple notes; they have been written for others to read, and are full of explanation and description. Here is a selection, framing a year in the life of Dr Penn, a campaigning doctor:

January . . .
After some pretty-big and long surgeries, I finished late and changed quickly to get to Llanboidy Hall where I was M.C. at the Y.F.C. dance. There was a marvellous crowd and everybody had a good time. I thought things didn't go badly for me but, after coffee with Mr Llewellyn, I didn't get home until 4 a.m.!

February . . .
I was in surgery most of the morning with Dr Hugh Philipps helping, before returning to the afternoon surgery until 3 p.m. Then home to watch the Wales-Scotland International Rugby match on T.V. – an exciting match won by Wales.

In April, Dr Penn and Peggy went on a rail excursion to London:

> We didn't take the children because Sarah had German measles . . . but mother was cross over our last minute decision. However, it was a good trip and we enjoyed it very much. We saw a film called *Language of Love*. We called in the Savoy Hotel for a bit of fun.

In May, Dr Penn had a meeting with two insurance agents who reminded him that his nine-year-old investment was due to mature:

> They advised me to take out another policy for about £100 per year. I could have a £1,000 policy for 10 years (becoming £1,300); or a £1,500 policy for 15 years (becoming £2,200); or a £2,000 policy for 20 years (becoming £3,800). I couldn't make up my mind which to do – but I sold them both a copy of the *Pembroke & Tenby Railway* booklet!

Shortly afterwards:

> I was called to a commune in the countryside for a confinement at about 9.35 a.m., so I went straight away and took my shaving tackle with me. The room was warm and cosy with a lovely log fire and everyone was there drinking tea, rolling their own cigarettes – sat around the lady who was naked on the couch in the middle of the room. They had all positively asked to witness the childbirth! A friend fetched herbs and natural scents and applied them to the lady's forehead. I had a shave in the kitchen while waiting – using an old mirror belonging to a washing stand. Both the midwife in attendance and I were very glad that everything went well. Then I was given a mug of tea, two glasses of Elderberry wine and a kiss from the mother!

As June approached, Dr Penn and Peggy were taking their family to London for a mini break:

> I was busy in the Bont country surgery, getting back in time for us all to catch the 3.45 p.m. train to London for our 3-day holiday – Peggy's family looking after Hillside. Auntie Katie came with us and got off at Cardiff, where my mother met the train. After Cardiff we had a marvellous meal in the carriage, soon arriving in London at 9 p.m. We had a taxi to Brecon Towers Hotel, Grays Inn Road, where we were well fixed up in one family room (costing £8).

The next day:

> We went to Hyde Park to hear an overture, then for dinner in Marble Arch. Afterwards we went to Victoria for a two-hour sight-seeing bus tour. Unfortunately, I fell asleep; it was stuffy inside, raining outside. We then caught the tube to Trafalgar Square, and had a meal at a Bernie Inn on the Strand. Then, we jumped aboard the 7 p.m. boat for a cruise on the Thames – seeing St Paul's Cathedral, the Festive Hall, London Bridge, *Gipsy Moth* (Sir Francis Chichester's boat), *Cutty Sark* and *The Discovery*. I was sad to see London's dockyard becoming scrapped. We heard a bit of an open-air concert at the Embankment Gardens, before going back to our hotel.

The following day:

> We caught a bus to Hyde Park Corner and walked along Constitution Hill and Buckingham Palace, seeing the 'Changing of the Guard'. Next we went to Victoria for lunch before returning to see a parade organised by the big stores of London, with lots of military bands. Then, into Hyde Park, rowing on the Serpentine, before rushing to the

Dominion Cinema to see *The Sound of Music*. From there, we walked back to our hotel: the weather glorious.

The final day:

> We went shopping, buying a dress for Peggy in Bourne and Hollingsworth, before keeping our appointment at the Top of the Tower Restaurant. We really enjoyed this, rotating three times an hour. It was most pleasant and the service was wonderful. The bill for the five of us (including a bottle of wine!) was over £16. Afterwards, we went to Selfridges and other shops, buying trousers for Roger, shoes for Sarah and Elizabeth.

And, to complete the holiday, Dr Penn managed a swim:

> We then dashed to the hotel by taxi and thence to the Serpentine – then to Paddington Station where I was disappointed to find no mention of Whitland or Carmarthen. We had a lovely meal on the train, and arrived home at 12.30.

Dr Penn did not have time to mention Whitland Week 1971 (all ten-days of it!), which was again action-packed, with Stan and Hilda from *Coronation Street* being the main guests on Carnival Day. Each year he took his annual leave to organise the events – with the support of Peggy, of course: wife, secretary, receptionist, best friend and, most definitely, unsung heroine. Here are more diary entries covering the latter stages of the year.

A visit to the De Valence Pavilion, Tenby, for a Fashion Show:

> I wanted to go because I thought we might put on a similar show in Whitland. I wasn't so impressed with this one: the catwalk was low meaning that we couldn't see well, and

there were no refreshments other than 'an interval' glass of sherry.

Displaying posters in Haverfordwest for a British Rail trip to Blackpool:

I dished-out as many as I could and found it a depressing experience. Nobody seemed to know about the trip. One café proprietor even refused to put one up, being unhappy with the present standards of British Rail.

Dropping more home-made advertisements in Pembroke:

I had lunch in a pub near Sageston and carried on with my rounds. I took my best suit, ready for the Farmers Union of Wales meeting in Crymych, which I chaired.

Attending a wedding:

It was a beautiful day for Jocelyn's wedding. I wore my new dark suit, but I wasn't all that happy with it. It was heavy and has Edwardian-type lapels.

Preparing a speech:

I got up at about 6.30 to finish writing my speech for the Installation dinner. I'd been asked to propose a toast to the Deputy Provincial Grand Master and the Provincial Grand Lodge Officers.

Attending a Parish Council Meeting:

This was depressing. We heard that British Railways were insisting on putting down Continental Barrier crossings – replacing the two existing signal boxes with one new one – as well as getting rid of four men, in spite of our objections.

Attending to railway business:

With difficulty I got up at 4.45 a.m. and got on with writing a speech for the railway meeting at Carmarthen. It was a somewhat starchy meeting and it was a job to get-in on it, but I managed to say my piece. I stated that we're within an ace of getting to the Beeching Plan. I suggested that a solution might be an all-Wales meeting, followed by the administrative separation of Welsh Railways from British Railways. The meeting 'idea' was accepted, but there wasn't much interest in the Welsh Railways concept. Nicholas Edwards was there and also Gwynoro Jones, who spoke well.

Making time for Neville:

Went to fetch Neville in time for dinner, and then slipped to the rugby club to fetch a drink for him. But regrettably, I stayed there a while: met a lot of people.

Travelling to London to defend rural railways:

I felt full of cold and dosed myself up with a couple of whiskies. I caught the train at Whitland for a railway meeting in London. We changed at Swansea and went into the Buffet car and had tea. I also had a couple of beers with 'Charlie Glogue,' who was with Percy Thomas going to London for a First Aid competition.

Fulfilling an official farming engagement:

I was fortunate to be at Withybush Hospital to make the presentation of a medical machine on behalf of the Farmers Union of Wales. Peggy kindly drove me there so that I could memorise my speech. There were reporters and photographers and we were all given tea – but sadly there was no Dr Eirian Williams; he had been called to London.

Welcoming an old friend:

> Of all the amazing things, Ben Ashton and his wife called on us. I was his best man about twenty-four years ago in Blakeney, East Anglia.

Dr Penn ended the year travelling to a farming function at Llwyngwair Manor in Newport, Pembrokeshire; being President of the 'Chrysanthemum, Horticulture and Handicraft Show' at the Memorial Hall, in Whitland; and speaking to the local Jalopy enthusiasts at their dinner in Kilgetty – before finding time for an important visitor to Whitland:

> Wednesday December 22nd
> I managed to fit in being at the station for Father Christmas' arrival at the station by train at 5.40 p.m. – presents being given to the children who came in spite of the rain.

Tea for Two at Buckingham Palace

SINCE MOVING TO Hillside in 1960, Dr Penn's appreciation for the beauty of Wales' villages, towns, scenery and farming landscape had continued to grow. Glancing out of his bedroom window he could see the full glory of the Taf valley spread out before his eyes, extending for miles to the distant Tavernspite Ridge. But now, as a member of Whitland Parish Council, he was trying to enhance the natural beauty of the area by attracting financial incentives for Whitland residents living near the A40 trunk road to grow cherry trees in their front gardens. It was another simple idea, but one that Dr Penn knew could make a big difference.

Dr Penn had also been persuaded by Colonel Man, a patient and a good friend, to join the Pembrokeshire branch of the Council for the Protection of Rural Wales. This seemed to go well with Dr Penn's enjoyment of his involvement with the Farmers Union of Wales; indeed after years of loyal service, he was now Chairman of the Pembrokeshire branch – a unique experience for a G.P., as he admitted at the F.U.W. presentation mentioned in his 1971 diary notes. Here are some extracts from his speech that day:

> I must say that I feel thrilled to have the honour of making this presentation.
>
> I joined the Farmer's Union of Wales on the suggestion of a friend, but I was pleased to do so, and my only justification for joining was the fact that I have a field adjacent to my house on which I keep a few beef cattle. As

a person who earns a living almost entirely as a practising doctor, I naturally felt uneasy about being nominated Chairman of the Pembrokeshire Branch. I felt guilty and frightened that soon I should be painfully aware of how much out of place I was.

However, at least two happenings have made me feel happy and comfortable in my position of Chairman at a time when health matters, with which I am concerned, have been prominent in the thoughts of the Farmers Union of Wales.

The first occurrence was our joint meeting with the Veterinary profession on the subject of eradicating the disease, Brucellosis. That was a happy and successful one, setting many farmers on the road to having Brucellosis-free cattle. As one who works closely with Dr Eirian Williams, who has been such a pioneer in combating Brucellosis, I felt proud to be playing a part – through the Farmers Union of Wales – in helping in this most important matter affecting human beings and cattle respectively.

The second reason for me being happy in my position as Chairman is that Dr Eirian Williams approached me and then the F.U.W. Executive committee about donating funds for the detection of lead poisoning – a condition that I have encountered in general practice, and which nearly cost a patient of mine his life. I was thrilled that the F.U.W. members were not deterred by the price of £1200 for this equipment but, instead, all members wholeheartedly gave their support.

We are all proud and pleased at possessing a National Health Service – yet we can still perform charitable deeds, and this is a wonderful thing to do. It pleases the people who are on the receiving end, and it gives satisfaction to the giver.

I have great pleasure in officially handing over this valuable piece of equipment and may it prove to be a useful acquisition.

David Davies, from Lampeter Velfrey, and Con Harries J.P., from Whitland, explained to me the circumstances of the lead poisoning to which Dr Penn referred in his speech. Having visited his patient on a number of occasions without seeing an improvement, Dr Penn called for the drinking water of his home to be examined. Here lay the problem and once this had been identified, the gentleman in question made a full recovery.

Goronwy Griffiths, photographed with Dr Penn at the presentation, was then president of the local branch, having already served as chairman. He remembers having a lot of fun with Dr Penn, as did Peggy and Thelma, Goronwy's wife, when they were together. Goronwy has a small secret to let out of the bag:

George had been a member for about four years before he was made chairman – and his attendance wasn't bad at all. In fact, he and I used to travel together to Aberystwyth for our executive meetings. He'd try to make them if he could.

On one occasion, we were passing through Aberaeron and George was feeling a bit hungry. 'Have we got time for a spot of lunch,' he said to me.

'We've got an hour, George,' I replied.

'Oh, let's pull up somewhere, Goronwy, and have a bite to eat.'

Well, I think we went the full hog that day. We had a starter and ended up with dessert and coffee. Of course, we were talking flat out, and when George started to talk, he got carried away. When we got round to checking our watches, we were running late – very late.

'Do you still think it's worth going?' asked George.

'I'm not so sure that it is, George,' I replied – so we had a few drinks instead and went home later!

George liked the traditional ways of farming, and he was dead against trees and hedges being cut down. He saw farming from the small farmer's point of view. He wanted things to move forward, but in the old ways. These were the ideals that he held onto.

Goronwy's words support the contents of an earlier speech by Dr Penn to a farming audience – possibly to members of the Young Farmers' Club at Whitland, who often invited him to speak at their meetings and dinners. This was an impassioned delivery, which explained his farming roots and demonstrated a preference for the traditional ways of the industry, as well as an awareness of the dangers of the more modern approach:

It is a sad state of affairs when we become ruled, not only by our politicians, but also by the economists on whom our politicians seem to depend. It is sad because the economists' deductions lead to large scale alterations in our pattern of living and also because the economists are not always right.

Our farmers, or some of them, have, in my opinion, been having an unfair time in the minds of economists, politicians and the public in recent years. I have always found this distasteful and upsetting, because of the high regard which I have always had for the farmer, especially the family farmer of small acreage.

Of course, in times of war and crisis, everybody turns to the farmers and they become the objects of flattery and wooing, because the nation knows how much it depends on them. But, when the nation can get food easily and cheaply from other countries, it is all so different for our traditional family farms, which are treated as expendable – just like our lately lamented traditional half crowns.

The 'Powers That Be' have not only been trying to oust the small farmer in favour of larger units, but they have also been trying to push forestry as being more important than farming – certainly in Wales. A journey through Wales, as seen, for instance, from the Central Wales railway line, shows how in recent years much farmland has been turned into soulless coniferous forests.

I think that what is worrying many of us is that, these days, under that persuasive banner of 'progress', there seems to be an obsession for changes – and quick changes at that. Even when changes are quietly taking place, the 'Powers That Be' see fit to give pushes and prods and inducements to win the day.

Dr Penn had always been cautious, if not dubious, about grants, feeling that sometimes they led applicants into the 'Promised Land'. Here he explains why:

> For instance, when somebody once found that it was advantageous to remove a hedge or two – then in no time at all, grants and inducements arrived to remove hedges almost everywhere, and almost to work against time to do so. We know that this process has been tragically overdone, especially in some parts of the country where resulting soil erosion has caused alarm. It might well have been wise to remove a few, here and there – but not the thousands of miles of hedges which have been removed so far because of prods and inducements.
>
> Then again, we have seen fantastic strides in getting milk parlours, pipelines, bulk tanks, covered yards – and they may well be laudable ideas if they are allowed to work their way in gradually. However, such is the outlook of the day,

that when the 'Powers That Be' say that they are good and necessary things to have, there develops a veritable frenzy of activity, spending and inducement to get farmers large financial grants. And, sometimes, these have proved too tempting for some people, who have 'gone under'. These grants have in many cases led not to help, but to financial ruin.

Dr Penn advocated a 'slowing down' of progress:

It seems that the 'progress craze' has had a good run and now 'common sense' must have a chance. In the medical world, the arrival of penicillin was soon felt, and its value was known about the world over: no fanfare, no laws and no inducements were required to get it used. We must not forget that a good discovery, or real piece of progress, soon proves itself and needs no pushes or prods from the 'Powers That Be'.

Here was Dr Penn speaking forthrightly in his desire to preserve the best of the past for the future. Goronwy earlier touched upon Dr Penn's love of trees, a subject that he liked to discuss with John Davies of Whitland, who once visited Highgrove, Gloucestershire, with Clynderwen Gardening Club. John explains:

I remember Dr Penn phoning me one night about eleven o'clock. Something was on his mind; probably he was writing a speech.

'John, do you think trees have feelings? And do they enjoy each other's company?'

'Well, of course they do,' I replied. 'They are living organisms; they do their thinking through their roots.'

For Whitland, down in the valley, we should have as many as possible, because during times of flooding trees absorb the water. They drink a terrific amount, far more than we realise. Dr Penn took time to understand trees, as well as appreciating their natural beauty and fruits. He was upset when they were cut down, and quite rightly, so. We both shared the same views, and we'd be talking for hours.

At the time of writing this chapter, it is proposed to invest substantial sums of money in planting trees and woodlands around Britain as part of the Queen's Diamond Jubilee Celebrations. Dr Penn would have cheered this news – and how fitting it was that he and Peggy, two keen supporters of the Royal Family, were rewarded by the Farmers Union of Wales with invitations to a Royal Garden Party in the early 1970s. Dr Penn and Peggy enjoyed their 'Tea for Two' at Buckingham Palace, travelling by train to Paddington Station. Goronwy and Thelma had already enjoyed this privilege and here they explain what lay in store for Dr Penn and Peggy:

> Our names were put forward by the County Office. It was a real honour for us to walk through the grounds of Buckingham Palace, seeing long marquees, and crowds everywhere. Quite a few of the Royal Family were present, including the Queen, who mingled with guests, also passing near to where we sat.

Thelma enjoyed staying overnight in London before the 'Big Day':

> We had a taxi from our hotel to Buckingham Palace, and we were taken to one of the outside courtyards. There were people everywhere, all looking smart, enjoying the wonderful weather and stunning scenery – although no one was allowed to take photographs.

I remember seeing a lot of guards when we arrived, but I was looking out for Prince Charles. I have always liked him, but he was nowhere to be seen. I heard later that he had tonsillitis. We had picked the wrong day!

Edinburgh-bound 'In our little Austin A35'

BY 1973, New Year's Eve parties at Hillside had become a law unto themselves. This was a night when Dr Penn and Peggy opened up their home to the people of Whitland. Everyone was invited and many accepted. Con Harries explains:

> I was sitting at home late one New Year's Eve. It was about half past one – and the phone rang. 'I know it's late, Con, but we're having a party. Come over,' said George. This was too good an opportunity to miss. When we arrived, half of Whitland was there, merrily drinking away. There was no room to move, and I remember sitting on the stairs. Of course, George was famous for his partying! One night at the end of a dinner dance, he suggested that we all go to Amroth for a dip – and we did! He led the way.

Brian Cook, mentioned earlier, is another who remembers these days:

> George's parties went on into the early hours of the morning. One night, I was up in Hillside and he was called out to Henllan Amgoed – in the middle of New Year celebrations. He was late coming back that time and Peggy was worried – so I went to look for him. I was approaching the bend of the road near the farm entrance, when suddenly a car shot out of the driveway. This was George; he was on his way back to the party. He couldn't get there quick enough.

In the clubs and pubs of Whitland, following the traditional singing of 'Auld Lang Syne', thoughts turned to the cosy fires and free flowing drinks at Hillside.

'Ble ti'n mynd wedyn?' (Where are you going afterwards?), one was saying to another.

'Dw i'n mynd lan i weld Dr Penn,' (I'm going up to see Dr Penn) was often the reply. And this is how it was: people arriving in droves at the doorstep of Hillside in the early hours of the frosty mornings, where Dr Penn and Peggy made everyone welcome, celebrating the New Year's arrival in style.

By now Dr Penn's cars had also become legendary. The Triumph Herald had now been replaced with a succession of A35 Austins, which were built like tanks and bounced uncomplainingly up and down the bumpy country lanes. Brian Brown recalls:

I was working in Rhydwen Bakery around the early 1970s. It was about nine o'clock in the morning. I suddenly saw Dr Penn running into the back of the house. I thought that the old lady had been taken seriously ill, but then he rushed into the bakery.

'Brian, come quickly,' he said. 'My car's on fire.'

In a flash, Dr Penn and I jumped into my van and we headed up the road, some 200 yards. But, by the time we got there, Ben Davies had seen the flames and had smothered them with Hessian sacks.

I can remember Dr Penn gathering together his medical equipment and bits and pieces, just doing what he could really in the circumstances. No doubt, he was shocked by what had happened, although he didn't show it, and was certainly relieved that nobody was hurt.

Then, before Dr Penn left the scene, a crane came down the road, its driver offering to lift the Triumph Herald back to the bakery. But, somehow, it collided with the Estate-car belonging to the bakery's owner. Rhydwen had not seen so much action in years!

Les Evans told me that he was the person who brought the Triumph back to Hillside:

I had a tow-bar on the back of my car and I borrowed a trailer. I brought it back slowly, the back wheels being on the road. And it wasn't an ordinary motor either; it had a twin carburettor. It would have made a good jalopy.

'Can I buy it from you, Dr Penn?' I asked, as I was racing at this time.

'Oh no, Les, I hope to do it up some day,' was Dr Penn's reply.

Brian Cook has a funny story to share concerning Dr Penn's A35s:

A few years earlier, George and Peggy were planning to take a friend to Heathrow Airport to catch a plane. They were preparing to go in the Austin car. I remember saying, 'Now look George, rather than taking your little car all the way, borrow mine.' At the time, I had a Daimler-66: a powerful motor.

'It will give you more speed and comfort,' I told him.

'Brian, I'll try it out,' he said reluctantly, before getting to like it.

Anyway, they took the Daimler, travelling all the way in the outside lane – a real change from the inside ones! – and George got to Heathrow and back in time to call on his mother in Cardiff; and he had a famous welcome.

'Well George, you've actually made it,' she said, always ambitious for George and thrilled to bits to see him arriving in the Daimler . . . But the funny part of this story is that

I borrowed his A35 for the day. Wherever I went, people were waving to me; they thought I was Dr Penn.

By now Dr Roy Allen was well established at Dolycwrt having arrived in Whitland in 1969. He, too, has a story about Dr Penn's cars:

> George was so funny with his old cars. I remember one Tuesday shortly after I arrived at the practice we were on our way home after he had taken me round the Tegryn area. We were in his little Austin and I remember the hooter was in the centre of the steering wheel – and all of a sudden it shot out of the socket, like a mini explosion. We must have gone over a bump – and I remember thinking what's going on; the car is falling apart.

Another well-known Whitland character had the difficult task of keeping Dr Penn's cars on the road. This was Iorry Griffiths. I asked Iorry why Dr Penn liked A35 cars so much:

> I don't know really. I think Dr Penn liked to hold fast to the old ways. The A35s suited him; they were practical and well designed. They were also made to last. What I liked was their small engine. There was plenty of room to get my hands around most of the parts.
>
> I was sometimes called into the country by Dr Penn when there was a problem with his cars, and usually I got them going again. I went to places like Llanboidy and Blaenwaun – although one day Dr Penn phoned me from Llangadog. He was heading up the Black Mountain: this being the furthest place I can remember going. That day the steering had packed in; it was serious – so I towed the car back with an A-Bar. But, by the time I arrived, Dr Penn wasn't there; he had gone. I have no idea where he was going, but he found his own way there – and his own way back.

Little stopped Dr Penn, of course, as a trip to Scotland in February 1973 to watch Wales play Scotland in the Five Nations Championship demonstrated. In the corresponding fixture, two years earlier, an outstanding rugby match had thrilled spectators that few will forget.

That day, with the game delicately poised and nearing its end, Dr Penn saw Peter Brown, the tall Scottish forward, missing the relatively easy conversion (for him) of Chris Rea's try. This would have clinched the game for Scotland. But then drama unfolded amidst excitement shortly after both sets of forwards converged for a lineout. As ever, Scotland's masterly commentator, the one and only Bill McLaren, was there to describe the action in his broad and honey-rich accent. Impartial as ever – he broke into his customary crescendo at the death knell of this intriguing encounter, when his own heart must have sunk:

> Scotland [are] four points ahead at 18-14 . . . Delme Thomas again . . . Edwards to Barry John . . . out to Dawes . . . John Williams . . . Gerald Davies . . . Can Ian Smith get him? . . . It's Gerald Davies for Wales!

With Scotland's lead cut to one point, Wales needed a difficult conversion to win. As euphoric Welsh celebrations switched to a deathly hush before the kick, Bill McLaren continued:

> This is John Taylor, kicking from, for him, the correct touch line . . . It's high enough . . . What a conversion!

Wales had won 19-18 and Dr Penn had not forgotten this terrific match. Indeed, he was now planning to take his son Roger to the next Edinburgh episode in February. However, there was an another, more selfless reason behind the planned trip. Dr Penn was by now known across the length and breadth of West Wales for his unique commitment to patient care. Nothing was too much trouble for him, as countless people who remember him staying half the night with seriously ill patients and always finding time to make hospital visits, can testify.

Mair (Kirk) Thomas:

> When my husband, Mel, was ill, Dr Penn called back at midnight to give him an injection. 'I'm staying now, Mair, to make sure that we see a positive effect,' he said to me. He was more than a doctor; he was a friend to everyone.
>
> It makes me laugh to think back to the late 1950s when we had Sunday surgeries at Dolycwrt. Dr Penn was carrying out a little operation on me – saving me having to go to the hospital, especially as my son, David, was a two-year-old at home. 'I'm sorry I took so long, Mair,' he said to me. Of course, I wasn't in the least worried, but by the time I left, the waiting room was full of eagerly awaiting patients who were wondering what the delay was!

Ruth Davies:

> When my mother wasn't well there was a function going on in the town which Dr Penn attended. When he saw a light on in our house on his way home, he called just to see how my mother was getting on.

Josie Wills:

> I remember Dr Penn ringing late one night asking my husband, Peter, 'Are you busy' – because he was visiting a patient near Cefn Brafle. They were away for more than an hour and, on the way home, Peter asked,
>
> 'What was the problem there, George?'
>
> 'Well there's nothing medical that I can do anymore,' he said. 'It's just a case of reassuring the patient.'

That night Dr Penn had taken Peter along purely to give the impression that someone above him (medically) was also taking an interest. This was at ten o'clock at night, when Dr Penn should have been in bed and it happened more than once.

Maurice Dunbar:

We were all staunch supporters of Dr Penn in my family. I was one of fifteen children and he did some sterling work with us all. And, when my grandson who lived in Carmarthen was ill, he asked for the little boy's parents to meet him. 'Phone me if there are any developments in the night,' said Dr Penn. 'And I'll have him admitted straight away.' With Dr Penn on the case, the little boy ended up going to Llandough, the Heath and a children's hospital in Bristol.

Ivy Phillips:

I can remember Dr Penn travelling to Tegryn, on the boundary of his practice.

It was a real emergency that day and although I was only small at the time, I remember he was desperate to get his patient to the nearest hospital.

'Do you want me to call an ambulance, Dr Penn?' someone asked.

'No,' he replied, 'we haven't got time.'

Then he took the patient to Glangwili himself, in his little car.

Dr Roy Allen:

The greatest thing about George was his devotion to patients – and, likewise, their devotion to him. I remember thinking that he was spending too long with those who

had family or personal problems – instead of moving on
– but he actually taught me to be more tolerant of human
weaknesses, and I was grateful for this.

Before setting off for Scotland, Dr Penn had made
arrangements for a patient to undertake a period of obser-
vation and treatment at Wythenshawe Hospital in South
Manchester and the proposed trip would provide him with
an opportunity to pay this person a visit. Indeed, if he could
coerce and manoeuvre his faithful A35 car along the packed
motorways of Manchester and the winding country roads
to Edinburgh and back, this would amount to his very own
Triple Crown. And, if he could dare to make a flying visit to
another patient at Cardiff Royal Infirmary on the way, then
he could justifiably record a personal Grand Slam.

Setting out on Thursday, 1st February, Dr Penn motored
for two hours in a south-easterly direction – hardly the best
of starts when heading for Scotland – but managed, at least,
to visit his patient in Cardiff. Then the serious trip north
began, hampered by thick fog in the Welsh Marches.

'Do you mind, Rog, if we stay the night in Ludlow? We'll
get off to an early start in the morning.'

At one of the town's finest hotels, Dr Penn insisted
on settling his account that evening, pointing out to the
receptionist that he intended leaving in the early morning.

'Oh, you won't be able to do that,' said the lady. 'The front
door is locked until seven-thirty.'

'Don't worry, Rog,' said Dr Penn upstairs. 'I noticed a little
window near the reception. We can climb out of that, and
we'll have breakfast on the way.'

This was easier said than done. There was an awkward
three-foot drop the other side. More importantly, Dr Penn
wanted to close the window properly, ensuring that the

metal lever dropped exactly onto the protruding prong. Having managed this, it was 'all missions go'. Then a roadside transport café provided breakfast, the A35 lost amongst a host of big container lorries in the car park.

After being overtaken on the road by another Dolycwrt patient, Manchester was the next stop. Wythenshawe was already a huge hospital in which Dr Penn seemed almost insignificant amongst the crowds who made their way around its wide corridors. Some two hours later, having seen his patient, he was preparing to launch his A35 onto the next stretch of motorway – but not before pulling up alongside the red and white pole of a barber's shop on the outskirts of the city. 'He's got no customers, Rog. We'll have a quick haircut; then we'll be on our way.'

It was well into the evening when Dr Penn pulled into Jedburgh in the Scottish Borders. After staying the night he and Roger moved on swiftly the next morning, to arrive in Edinburgh for the afternoon kick-off.

With time to spare they joined the queue moving quickly towards Murrayfield. As they approached the ground a small doorway broke open at the back of the terraces. Caught up in a *mêlée*, they were amongst the crowd entering through this doorway, still holding their ticket money and feeling full of guilt, for not having paid.

The match could not possibly live up to the excellence of the last encounter, with Wales losing narrowly. Then, after returning to Jedburgh for the night, visiting Blackpool the next day and booking into a city-centre hotel in Liverpool on Sunday evening, Dr Penn's ever-reliable A35 pulled into the driveway of Hillside late on Monday afternoon.

Dr Penn's partner, Dr Malcolm Holding, a devotee of modern cars, could not believe that Dr Penn had managed to get to Edinburgh and back in his A35. In his retirement speech, Dr Penn – who incidentally sent his ticket money to the Scottish Rugby Union with a belated explanation and apology – recalled his partner's reaction on their return:

> When I reported back on the Tuesday morning surgery . . .
> Malcolm said, 'You didn't get to Edinburgh did you?'
>   And I said, 'Oh, yes we did.'
>   And he said, 'Not in that A35?' – to which I replied,
> 'Yes we did, and we had no problem at all.'
>   Then he looked shocked and said, 'Well, I've seen everything now: Hillary got to the top of Everest, Armstrong got to the Moon, and you've got to Edinburgh in your A35!'

Later that year, Dr Penn was again driving north in his A35, this time on his way to Cardigan. He and Peggy were attending an important ceremony at Teifi (Hall Stone) Lodge. Thursday, 11th October 1973 was the night Dr George Penn was appointed Worshipful Master in the lodge – the highest honour it could confer upon him – by his predecessor in the role, W. Bro. George Alvery Cove. Following the ceremony, there was a six-course banquet at the Cliff Hotel, Gwbert on Sea. Teifi Lodge does things in style, and its members are still proud of Worshipful Brother George Penn. The following is an extract from their *50th Anniversary Booklet* of 1974:

> W. Bro. Penn is singularly proud of the fact that he is the product of the Masonic Boys' School. He is a man of wide and varied interests, which includes conservation and the preservation of railways threatened by closure.
>   Despite the heavy demands of a large practice, W. Bro. Dr Penn has managed to attend Teifi Lodge meetings with praiseworthy regularity, and is keen to improve facilities in the lodge which add to the comfort and pleasure of the members.

W. Bro. Jestyn Edwards, mentioned earlier, has another story to tell:

> George's time as Worshipful Master was extremely busy. He travelled extensively around our local counties, visiting neighbouring lodges and attending Installation Nights. Of course, George enjoyed meeting people and he made many friends along the way. And, when he got up to speak, he was usually humorous. We all acknowledged his generous community work, and I was pleased to judge for him at Whitland Carnival one year. As usual, he was kept busy that day, but we still found time for a bit of fun.
>
> On another occasion, I was going home from Lodge rather late one evening and ahead of me was George in his car. I noticed that his reversing light was on and I flashed to let him know that something was wrong. George couldn't go fast and the road was narrow, so I stayed behind him. A bit further on, we came to Blaenffos, where there was a petrol station at the time, and this is where George pulled aside to let me pass. But when he saw my car stop, he panicked – until I stepped out. 'Thank goodness it's you, Jestyn,' he said, 'I thought you were the police.'

The Beginning of the Teifi Valley Railway

To the credit of Dr Penn and members of the hard-working West Wales Railway Action Committee, they never took their foot off the throttle when it came to promoting and defending the railway lines of Wales. They stood defiant, opposing line cuts, demanding to examine the rationale for such proposals and, slowly but surely, enlisting the support of a sympathetic Welsh population and its public bodies. Dr Penn continued to fly the flag of a committee that had by now also gained respect in the eyes of British Railways and Westminster, by virtue of its *bona fide* intentions and sheer determination.

Meeting fire with fire, they slowed down the demise of the network, whilst advocating its growth, by launching credible campaigns to reopen St Clears, and later Templeton, stations. Although these ultimately failed, they provided invaluable publicity for the committee and its aims. For Dr Penn, such work was a respite from an increasingly hectic medical schedule; it invigorated and challenged him, providing that certain 'something' to strive for he had once described in his little black book at Bushey School. The committee continued to charter trains to Builth Wells, Shrewsbury, Kidderminster (an important railway junction) and Swansea, where a boat trip to Lundy offered another popular outing. And despite setbacks, and all odds being stacked against it, momentum seemed to be on the committee's side.

It is this spirited momentum that Dr Penn and his 'Action Committee' took into another highly ambitious challenge, to keep alive the Carmarthen branch line to Newcastle Emlyn and Lampeter. By the early 1970s passenger services on this line – which provided a connection to the university town of Lampeter – had long gone, but now the line's important freight service, which carried coal, milk, wool, cattle and other livestock was also threatened with closure. Working hard alongside coal merchants and other tradesmen, Dr Penn deployed all manner of political tactics to prevent the closure of this important country line. The *Cardigan & Tivy-side Advertiser* for Friday, 29th December 1972, carried a headline which indicated the enormity of the task:

> Teifi Valley line gets 28-day reprieve to help local coal merchants: little hope held out after January 27th.

Clearly, it was a tremendous effort on the part of the 'Action Committee' and others to force a further reprieve in the face of such adversity. Their message – that people actually cared about this serious railway carve-up and that it had to stop – was obviously getting through to those in power. By the 23rd March 1973, the *Western Mail* was reporting:

> Teifi Valley railway escapes the axe – Councils agree today £100,000 a year to keep the line going.

Exuberance at this good news was short-lived, however; with echoes of the Cardi Bach closure of 1962, the rail service came to an end in late 1973.

In the run-up to this, the Teifi Valley Railway Preservation Society was established in October 1972 with a view to buying the stretch of line between Carmarthen and Newcastle Emlyn in order to run a tourist steam train attraction. The members of this society were another highly ambitious group of enthusiasts, who dreaded the thought that trains would stop running through this picturesque valley. The group moved quickly, opening negotiations with British Railways to buy the track bed and lines, and excursion trips for passengers were soon being organised along its course.

Such campaigns served to stop the physical lines – much in demand because of the rising cost of steel – from being lifted, whilst also attracting considerable media publicity. This was good news for Dr Penn and his 'Action Committee' who added their support to the work of the society, as minutes – handwritten by Dr Penn – from a committee meeting, held at the Fishers Hotel, Whitland on Friday, 18th January 1974 make clear:

> Carmarthen-Lampeter-Newcastle Emlyn
> The recent events and efforts regarding this line were mentioned and the secretary made the point that our members ought to join the Teifi Valley Railway Preservation Society because of the great efforts being made by that Society.

Roger Padfield and Barrie Burgess' book, *The Teifi Valley Railway*, notes the considerable difficulties facing the 'Preservation Society' in a rural area so different from populated industrial regions such as the Midlands, where preservation work of this nature could attract the support of numerous enthusiasts. The book was, nevertheless, optimistic about the future:

> Despite these problems, two small groups are determined to see that at least a little of the Teifi Valley Railway remains for posterity. The Preservation Society has now turned its attention to the station site at Lampeter, and the Dyfed Railway Company, an offshoot of the Society, maintains an interest in the southern section of the line.

Spearheading 'interest in the southern section of the line' was none other than Dr Penn, whose 'Action Committee' was now turning its attention to another important railway project. This was the Teifi Valley Narrow Gauge Railway Society – with Dr Penn as secretary – which was established to pioneer a small steam venture along some of its length: a strategic move that offered slight hope of safeguarding the reopening of the full line at a later date. After putting proposals together the committee was advised to form a limited company to help achieve its goal. An account of the meeting organised by the West Wales Railway Action Committee in Lampeter early in 1974 was reported in the *Cardigan & Tivy-side Advertiser,* under the headline 'Company to be formed to buy and run Teifi Valley Railway':

> The chairman of the proposed new company will be Dr G. K. Penn of Whitland, who told the *Tivy-side* that it was hoped to have the company legally in being very soon. Then an appeal would be made for financial support not only to all interested organisations and private individuals throughout Wales, but throughout Britain as well.
>
> 'We consider this line absolutely essential to Dyfed and to Wales and that it may in the future have to be re-extended to Aberystwyth in order to provide a north to south rail link in Wales' [said Dr Penn].
>
> 'This line has a greater significance than any other branch line which has hitherto been closed.'

Dr Penn's immediate objective was less ambitious than the article suggests. Although the re-opening of the line to Aberystwyth was a long-term aim, the primary focus was on opening nine miles of track in the Teifi Valley to provide rides to enthusiasts and tourists. The early meetings of the new concern, Dyfed Railway Company Limited (trading as The Vale of Teifi Narrow Gauge Railway Society), were held at

Dolycwrt Surgery in Whitland in late 1974 – once Dr Penn's last patient had walked out of the front door. John Llewellyn, who was a vital part of the group for years, explains:

> Unlike the Cardi Bach, George knew that we had a chance to do something here. The line was still in place; it was in the hands of British Rail. He was raring to go, he was the instigator and he dragged me, and others, in. We began our meetings in Dolycwrt – this being convenient for George, and all of us really – but I remember saying that we should be meeting where the railway line was, around Newcastle Emlyn or Henllan, so we moved.

When Liz Perry came to live in West Wales in 1975 she noticed posters around Newcastle Emlyn inviting people to attend a public meeting about this new steam venture:

> I had no idea that the town once had a railway station. In earlier years, I had been involved with research into railway systems in East Africa – so I thought I'd go along to see if I could help.
>
> The next meeting was at the Bunch of Grapes pub in Newcastle Emlyn. A room had been hired upstairs and, being a pub, it was a social affair. I remember seeing members folding raffle tickets and putting them into a large drum, ready to be drawn. Dr Penn, the driving force, came in late; he had been writing the minutes in the car park.
>
> The outline, in brief, was that money had to be raised for the track bed and the Light Railway Order, and this was the start of some serious fundraising on the part of the members. Soon it became clear to us that we had entered into a big project. Dr Penn had for some time been locked in talks with British Rail, negotiating on behalf of the

group. We had deadlines to work to, but Dr Penn wrote furiously on our behalf – his eloquence staving off many an evil day! Dr Penn also knew everybody, which was an enormous help, and then he actively wrote for donations and subscriptions. He was very determined that we would succeed.

John Llewellyn remembers the excursion trains that Dr Penn organised from Pembrokeshire as part of the fund-raising effort:

I can remember having to get up around three o'clock in the morning to accompany George to catch the train as it came through Whitland on its way down to Pembroke Dock – this being where the excursion started. George insisted that we be on the train from the first pick-up point. Of course, it was totally empty when we jumped aboard. It was a long day, extremely tiring, but we had a lot of fun. Very often the train was full, jam-packed. It was a big responsibility, but we needed the funds.

Of course, it is not easy to persuade people to part with their hard-earned money, especially to support a modest concern at the infancy of its being. The following letter provides a good example of how Dr Penn tried to bridge the gap between a man and his wallet:

Dear Sir,

I am writing on behalf of the Vale of Teifi Narrow Gauge Railway Society, which has been formed during the past three years to buy the track bed of the former British Railways line between Newcastle Emlyn and Pencader junction – a distance of nine miles – with a view to operating a tourist railway in this delightful part of rural Wales.

We require £15,000 to complete the purchase, which includes the cost of a Light Railway Order which we are required to have if the scheme is to continue.

So far, we have reached the halfway point in our target, which we are supposed to attain by February 1979. We have a very enthusiastic and active committee and one of our members *A. N. Other*, in fact, suggested that I write to you to tell you of our hopes and aspirations – as he thought that you might wish to support us in our endeavours and perhaps might like to make a contribution!

Clearly, this was only one means of raising money. The train excursions continued, as well as the raffles, concerts, film shows and dinners. Dr Penn enlisted the support of friends in Whitland to help arrange social events, John Llewellyn being one of these. For years, an annual New Year's Eve function was held at Llanboidy Village Hall, or sometimes at Whitland Grammar School – thankfully taking over from the New Year's Eve parties at Hillside! – and sometimes Danny Stephens and his wife, Mabel, led the Whitland Male Choir for concerts such as the one held at Ebenezer Chapel, Newcastle Emlyn in 1979. Elizabeth, Dr Penn's eldest daughter, remembers these busy days, especially the rail excursions:

The train trips were always family events for us and during the early 1970s we regularly travelled on the Central Wales line, firstly to Builth Wells for the Royal Welsh Show and then to Shrewsbury for the flower show. Each time we took a big urn full of hot water into the guard's van where we made tea and coffee for the passengers, and I remember we were kept busy all the way. But we enjoyed the scenery and the occasion and there was a lot of fun – even though we were usually too tired to make the most of the show.

It's true to say that the day didn't always go by without an incident. One year someone got on the train near Llandeilo believing that it was the regular passenger service – and when it didn't stop at the next station – he pulled the Emergency Cord thinking something was wrong. Of course, this caused a bit of an upheaval, and I'm sure Dad was in the middle of it all, sorting things out.

All the while, the hard work of the faithful committee members never waned. Richard Nicholl, the youngest, had worked alongside Dr Penn since the early 1970s. He had high ambitions for the railway and still does today. He told me that a few years into the project the committee started to really understand just what they had taken on. A 'Bridges Fund' was required to satisfy the requirements of the local authority and a survey was also arranged, both substantial financial demands that fell upon the committee. In addition, there was the cost and other implications of the Light Railway Order. In the end, it was deemed prudent to concentrate on developing a much smaller one-mile stretch of the old line. This made the project more feasible, though the committee still hoped to extend the railway line at some later date. Richard saw a lot of Dr Penn during these years:

I met Dr Penn when I joined the 'Action Committee' shortly after the 'Pembroke and Tenby' line had been saved. We held some of our meetings in the Yelverton Hotel in Whitland then, and I can remember us waiting around for Dr Penn. He was so busy; he was often late. Railways were going down like nine-pins, and we all realised exactly what Dr Penn had done in saving that line. More to the point he had raised the profile of railways by making such a defiant and successful stand. The message was that the people actually wanted the rail services to remain. This was vital at the time.

Because of his enormous connections, he'd be able to sell the vast majority of tickets for our train trips. Peggy was always supportive, too. She had a lot to contend with, but she saw the bright side of it all. They were the perfect match; they understood each other.

Dr Penn would be out on his busy rounds, but he'd also be selling our tickets. Sometimes he'd go as far as Llanelli or further. He had a good working relationship with the travel agents; he got everybody involved. On the morning of the excursion, he'd be in Hillside, hurrying to get ready, leaving some things to the last minute.

'Hurry up, George,' Peggy would say. 'We'll miss the train!'

Then we'd go down to Milford Haven to ensure the carriages were properly filled. Sometimes, we'd have ten carriages, so utilising every seat was important.

In the early days, Dr Penn and I went on several trips, such as to the Tal-y-Llyn Railway in North Wales, purely to learn more about steam ventures. That morning we travelled to Shrewsbury in his A35, passing the Sugar Loaf Mountain by breakfast time. Then we took a train from Shrewsbury to Towyn – later riding up and down the Tal-y-Llyn line. Dr Penn was friendly with Mervyn Matthews, who lived nearby. He chaired the *Welsh* Railways Action Group which George was also connected with.

I remember late one night – it was about midnight – when we were returning from the Henllan Falls Hotel. This had been a long meeting and Dr Penn was feeling thirsty. As we were getting nearer to Blaenwaun, he turned to me:

'Shall we stop the car, Richard, and have a drink?'

'No, George,' I replied. 'It's gone twelve now; we've both got to get back.'

A few minutes later, we were getting nearer to a pub.

'I think we'll have a quick drink, Richard. Don't you agree?'

So we stopped outside the pub, which was all in darkness now.

'I think everyone's gone to bed, George,' I said – as he shot out of the car.

I remember seeing him banging on the door. Then the upstairs window opened. Here goes, I thought. He's going to get a mouthful now – but I was so wrong. The lady took one look to see who it was, saying 'Oh, Dr Penn, I'll be down now,' before opening the door.

Wherever we stopped, the local people suddenly came alive when Dr Penn called. He'd walk through the door and I guarantee they'd spring to life. They would exchange a few Welsh words with him and then he usually bought a round. After a bit of a discussion, some medical issue would arise. Then Dr Penn disappeared to his car for a prescription pad – there were usually a few of these around in the different compartments – and then he'd be writing one out for a patient. Of course, Dr Penn's car was also an interesting feature – Liz Perry likening it to travelling around in a glorified doctor's bag!

The Death of a Father-Figure – as Dr Penn's Spirits Drop

I N DECEMBER 1976, Dr Hugh Philipps died aged 79. His obituary occupied a central column in the *Carmarthen Journal* during Christmas week. Survived by his grandchildren, he was remembered for being High Sheriff of Carmarthen, a Justice of the Peace, a holder of the Royal British Legion 'Gold Badge', a survivor of World War II and, of course, for being a long serving general practitioner.

His death had a profound effect on Dr Penn. The two doctors had known each other well and had shared a close friendship. Dr Hugh Philipps had also helped to ease Dr Penn's medical load by attending to surgeries and visiting patients when he had bitten off more than he could chew.

On the day of Dr Hugh Philipps' burial, Dr Penn would have stood in the graveyard of the ancient church in Llanboidy and noticed the pleasant green countryside in the distance. Yet, a big black cloud threatened to engulf his own peaceful world. As with all his ailing patients, Dr Penn had been attentive to Dr Hugh Philipps to the end and, only weeks earlier he had been telephoned by the gentleman's housekeeper asking him to call. Barry Burgess, a close colleague on the railway committee explains:

> For some time, George was going back and fore regularly to his home, Clyngwynne. But, by now, things were pretty serious; the great man was desperately ill, not far off the end. 'The doctor would like a word with you, Dr Penn,' said

the lady, directing him upstairs, to a seat close to Dr Hugh Philipps in his bed.

'Will you do something for me, George?' he asked – as if to suggest he had something major to request, something profound to say.

'Of course I will,' answered Dr Penn, 'and what is that, Dr Hugh?'

'Get yourself a haircut, George!'

By now, Dr Penn had another problem which had slowly taken hold of him over the years. This was his love of whisky – at one time a medicine prescribed to patients in the old infirmary wards. For years he had participated in a 'drop or two' on his rounds at the kind behest of his patients. But his drinking had latterly become excessive, although outwardly there was little real indication of this. By choice, Dr Penn had filled his life with responsibilities, but increasingly it seemed that these could only be fulfilled with the aid of whisky.

At home in Hillside, he was encouraged to drink less – but here was a man under great pressure, fighting hard on too many fronts, and a glass of whisky had become his escape. The human body has amazing powers of recovery and Dr Penn's body was, no doubt, accommodating the alcohol whilst appearing to function as normal.

By the summer of 1978 – a special time of the year when Dr Penn escaped to Amroth or Pendine for a swim and when he prepared for his annual fortnight's leave to run Whitland Week – his daily routines were just as full and much the same. Thankfully, he had been excused some of his earlier commitments to the Masonic Lodge and to the Farmers Union of Wales, yet now he had picked up another long-term responsibility, working for Whitland Town Hall. Dr Penn, alongside Grismond Jenkins and one or two others, had successfully campaigned for the town to purchase this grand Edwardian Hall – built in 1904 and, at the time, a social venue for the personnel of Whitland Creamery.

This pleased Dr Penn greatly who was happy to serve as the Management Committee's secretary. This involved monthly meetings and administration work, as well as organising functions to pay for the building and its bills. Despite being engrossed in commitments further afield, Dr Penn never forgot Whitland's interests and he took great pleasure in this project, as he had done ten years earlier in similar circumstances when helping to secure Whitland Rugby Club.

On the evening of Monday, 3rd July 1978, however, he was heading to Newcastle Emlyn to attend to various business matters concerning the Teifi Valley Railway. With him was Denzil Davies from Whitland who also contributed towards this steam venture. After visiting patients in Clynderwen and Efailwen on the way up, Dr Penn and Denzil proceeded to Newcastle Emlyn, stopping on route for drinks. After accomplishing all that they had intended, including liaising with a committee member and later meeting a Councillor, they called at the town's Ivy Bush pub. At the end of the evening, they were two of only four people left in the premises. Upon leaving to go home, they chose the direct road through Penrherber, Cwm Cych, Pantyblaidd and Blaenwaun. Dr Penn was behind the wheel and now continues the story:

> We had scarcely turned left into the narrow road to Cwm Cych when a car appeared behind me. It stayed right behind, within a distance of about five-yards, or perhaps less at times . . . I would hazard a strong guess that the headlights were full-on, because I was dazzled . . . Eventually, I said to Denzil, 'The person behind us is obviously in a bigger

hurry than we are, so I'll pull in to let him pass.' I came to
a wide grass verge which would accommodate my small
Austin A35 car . . . Much to my horror, instead of passing
me, the car stopped and out popped a policeman.

Suffice to say, Dr Penn failed the breathalyser test and was in
real trouble. 'Doctor, you are under arrest,' were the words,
delivered sternly. He was driven to a convenient police
station for a second test – which, again, he failed. This meant
that medical officers were summoned to take a sample of his
blood, which, luckily for Dr Penn, proved to be fully within
the accepted tolerances.

Emerging by the skin of his teeth, Dr Penn had learnt
a hard lesson in life and, in fairness, it was overdue. 'Penn,
you are inclined to be individualistic,' his housemaster had
told him at Bushey School in 1944 – and how true. For all
Dr Penn's exceptional qualities and outstanding offerings, he
could not escape the law on this occasion, and neither could
he really complain. Despite feeling uneasy and downcast
to begin with, his moods fluctuated from feeling guilty
to innocent; saddened to heartened; annoyed to grateful,
publicly demoralised to privately triumphant.

The important thing – and let us thank the policeman
unreservedly for this – is that he would think twice about
accepting another drink. In the Penn household at Hillside,
the initial shock had given way to feelings of relief and hope.
From now on things would start to change – despite continued
feelings of despondency from Dr Penn, as are clearly evident
from his diary entries over the next year or two:

Sunday January 14th 1979
I phoned Neville to ask if he'd like to come to Barry with me
today, and he said that he wouldn't. I bought some flowers
for Auntie Mattie and Auntie Margot, and when I called on

Neville, he decided to come. Whilst in the hospital I loaded up all the beer-empties following my drinks delivery to the ward at Christmas. We went to Morriston and I visited two patients. This was a depressing experience, and I was frightened when I got back to the car, because Neville wasn't in it! However, he wasn't far away: in the hospital looking for toilets.

We then went into Swansea and had gammon, egg and chips at the Three Lamps. Then off to Barry – asking if I could be excused to go down to the sea. It was gorgeous down in 'The Knap.' I washed my face in the sea and gathered firewood. There were crowds of fishermen on the beach and they were all gathering their lines and rods and packing up. I discovered that they were having a 'big day' and were to meet in the Water Cliff Hotel – so I, too, went in there and had a pint and enjoyed mingling with the anglers for a while.

Later, I dropped Neville off at St David's Hospital, after buying him a drink in Briton Ferry. He said that he had enjoyed an interesting day. In the main, it had been successful, but I had been feeling depressed: I'd seen Neville insulted at St David's Hospital; I'd seen my mother confused; I'd seen those wretched motorways again; I'd seen two patients in a bad way in Morriston, and both Auntie Mattie and Auntie Margot were getting old.

Thursday July 12th 1979
After putting quite a few posters out in Saundersfoot with Roger – Peggy and I went to Llandysul to the film show, arranged by the Entertainments sub-committee of the Vale of Teifi Railway. Unfortunately, hardly anyone was present and everyone was fed up about it. Afterwards we went to the Porth Hotel for a drink and some of the committee

were with us, and seemed to be full of concern about the Royal Welsh Show trip, which they couldn't see succeeding somehow. Then it was mentioned that the intermediate bit of line [where Dr Penn eventually hoped to extend the railway] was being built on – so I was fed up between everything.

Thursday November 22nd 1979
At 4 p.m., I sallied forth to Llandysul to do some work for the railway. I called at Gwasg Gomer and bought a birthday card for Neville and posted it. I called on a gentleman regarding a railway contribution and he was very interested, but firstly had to speak to his wife. I then visited a businessman, who just listened impassively and displayed no interest. Then I went to the Porth Hotel to speak to someone who wasn't there, onwards to another business person who was away – before travelling to the Half Moon, where John Llewellyn and others had agreed to meet me.

The death of his mother, Beatrice, compounded Dr Penn's miseries. In the years prior to her passing, at a time when her memory began to fade, Beatrice stayed for long periods at Hillside. Beatrice was fond of the grounds and her main love was to go into the garden where she'd spend hours, often weeding on her hands and knees. Still a keen smoker, it was amusing to see her approaching the end of a long row of onions with a cigarette in her mouth, an inch or more of ash clinging delicately to its end. 'Fags are my only vice,' she often said, and she certainly had no intention of giving them up.

When one day Dr Penn suggested to his Aunty Margot in Bridgend that Beatrice, who was now in her eighties, go there for a break, she was made welcome – in fact, so welcome that she stayed for two years. Following this, she spent some time before her death in a home for the elderly in Sully. Beatrice was cremated in Coychurch, Bridgend.

As the months rolled on, Dr Penn's diary entries continued in the same vein, sadly one of at least mild depression:

Wednesday June 11th 1980
A 'no peace for the wicked' sort of day – busy all afternoon, right up to the Dairies surgery, where I arrived late at 4 p.m., and then busy all evening, with two extra evening calls. Then I was called out of bed at 3.30 a.m. to go to Henllan. I suppose, with so much to think about besides work – the narrow Gauge Railway, the Town Hall, Whitland Week, Neville, Aunty Mattie, Auntie Margo and Elizabeth's wedding – it's disappointing to be unable to make a phone call or to do something besides practice work.

Thursday June 12th 1980
I was feeling downright miserable, weary, limp and without much will or morale – but I felt I've got to keep trying. I called to deliver raffle tickets, but the person was out . . . and then to my next call, but I found they had already been given tickets to sell: the gentleman complaining that he had too many. This caused me to buy some of his back . . . !

With the Teifi Valley railway fast approaching a critical and defining moment in its history, Dr Penn was now frantically trying to secure the Light Railway Order – a major obstacle and daunting process in its own right – so that the purchase of the track bed could duly follow. Some six years had passed since the early meetings at Dolycwrt and, understandably, anxiety was beginning to creep in. Of course, there was a limit as to how long British Railways could wait – prompting Dr Penn to demonstrate the strength of his convictions by offering a personal financial guarantee. This would hasten progress, he thought – but, when this was deemed to be unacceptable to some of the parties concerned, he was saddened to the core:

> How awful I felt going down the County Hall steps? I could have cried. I'd have loved to have drowned my sorrows or at least to have had a couple of drinks, but as I'm still off drinking, I didn't bother. And with a heavy heart I made my way homeward.
>
> When I got to Hillside, I was so depressed. I could hardly eat dinner and I couldn't help the tears and thickness and fullness of my throat. I felt really terrible, thinking that we may have lost everything.

John Llewellyn explained:

> The thing about George is that he had the difficult task all along of negotiating with British Railways. He was the man in the middle, and this really wasn't easy. More than anything else, he wanted to secure the Light Railway Order – a huge administrative task which involved presenting our case to Parliament and seeking legal representation to overcome the statutory requirements. These things were not granted lightly, and employing parliamentary agents was a costly business. We had to demonstrate our competency and we forever needed money; it was almost impossible to make ends meet. We also had to play our part in maintaining the bridges and the embankments. It was a real trial, a very tough time – but George knew that if we could get over this one big hurdle, the track purchase would quickly follow. The pressure was mounting. We relied on George to keep all respective parties happy – including subscribers. It was a worrying time.

Wedding Bells and a Little Red Book

A s the warm weeks of the summer months went by, Dr Penn emerged from his dark tunnel. In fact, he was soon stepping onto the stage and into the limelight – in front of a large gathering of happy people at Nant-y-Ffin Motel, Llandissilio. This was the occasion of the wedding reception of Dr Penn and Peggy's first daughter, Elizabeth, to Kenneth Bevan. He was never happier than when enthralling a capacity audience and this had not been possible lately when challenging the railway authorities. Putting campaigning aside for the day, he intended to enjoy himself, despite having greatly reduced his drinking. Here is Dr Penn, the entertainer: self-deprecating and thoroughly amusing. This is a small part of his speech that day describing his early upbringing:

> I look back on Brynmenyn and I am really sure that the seeds were sown there for me to want to be a doctor, and certainly my memories are a bit medical.
>
> For instance, I remember I first heard the word 'migraine' when my Auntie Katie used to return to bed and draw the wooden Venetian blinds, because of her blinding headaches. And I was a bit of a nuisance going up to see her, to ask how she was feeling, and she wanted to get rid of me in a way – and said,
>
> 'Look George, on the dressing table over there, you'll find a little red book. Learn a few verses out of it.'
>
> It was only the size of a book of stamps and was made up of Bible quotations.

On the following Sunday service in Betharan Chapel, I could see all the children going up to the Big Seat to say a verse – mostly in Welsh and mostly well-known verses – and I started to head towards the Big Seat, my family trying to restrain me. When I got there, I wanted my turn, and said proudly,

'And they shall be mine, saith the Lord, in that day when I shall gather up my jewels.'

And the minister, who had a deep, reverberating voice said,

'Well done, George, and what part of the Bible does that come from?'

'Oh,' I replied, 'it doesn't come from the Bible. It was in my auntie's little red book!'

My grandmother had the most drastic treatment for my croup and bronchitis – rubbing goose grease immediately into my chest, and covering it with hot Welsh flannel and even making me swallow the goose grease. And there was elderflower wine, and all the neighbours knew when the wine was ready. They used to call around under the pretext of waiting for the magical moment when my Auntie Mattie would say, 'And would you like a taste of my new elderflower wine?'

This subject steered Dr Penn's train of thought back to some of the farms around Whitland, which were particularly popular places to visit during times of brewing. He was amused to recall one lady who gave him a glass of home-brewed beer 'with her apologies for having to rush off, to play the organ in a chapel Temperance Service!'

To come back to Brynmenyn, I was always with the doctor. I once had a greenstick fracture of my forearm, which was all out of shape; and he put my arm across his knee, and pulled it, as if breaking a stick. And, of course, I howled mightily, and he gave me a sixpence – which was reckoned to be fantastic at the time.

I remember falling off my bicycle, and I was in quite a mess – with bandages everywhere, including both hands and wrists, and both knees. And they were feeling sorry for me and they thought it would cheer me up to go to Abergarw farm for the hay-making – where we children used to have the much looked-forward-to ride on the *gambo* when it was going up to the field, empty, to fetch more hay.

The only trouble was that I couldn't get on the gambo without help, because I was all bandages. And I was waiting for a pull-up when Rover, the farm dog, very excited with all the fuss, was barking about the place – and, amused that I was the only one not on the cart, he came up to me excitedly and found the only un-bandaged part of me . . . and bit my behind! I went howling back to Bryn Haf and, there, my aunt had to attend to a bit more of me.

The family doctor was a frequent visitor for professional and other reasons and I remember my grandmother, who was a teetotaller and against anyone having a drink, keeping a bottle of whisky in the sideboard, especially for the doctor! I think I got interested in the idea of being a doctor in those days!

Then Dr Penn shared his amusement about a little dig that had been directed his way regarding his past drinking:

I was mightily thrilled when I qualified and I couldn't get over it! A chap asked me in a British Legion dinner recently if I liked being a doctor. I replied that, in the main, I did, and that I was so thrilled when I got through, I don't think the thrill has ever worn off. And he replied,

'Oh, I see; that explains why you have never stopped celebrating!'

Elizabeth has not forgotten her father's entertaining performance that day, which continued for over forty minutes:

> It was the funniest wedding speech that I can remember and Dad kept everyone amused throughout. Then, at the end, it dawned on him that he had to propose a toast. His humour was really appreciated and he had a wonderful round of applause. But what amused me most was that before he had finished speaking, guests had already started to arrive for the evening party.

Only a few months later at the end of that same year, 1980, Dr Penn could reflect upon another job well done. The Light Railway Order was granted, heralding a time of relief and peacefulness over the Christmas period. The track bed exchanged hands the following year; and now it really was full steam ahead for the Teifi Valley Railway Society. It had been a traumatic start with committee members having to overcome one setback after another – but now things were moving. Richard Nicholl outlines Dr Penn's next proposal:

> We knew someone who had rather a lot of railway knowledge, and he had heard that a steam engine was for sale in Leeds. This was the *Alan George* locomotive, built by a well-known firm, 'Hunslet of Leeds', in the 1890s. It had been used at the Penrhyn slate quarries of North Wales, and seemed to suit our purposes for a two-foot gauge.
>
> Dr Penn was determined to find out more about it and nominated me and two others to travel to Leeds. We got there by car and stayed in a Bed and Breakfast house. I remember the bidding took place in a person's garage. Fortunately, few people had heard about it, so we were able

to secure the engine at a favourable price – and, in the end, we also managed to buy a little diesel locomotive (called *Sholto*) and the portable garage where the bidding took place: this being our first engine shed!

Dr Penn put a lot of money into this, but the main thing is that it worked for us. Everyone seemed happy with it.

There were now tangible rewards which drove the committee onwards, but it soon had to cope without its inspirational leader. Dr Penn's life was over-full and as events were overtaking him he decided that he had to 'step down from the footplate' and take up a more passive, supportive role. A new era was dawning for the railway with which Dr Penn no longer felt entirely comfortable. As John Llewellyn said:

> George always had the vision of us getting the railway going under our own head of steam. But others realised that to make progress we needed the financial backing of bigger concerns, such as the Local Authorities and the Welsh Development Agency. George admitted that this wasn't totally his scene. He didn't seem to favour grants. We parted company in a way, although he remained supportive throughout, and friendly on a personal basis.

In 1983 Dr Penn took delight when the track to nearby Pontpreshitw was in place, soon to carry passengers behind the little *Alan George* engine – as well as extending further in later years to Llandyfriog. In this area, he is still remembered as a founder member of the railway committee. Richard Nicholl's opinion was that Dr Penn was a practical politician who could have stood for Parliament. Richard Parker called him the 'Redoubtable Dr Penn of Whitland', whilst another of his colleagues simply described him as the 'Great Railway Champion of West Wales'.

Barry Burgess, mentioned earlier as a member of this railway committee, has a few stories:

I first spoke to George when I phoned him for advice about running a train trip. He had been in the business of chartering trains for a while; probably the only man in Wales – certainly in a personal capacity. He was a one-off. He lived his life the way he believed. Lots of people were absolutely devoted to him. I was at a meeting with George once when he arrived late – having been called away to see a patient, as he so often was. When he walked in, we all got up and clapped him. People worshipped him. And the thing about George was that he didn't flaunt the old doctor bit.

George could be very funny when he made his presentations. I think he was a shy man, a reluctant speaker – but he had terrific courage and spoke with innocence. If there was something he wanted to do, he did it; nothing troubled him. I remember he made us laugh when he described the time he was called to Crymych to see somebody who had been injured in a motorbike scramble. Some poor chap had been laid out on a table in a saloon bar by enthusiastic helpers – covered from head to foot in bandages, like an Egyptian mummy. I'm not sure if he could breathe! By the time George undid all of this to get to the man, he had had enough; he was ready to take off like a shot. 'Thank goodness you're here doctor!' he said. Otherwise he'd have disappeared like a scolded rabbit!

I remember the time we went on a Campbell Steamer to Lundy Island. When we got out of the boat, there was a long climb up the hill, and a lady twisted her ankle. At the time, George was in no hurry to leave the boat. I think his attitude was to let everybody go ahead while he had a snooze on deck. Then, there was a loudspeaker message: 'Is there anyone who can help?'

In no time, members of a voluntary first aid group were assisting, and there was a stretcher involved and a big procession of helpers commandeering the lady back onto the boat.

'George, do you think you ought to do something?' asked Peggy, 'You're probably the only doctor on the boat.'

Of course, George was wise enough to know that she was alright. But Peggy nudged him, so he stepped forward:

'Excuse me, I'm Dr Penn. Is everything alright?'

'Well yes doctor,' she replied quietly, 'I've never had so much fuss made of me in all my life.'

We were once in a railway meeting near Henllan – I believe it was the Henllan Falls. We were chatting away, and a chap came up to Dr Penn:

'Are you Dr Penn?' he asked. 'Can I have a word with you – because a mate of mine is in the back room and is in trouble?'

So they went into a little huddle.

'He's done something to his leg some months ago,' said the man. 'He will not go to see a doctor; he is dead-scared. He can barely walk; it's quite serious.'

Of course, a lot of doctors wouldn't get involved; protocol interfered. But with George it was all about getting someone better. So he disappeared with the guy to see his friend.

George was missing quite a long time, maybe up to an hour, but he eventually came back. It transpired that the old boy's leg was gangrenous and weeping. George had sat down with him and spoke to him person to person, not doctor to patient – as if he was a good friend. He convinced this old boy that he had to do something quickly. He told him that his only chance was to have the leg removed. George succeeded in convincing the man that he had to see his doctor and get it done. He explained how successful false legs are today, and that he would be able to get around, that he had nothing to fear. Then George made a point of speaking to the man's doctor the next day.

It was about six months later, when this same person walked back into the pub on his false leg – making for George to shake him warmly by the hand. 'Dr Penn, you saved my life.'

PART X
SOLE PRACTITIONER AT DOLYCWRT

A Love of all Things Traditional –
as the Tributes Flow

D R PENN WAS now going through a transitional period as he prepared for the last passage of his medical career. It was to be a fourteen-year journey to the distant destination of 'retirement' – the 'Promised Land' for most, but a rather unknown quantity for Dr Penn, and to be delayed until the last. This journey had to be planned carefully, and given that Dr Penn was soon to start work as a sole practitioner he needed to relinquish some of the commitments that had hitherto taken up his time. Dr Malcolm Holding, a close working partner since 1962, explains:

> The thing about George is that he tried to fit so many things into one day. He was on call from all sorts of places – and, if he had a few minutes, he'd be dipping into his Masonic book to learn a few more lines. He was heavily involved in so many committees. I'm sure George attended more meetings per week than there were nights in the week.

Whitland Week was one of Dr Penn's biggest commitments in the town. Eddie Fussell knew this well:

> When Whitland Week came round, Dr Penn was full of it. He made it all tick. When others were going abroad to find the sun, he and Peggy were spending their fortnight

organising the events. I can remember artists like Ryan and Ronnie coming to the town. They stayed overnight in one of the hotels. We all had a riot; nobody wanted to go home. Dr Penn was there; he was in the middle of it all, as usual.

I used to arrange the barbecue on carnival day. And very often, I'd stay until the early evening for the carnival dance. There were people everywhere then, all enjoying themselves. On one occasion, Dr Penn helped me; he was doing the cooking. I have a photo of him in a typical butcher's apron and straw hat, and certainly looking the part. Dr Penn was always searching for something new to bring to the 'Week.' One year we had a *Generation Game*, just like Bruce Forsyth's T.V. programme. I was demonstrating how to link a string of sausages. Then two teams of competitors had a go on the stage. We were in the Town Hall, and the place was full. We had some fun that day, and we saw some shapes and sizes, too.

Over the years, Dr Penn whipped up Whitland Week into such a frenzy of activity that on one occasion the local boys kidnapped him. It happened on a carnival day, creating quite a stir. Len Shipton, a masked man on the day, recalls the event:

We could only do that to Dr Penn. We all had a lot of fun with Dr Penn; he was such a character.

I remember him stitching my finger once and I said to him. 'Tell me straight now, doctor. Will I be able to play the piano when I go from here?'

'Well, I don't see why not,' he said thoughtfully, yet looking a little surprised.

'Well that's strange,' said Len, 'Because I couldn't play it before I came in!'

Dr Penn often reminded people about that. On another

occasion, he was examining me on his medical couch. Then suddenly he said:

'Oh dear, oh dear. Hold on a minute, Len' and disappeared for a few minutes – although it seemed more like a lifetime to me.

'Is there anything the matter, doctor? I asked when he returned.

'No, no,' he said. 'I just remembered about the constellation of the stars. Sorry, Len, I should have told you that I was nipping outside.'

John Seeley has a similar story to tell:

I went along to Dolycwrt one day and after waiting the usual length of time for Dr Penn I was invited into his consulting room. I explained that I had a bad back and, as he examined me, he looked up:

'What do you think, John?'

'Well you're the doctor, Dr Penn; you tell me,' I replied.

'No, no. Forget about your back. I was going to say, "What do you think . . . about doing a disco at the Town Hall next Friday?" Are you available, and do you think you can arrange it for me?'

These two stories typify how relaxed Dr Penn was when treating patients, rarely ruffled, totally in control. He was more worried about resigning his position as Secretary of Whitland Town Hall, which happened a year after stepping away from Whitland Week in 1982. This had been another rock of a commitment that he had honoured for many years. Jean Jenkins was a member of the hardworking committee at the time:

When George heard that the hall premises were being offered for sale to the town by the Dairies in 1973, he went around twenty-seven organisations in Whitland asking for their support by using the hall.

Then there was a public meeting. George offered to be the Secretary, Grismond, my husband, became Chairman, and Cyril Evans, as the new treasurer, arranged for the Rugby Club to pay the deposit. That's how it all started. George liked the hall because it was a place where we could hold a dance; it was also a licensed premises. But it was hard work. Every Saturday night George was arranging discos to raise money.

I remember on one occasion, after he had finished as Secretary, he came along to one of our pantomimes. George appreciated it so much that he took the entire cast – including committee members, such as Madeline Phillips, our wardrobe mistress – over to the Station House for food and drinks. This is how generous he was.

Committee meetings were, no doubt, different after he left. Con Harries, mentioned earlier, has a story to share:

George worked hard with us all, but he was also his own man.

'Do you think it would be a good idea to get the Pendyrus Male Voice Choir?' he asked one day. Then, when everyone agreed, he said with a relieved, but naughty-boy smile, 'Good, I'm glad about that, because I booked them last week!'

We all made a big effort for the carnival; it was the highlight of the 'Week'. I remember George hiring costumes for us all from Bristol. He dressed up as an Indian chieftain named Geronimo George. He used to go around the houses asking for help and, wherever he went, there was a welcome.

'Will you have a cup of tea, doctor?' they asked, 'or something?'

'I'll have something!' is what he used to say!

Dr Penn's railway work was also beginning to draw to a close, although not completely. In the summer of this same year, 1982, at a time of industrial action, he wrote to Mr Enoch Powell, M.P., a man he greatly admired, seeking support. He felt that political organisations were lobbying hard against the railway network, further endangering the future effectiveness of the railways. Here is an extract outlining his concerns:

> I really believe that the present strike on the railways suits an awful lot of people – people who are not worried about Wales and much of England and Scotland being railway-less.
>
> I even wonder if perpetrators of the strike – which applies to both sides of the nonexistent negotiating table – are being encouraged to keep the strike going. Those who would seek to keep the strike going fall into varying and differently motivated groups of people – whilst the almost-universally elected victims for almost-ritualistic sacrifice are Britain's railways.
>
> The ill-informed, demoralised railway workers are mere pawns in a mighty game of Railway chess.

Although stepping back from many commitments in his life, Dr Penn was now ready for another huge challenge. In March 1983, the eagerly awaited opening of the Meddygfa Taf Surgery, in North Road, took place: essentially a modern health centre in Whitland, similar to others established across the country. This is where Dr Penn's two partners, Dr Malcolm Holding and Dr Roy Allen would in future practice medicine. Initially Dr Penn had been part of the great plan to move, but something held him back. That 'something' was 'tradition'.

Over the years, Dolycwrt had been a medical fortress protecting the old ways of medicine. Now it would protect all things traditional, including medicine. In a future medical publication, the *Doctor* magazine, Dr Penn was soon to be described under the heading 'G.P takes to the hills to plough lone furrow'. How true – but he was also entering into life's great wide oceans, relishing the bracing sea air of sailing beyond the call of duty. It was to be a remarkable and much-celebrated voyage, and even Dr Penn's foresight could never have foreseen the adulation and publicity that awaited him at his destination port. As Secretary of Whitland Week, he had once invited Sir Francis Chichester to the carnival; one day they would have 'similar memories'. Here are some of his thoughts concerning this period of change:

> Dolycwrt had been the doctor's headquarters in Whitland for so many years that I was loath to leave it in 1983 when my two partners moved to a purpose-built surgery. So I stayed in Dolycwrt on my own with a smaller practice. However, our splitting was entirely amicable and only due to that 'blinking new surgery!'

Dr Penn loved Dolycwrt and his long hours there were happy ones. The surgery linked his work to that of Dr Gibbin and earlier doctors, and shaped his own personality and ideals. Dr Penn's former partners would miss him as he, too, would miss them; future work would not be quite the same. Dr Roy Allen shares an amusing story that typifies Dr Penn:

> When we were together, we didn't know all of George's whereabouts – and understandably so – but when he returned to the surgery and the stories came out,

sometimes in greater detail at social events, he was highly amusing. I remember on one occasion he tackled a difficult delivery in the confined spaces of a Romany caravan. He was entering into unknown territory here; most wouldn't have entertained this. To make matters worse there was an Alsatian dog running around which either attacked George or the midwife or both. But George took it in his stride . . . delivering the child, attending to the midwife, and all was well!

Dolycwrt's medical days started in 1898, when the esteemed Dr John Thomas Creswick Williams arrived at the premises. Upon his retirement in 1913, Dr William David Owen took over – making room for Dr Phillip Gibbin to assist him from around 1932 onwards. Already, Dr Penn had overtaken Dr Gibbin's long reign that ended in 1959; he was now the longest serving general practitioner in Dolycwrt's history – and he was returning it to a sole practitioner's outfit, as it had been with Dr Creswick Williams in the days of his horse and cart. In the little surgery's intriguing history, this changeover represented a real watershed in time, one that saw the present staff moving across to Meddygfa Taf. Clearly, Dr Penn's first task was to bring in a new team. Esme Williams, one of the receptionists making the move, reflects upon her feelings at the time:

> I remember being sad to leave Dolycwrt, because we were such a close working team and because I was saying 'goodbye' to Dr Penn. But, equally, I was excited about working in the new health centre. This was something completely different, a new challenge.
>
> Dr Penn was always so kind. I still have the letters that he wrote to me, and he once gave me a china bell, which I treasure today. When we were in Dolycwrt, he bought

everyone a bunch of flowers at Christmas – and I even remember him coming to Meddygfa Taf in our first year there, in 1983, with flowers for me. He also had a bouquet for Leila and Meinir. I can see him now, coming through the back door with flowers in his hands.

I can also remember the time when I phoned him many years earlier when my mother wasn't well. It was about 11 o'clock at night; clearly I was concerned:

'Would you like me to come up?' he asked.

When he arrived, he put us all at ease, and stayed until my mother was better. He was lovely.

As Esme left, Beryl Campbell arrived:

I started as a receptionist, before taking on the nursing role. I hadn't been in work for ten years and I was just delighted to have the job. And I was soon to learn so much from Dr Penn.

When someone came into the surgery – no matter what the complaint was – if it was within his limitations, he wanted to personally help them. This is what general practice meant to Dr Penn. He was hands-on and he loved to pass on his knowledge, too. His application to medicine and patient care was unique.

Clinging to the tried and trusted ways of old, Dr Penn was not burdened with computers, appointments and the various modern gadgets that afflict larger group practices. To a great extent, he was free to enjoy himself, serving patients with a level of commitment and personal care that typified his type. 'Just to see you, makes me feel better,' someone once wrote to Dr Penn, 'even without a prescription.' A similar message stated: 'Every time I saw your face, Dr Penn, and you opened your case, the pain disappeared.' Someone else went further:

'My mother thinks you are the nicest man to have taken the Hippocratic Oath.'

Dr Penn also had more time for surgery – and the bigger the job the better. Again Beryl explains:

> He did so many operations; he really couldn't do enough surgery. He would take his time and, without exception, his work was wonderful. I remember him doing a sebaceous cyst once and I was with him until nine o'clock in the night. And this was a really big job; it was a very big cyst.
>
> 'Oh my goodness, Dr Penn, you shouldn't be doing this,' I was saying to myself – but he did an amazing job. That day the patient was on the operating table for three hours. Dr Penn took great delight from the job – despite the patient complaining of a stiff neck when he left! 'He'll be pleased,' Dr Penn smiled; nothing got the better of him.

Pleasantly surprised by the few calls he had at night, Dr Penn mixed work with recreation, finding time to attend funerals, regardless of whose surgery the deceased had attended. Strangely, in his new circumstances, funerals kept him in touch with former patients, whilst attending medical lectures brought him into contact with professional colleagues. In former days, he rarely missed these talks, sometimes being asked to propose a vote of thanks, as we see in the following extract:

> Mr Chairman, Dr Brigden, Ladies and Gentleman,
> I remember hearing a specialist say that a doctor is either getting a better doctor or a worse one every day – and I believe it because I know that, as a G.P., I find myself continually oscillating from thinking I'm quite good, to thinking I'm pretty hopeless; and from believing that I know quite a bit, to recognising that I know very little.

Whilst it is difficult to keep our knowledge up to the minute, luckily it is, perhaps, just as important to keep up our interest – and I do believe that herein lies the great value of these Pembrokeshire Medical Society meetings, and we must surely be glad of the efforts of our Chairman and Secretary in laying on a night like tonight.

I am sure that we are all very grateful to Mr Brigden for coming from London to enthuse us with this ever present problem of Ischemic Heart Disease. We have enjoyed the talk, we have gained in knowledge, and we have been stimulated to fresh endeavour – and we have also been quickened by the fact that a London doctor has made time to come to this little corner of the country for the furtherance of medicine amongst us.

These were the words of a young, and equally modest Dr Penn. Time had marched on, but words of appreciation about his manner, attitude and great works were already pouring in. What is more, Dr Penn was such a character that most people, by now, had a few stories about him tucked away. Nancy Davies, aged ninety-four, was, and still is, one of his greatest admirers:

We had an A35 just the same as Dr Penn. We loved it. They were nippy little cars; they took us everywhere. We used to pull the window down manually. There was a little grip for this. The indicator was like a yellow rod that jutted out from each side. These cars were different from today, and so was Dr Penn different. They were his trademark.

I used to like the cap he wore to keep his head warm.

'How sensible you are to wear the cap, doctor,' I said to him once.

'Yes,' he said. 'Our body heat goes out through our head.'

The flaps came down over his ears. They were strapped

under his chin. It was comfy for him. Whenever he passed in the car, he doffed his hat. He was humorous also, and had a lovely laugh.

We went on that last Cardi Bach trip, Wil and I. I remember seeing Dr Penn on the platform. The train was packed. It was lovely weather. I also went to Shrewsbury on Dr Penn's train. It was my first and last trip there; I wouldn't have missed it for the world. We went to support Dr Penn; it was to keep the railway line active.

I remember on one occasion, Wil's mother had caught her hand opening the window. She was always afraid to leave it open at night because of bats. She needed stitches. It happened that she stretched up to reach the hook. The chord broke; it was a critical shock. Dr Penn, bless him, came up. He stayed there in the bedroom for hours. His stitching was a work of art. He was just meticulous.

I will never forget the day he went up to see my mother. 'I want to go up to see Mary,' he said but, when he was half way up the stairs, he said he could not face it and turned back. My mother had a charming way about her; he thought a lot about her; she had passed away earlier in the day.

The three of us – Wil also – were talking into the night. He had a whisky and a few cups of tea. It was late. It was one o'clock when he arrived. We were expecting him – he had been called out to Crymych late on. It was four o'clock when he left. Bless him.

And Peggy was a charming lady: always friendly and kind to everyone. I can say he wouldn't have been the man without Peggy behind him. She had terrific patience. He was out on calls all night and, bless her, she wouldn't know when to prepare a meal for him.

Doreen Adams was another patient and friend of George and Peggy:

I have tears in my eyes when I think how kind he was when my son, Aled, was born. He called with me twice a day for weeks before I entered hospital. He even took me into hospital in his car – and held my hand most of the way. He knew I needed his support. The next day he was back visiting me with Peggy. That day, Dr Penn's mother was outside waiting in the car – and she was 84! And I can recall the words of the ward's sister. 'More like Dr Penn, is what we need.'

He was ever so kind. Every Christmas, he brought me flowers; and, each year on 26th February, Peggy brought a present for Aled. This happened to be Peggy's birthday, too; they shared the same date. I felt safe in Dr Penn's hands. My father was unwell once, in the Priory Street Hospital, Carmarthen. I was concerned about him; he didn't seem to be improving. When I mentioned this to Dr Penn, he said, 'I'll call in to see him, Doreen,' and he did.

If ever I was worried, he would say, 'Come over Doreen. We'll have a chat about it.' Peggy was there and we'd be in the sitting room on the right of the hallway. I will never forget the stand-back fire. My face always went red; it threw out so much heat. When I walked back down the driveway, I felt better straight away. I was so fond of my visits to Hillside. Sometimes we sat outside, and Dr Penn and Peggy showed me the garden.

And he was so funny about his cars. He really didn't want a modern one. It makes me laugh when I think of the time he took his car into Eifion Morgan's garage in Tegryn. He asked Eifion to do some repairs whilst he attended to the village surgery. If Eifion needed to keep the car for a day or so, he usually gave Dr Penn a spare van to use – but this time, I was already using it.

'Oh, I'll get round Doreen,' he said. 'I'm sure she won't mind.'

Then his next move was to call into the milk factory, where I was working, to see me.

This extract from a bereavement message in a local newspaper uses the five words that followed Dr Penn everywhere:

> Special thanks go to Dr Penn and his nurses, whose dedication goes far ... *beyond the call of duty.*

Glan Thomas, formerly of Whitland, once said, 'The thing about Dr Penn is that he was so ... so ... nice.' Glan remembers Dr Penn buying a drink for everybody – literally going around the room, as he liked to do – in one of the packed local pubs of the town, despite having given up alcohol himself.

> I was sitting in the Taf Hotel at the time. It was the occasion of the Whitland Week coffee morning and Dr Penn was buying everyone a half. There must have been fifteen or twenty people there and he was taking their orders. I remember thinking that I hadn't seen Dr Penn for quite some time because I was working away – and when he turned to me, he asked,
>
> 'You're Glan, aren't you? Oh, it had better be a pint for Glan,' he said to the barman – remembering that I enjoyed a drop of beer in my younger days. I'll never forget that – especially as everybody in the room looked up and stared at me.

This next letter from Dr Penn underlines Glan's message about him being so 'nice'. It is to a patient, who was also a dear friend:

Dear Colonel Andrew Man,

What pleasure we have in extending our greetings and best wishes to you and Ursula and family on your 80th birthday – and we have further pleasure in presenting this little gift. You can be thrilled with the high esteem in which you are rightly held by all . . .

Gwilym Reynolds explains what Dr Penn meant to his family:

One night we sent for Dr Penn because my mother-in-law was bad. Oh, she was unwell; we didn't know how to help her. But when Dr Penn went upstairs and called out, 'How are you tonight Mrs Davies?' she replied, 'I'm very well thank you doctor.' She was better straight away! I remember we had a big laugh about that when he came back down the stairs.

My brother-in-law was also big friends with Dr Penn. He had a nice-sized farm and they both liked to talk about the animals.

'One of my cows isn't well,' said Dr Penn one day. 'Can I give her a drop of whisky?'

'Well you can try it doctor,' was his reply.

'What do you think?' asked Dr Penn.

'Well a drop wouldn't harm. It could be a good job,' said my brother-in-law.

So when he went home, Dr Penn gave the cow a drink. Then, when they next met, they were both laughing because the cow was well again. It had been a good job; Dr Penn's whisky had made it better.

Whitland's Jeff Court has a story to share about Dr Penn relating to an event that occurred outside Dolycwrt towards the end of 1986:

Dr Penn telephoned me to explain that a gentleman from Ireland, accompanied by his son and daughter, had broken down in their car outside Dolycwrt surgery. They had stopped for a sandwich while on their way home – but the car failed to restart. Dr Penn asked me to come over and try to get the car going. Dr Penn promised to pay me, whilst he waited to be reimbursed over the coming weeks.

When I got under the bonnet, I knew it was not straightforward; he needed a new engine. So I had his car on my lorry and I took the three of them down to Fishguard to catch the ferry.

About three months later, I received a beautiful box of Irish biscuits with a really nice letter.

That day, Dr Penn had initially been disturbed to see the man's car parked right outside the surgery front door: a small matter, but something that mildly irritated him. But, when he found out that the visitor was in trouble, he arranged for him and his children to go to Mr Ferris at Waungron Mansion for a meal, as well as for Jeff to attend to his car. Here are just a few sentences from a note that Dr Penn also received from this thoroughly appreciative gentleman:

> In your kindness, you set up such a sequence of help that after leaving your house, we never had as much as one moment's worry. I can smile now to think back on my confrontation with a fiery Welsh dragon, who was really a loveable G.P. defending the safe and free passage of his clients.

The gentleman was not wrong; equally Dr Penn liked to look after his colleagues such as Celia Leggatt:

We had most fun with the patients when Dr Penn was, shall we say, running a little late! There were some choice comments, especially from the older country patients who knew Dr Penn intimately. But it was all good, wholesome fun.

And we used to have some lovely parties after work. Often we'd gather in the kitchen of Dolycwrt, which was a really friendly place, the Rayburn keeping the room nice and warm. Sometimes we went to the Fishers Hotel for a meal and we had a really nice night in Trelech once. There were instrumentalists and artists entertaining us and we were all singing along to them. As for Dr Penn, he was the centre around which everything revolved.

Throughout his rather hectic life, Dr Penn had unfailingly made time for Neville, his older brother, who, being of a gentle, retiring and, sometimes, nervous disposition, was destined for an altogether different life. As a young man, briefly in the Royal Air Force, he enjoyed travelling. Later, as a civil servant, he spent time in Liverpool before setting sail for Australia and a taste of another world. At the Wyndham Hotel in Cardiff, Neville was a terrific help to his mother, Beatrice, and, whenever time allowed, he enjoyed visiting new places, Ireland being one of his favourites, especially Tramore in County Waterford. Sadly, days as an out patient in Whitchurch hospital led to a lengthy stay at St David's Hospital, Carmarthen, where his quiet and inoffensive nature made him popular.

It was at this supportive establishment that Neville entered into the spirit of a quieter life, whilst making the best of the opportunities that came his way, including attending church, organised concerts and outings. Dr Penn and his family regularly called to see Neville and to take him out to

Llansteffan, a favourite and convenient place, where he was fond of the beachfront café. It was a regular event for Neville to go back to Glamorgan with Dr Penn, stopping for food and drinks along the way, and every Christmas day, Neville was one of many who indulged in the drinks that Dr Penn delivered to accompany the festive lunch.

However, on June 15th 1987, Neville was himself called to rest, aged 65, whilst living at Ferry Park Home, Ferryside. The funeral was conducted at the Chapel of St David's Hospital. The first hymn that day was 'Eternal Father Strong to Save', well known for its refrain, 'Oh, hear us when we cry to Thee, For those in peril on the sea!' On the reverse of the Order of Service, Dr Penn thanked the ministers who officiated and 'the staff of St David's Hospital and Ferry Park Home for their wonderful care and kindness to Neville, and to friends for their support and sympathy'.

Neville Howell Kempton Penn, formerly of Cardiff, is buried on the gentle slopes of Carmarthen's beautiful 'countryside' cemetery, with a headstone of grey slate – traditional grey slate.

Sarah's Wedding – and Memories of Waungron Mansion

IN THE SUMMER of 1988, in the quiet countryside of Dr Penn's Dolycwrt practice, excitement was mounting; his daughter, Sarah was to marry Marek Wyspianski at St Mary's Church, Whitland. Dr Penn arrived at the wedding in a horse-drawn cart driven by Mr Ferris of the nearby Waungron Mansion Country Hotel. Later, in the comfortable surroundings of a packed reception at this same location, Dr Penn stood proudly in front of his audience, explaining how Sarah had become a devoted fan of the Swedish pop group, Abba.

Mentioning that he had often returned home to Hillside to hear the sounds of 'Fernando' and 'Dancing Queen' emerging from the upstairs windows, he also picked out another of their famous classics 'Take a Chance on Me'. Dr Penn related the words of this popular song to something that Peggy had done thirty five years earlier at Maes-yr-Haf chapel, Neath.

'I persuaded Peggy to "Take a Chance on Me",' he smiled. 'And it is because of Peggy's acceptance that we are here today.'

There is another reason why the Waungron Mansion Country Hotel was chosen for this occasion. Dr Penn had, over the past four or more years, struck up a friendship with its proprietor, Mr Ferris, who had transformed Waungron into a stunning hotel and restaurant. Now it was a high-class venue; traditional, pleasing, with roaring open fires, expansive lawns, superb food and accommodation. This excited Dr Penn and, above all else, he knew that Mr Ferris supported the town's butchers, bakers and other local traders. This is what capped it for Dr Penn; he liked to see the townspeople giving their custom to the town, especially as he was now 'Whitland through-and-through'. Whenever he had a spare five minutes, he promoted Waungron Mansion: dropping its name into conversations as well as distributing Mr Ferris' brochures here and there. Wally Rainbow, photographer, knew exactly why:

Dr Penn was just proud of what he could be proud of, and what we all should have been proud of, too. Over the years, I took many photos of Dr Penn – at his desk in Dolycwrt; outside his surgery; at Hillside with the family, at weddings and various events – but I was never busier than at Waungron Mansion. This is where Dr Penn liked to hold regular staff parties. Being on a slightly elevated pitch near the top of Velfrey Road, it had wide open views of Whitland and the Taf valley – as well as having a relaxing old-feel, a friendly ambience.

I looked forward to my work with Dr Penn, and I remember he quite took me by surprise one day.

'I'd like to have another official photograph,' he explained. 'Can I come up?' So he called at my home.

'And what's this one for, Dr Penn?' I asked.

'It's for my shotgun license,' he replied.

'Your shotgun license,' I said, hardly believing my ears. 'Dr Penn, when did you last kill anything?'

On another occasion, he asked me to take photographs of Trevaughan Bridge to help him save it from being demolished. This was also around 1988, a time when Whitland was having a new road bridge. It wasn't the easiest of tasks, I might say, especially trying to find the original stone giving the date when it was rebuilt, way back in 1767.

But I managed what Dr Penn wanted in order to give the old bridge much needed publicity. And when I see it today, I think back to that occasion, finding it hard to believe that, not long ago, it was the main road to Tavernspite.

It was around this time that Wally captured what is generally accepted as being a very fine photograph of Dr Penn that appears, with his kind permission, on the front cover of this book. It is a perfectly natural photograph of Dr Penn as we remember him best – and herein lies another story:

A lady contacted me from Canada, saying that she wanted a special photograph of Dr Penn. 'Could I arrange it?' I decided that I wanted to see him doffing his hat, carrying his Gladstone medical case, and with his old car in the background.

So I asked Bronwen and John Llewellyn, who were living in Cwmfelin Boeth at the time, to help me. They invited Dr Penn to call round one morning for coffee, asking Dr Penn to park his Morris-Minor at the side of the house. Then he walked into the doorway of the conservatory, raised his hat, and smiled. I was waiting for him behind the camera lens. It was the perfect photo, and we see it in the public halls of Whitland today.

By now, Dr Penn's cars had been a talking point for many years. Not content to keep a few of his tried and trusted models on the road – usually A35s, but more recently Morris-Minors as well – he was now building up a fleet. He had acquired these mostly from patients, simply because he couldn't say 'No' when they were offered for sale. The Reverend Nigel Griffin was, at the time, preparing to depart from the Whitland scene, but two memories of his first week in Whitland ten years earlier never left him; one concerned Dr Penn's cars:

When I came to Whitland in 1979, dear old Dr Penn was already a legend. In my first week, Tom Phillips, churchwarden, was very ill, and I called to see him rather late one night, about 10 o'clock, at his home in North Road. Then, an hour later, there was a tap on the door.

'Don't worry; that will be Dr Penn,' I was told.

Now, I had already heard about Dr Penn, but I had not yet met him.

In no time, out came the bottle of whisky reserved for Dr Penn, for his little tot!

And there we all stayed talking until 2 o'clock in the morning. What a wonderful introduction into the parish.

About a week later as I passed Hillside, I glanced up the driveway and saw cars all around the house. I thought that, perhaps, there was bereavement in the family, so I decided to knock on the door to say 'Hello,' Dr Penn answered.

'Sorry to disturb you, Dr Penn,' I said.

'Not at all, Vicar; I'm on my own.'

Then he spent a good half-an-hour explaining about each car. I had a story from him about them all. Dr Penn was simply wonderful. He was the most dedicated of country doctors. He knew his flock and he had nothing but love for everyone. And Peggy, she was a saint.

Gwilym, from Brynmenyn, now Dr Gwilym Rees, was caught by surprise when he visited Hillside with his wife, Anne. He was amazed to see all the cars 'tucked into the grass'. 'It was like a Morris Minor Preservation Society,' joked Gwilym, 'let alone the A35s!' Gwilym was no different to many others who had a funny story about Dr Penn's cars. One day, I spoke to a group of men in Hermon as they repaired an old engine. This is what one of them had to say:

We had heavy snow up here one year and although the roads had been cleared, conditions were still bad. Somebody had bumped into the hedge on a nasty bend and a few of us had put his car back onto the road – when along came Dr Penn in his A35. He smiled and waved and continued quietly round this same corner – without the slightest problem. We were amused by this: Dr Penn coping better with the conditions in his A35 than people in their modern cars. This prompted one of the boys to say,

'Wel, wel, bois bach, mae'n rhaid i mi brynu un fel yna!' ('I must buy one like that!')

It wasn't only local journeys that Dr Penn was making, of course. His old cars were taking him far and wide. On one occasion, he drove a patient to St Lawrence Hospital in Chepstow on his day off – not quite as far as Edinburgh, but still a long way on the old roads. And all these kind deeds throughout his medical life were not going unnoticed – prompting the Reverend David Faulkner, newly appointed to St Mary's Church, to propose that Dr Penn be recognised in the New Year's honours list. After asking various members of the community to write testimonials, Reverend Faulkner then submitted Dr Penn's case to higher authorities for consideration, as he explains:

We wanted George to be recognised, and we felt strongly about it. What I did was to moot the idea and approach leading people in Whitland for their thoughts. Most agreed that it was a good idea and wrote accordingly; everyone knew that it was well deserved – but, in the end, nothing came of it. I wondered whether an intimation had been made to George, which he had refused. He was so different that it was not out of character for him to refuse an official honour.

On one occasion, we gave George and Peggy a lift to a wedding reception at Llansteffan. When we approached the roundabout at St Clears, George asked. 'Do you mind if I make one quick call?' He wanted to check on a patient's progress, having recently carried out surgery on this person. I remember him saying that although the operation had been a complete success, it was not recognised by his senior consultants at the hospital. Probably, George had strayed across the line in his conscientiousness and this was not appreciated. I could see that he was upset about this: sensitive to being hurt, especially as his surgical work was so good. In fact, people often said he'd have made a wonderful specialist surgeon.

Equally, George was sensitive to the feelings of others. Someone told me that he once sat for half an hour in his car outside a patient's house before he went inside to deliver bad news. And people respected his word in absolute terms. If he said they would get better, they believed this fully. And with those whose lives were ebbing away, he would sit with them all night.

Strangely, I can remember crossing paths with George when we were looking to sell the Church Hall. I felt that a sale was a good thing, especially as Whitland had enough halls at the time. They were falling into disrepair. Why not move it on, I thought? With a change-of-use planning sanction, the hall could make a nice house. But George opposed me all the way. We had a meeting of the Parochial Church Council and I was overwhelmed by the number of people who came along to support him. People were pouring in from everywhere. George had certainly rounded up the troops. He'd been around town explaining about its heritage. People listened to him and came along especially for him – even though a majority had no right to be there!

In the end I thought it best to let sleeping dogs lie. And I certainly wasn't offended, not by George. I knew that he was doing his best: a lovely man. He didn't want to let go of the past. With George, it was a case of . . . 'as it was in the beginning, is now and ever shall be . . . world without end'.

Keith Thomas, former manager of Whitland Creamery, was one of many who wrote supporting Reverend Faulkner in his attempt to see Dr Penn honoured. Now he refers to a well-known story from 1982, when Dr Penn found his way through snowdrifts in an emergency – resulting in a helicopter being commissioned to take his patient to hospital:

I, for one, strongly believe that Dr Penn should have been rewarded for his bravery on that occasion. I don't think many would have ventured beyond their front doors that night. Things were bad in Whitland down in the valley, but they were a lot worse on the foothills of the Preseli [Mountains], where Dr Penn was going. He was out throughout the night; it was serious stuff and he was risking his life. It was a long journey, and he was going way beyond the call of duty. He should have been officially rewarded for that alone, besides all his other community work.

The great thing about Dr Penn was that he found time for people – and if someone needed him urgently at the last minute, he was always available. Many years ago we had friends staying with us and their little boy fell and had a nasty cut above his eye. Immediately I thought about Dr Penn. It was Sunday lunchtime when I telephoned:

'I'm terribly sorry to trouble you . . .'

'Not at all Keith, bring him down,' he replied – and it was all done in no time, five stitches, no qualms whatsoever.

This story is so typical of him. Patients came first every time.

At around this time, the early 1990s, Vivienne Morris, Whitland's former Lady Mayor, was returning to Whitland with her family. She, too, has a few tales to tell:

I can remember the time my son, Gruffydd, and I were staying at a school holiday camp in Llangrannog. In our room there was a tall wardrobe with open space near the top. Of course, Gruffydd climbed onto it when we left the room, and fell heavily onto the hard stone floor. Worse still, he hit his head as he landed, and was concussed.

We were very grateful that the local doctor, a modern physician, called and examined Gruffydd with his compact pen-sized torch. But as soon as we returned to Whitland, we thought it was a good idea to have Gruffydd checked out by a local doctor. Dr Penn was available at that time, so he called.

I'll never forget his arrival on the doorstep, his presence filling the doorway. 'Isn't it wonderful up here,' he said.

In his hand was a big red torch, with a large square battery, which he used when he examined Gruffydd, without having a little pen-torch himself. Of course, he knew what he was doing, but this was just so typical of Dr Penn. Then he stayed to have a chat, enjoying the children's company.

Sometime later, I was sitting in his packed waiting room at Dolycwrt, where Gruffydd was fascinated by an old painting on the wall. When Dr Penn realised this, he invited him into his consulting room to see his main collection, being away for a while before returning. Dr Penn was just so relaxed; he wasn't worried that people were waiting to see him – and, surprisingly, neither were they!

Now that he knew the children, when Dr Penn one day spotted Gruffydd and his sister, Megan, in Mother

Hubbard's Café in Whitland as he walked by, he decided to have something to eat himself, sitting down with them both for a chat. They were thrilled, saying that they had an amazing conversation.

Of course, Dr Penn lived his life with the relaxed manner of a G.P. from earlier days. Tony Hughes, Whitland's former chemist, dealt with Dr Penn's prescriptions:

> Dr Penn had a range of favourite remedies at his fingertips. These included mixtures for dry-coughs, indigestion, various tonics and even ointments – all inherited from Dr Gibbin with subtle changes of his own. These remedies remained in demand and it gave me great personal satisfaction to continue dispensing them – despite the ingredients being difficult to find and time consuming to obtain.
>
> Incredibly, but not surprisingly, Dr Penn managed to ignore metric measurements altogether, continuing instead to be true to the old apothecary system of prescribing! Of course, this meant converting from grains, scruples, drachms, and minims to grams and mils – something I did rather a lot of, especially as the younger pharmacists were not so conversant with this.
>
> Of course, all these changes were incidental to Dr Penn because patient care was always his priority. In medicine, and in life, he was a law unto himself and nothing could change the way he saw things.

Indeed, Dr Penn felt sufficiently upset about such wholesale changes as metrication that he wrote, at the time, to senior politicians and public figures expressing his concerns and had many a polite reply. David Kuhl was another who experienced the laid-back, relaxed and unflappable Dr Penn in the twilight of his shining career:

I remember working alongside the big tankers at the Milk factory. We were near the condensery, moving pallets around. I jumped off the lorry and one of the pallets was broken and I landed on a nail that was sticking up. In those days, Dolycwrt was part of a nearby row of houses, where Mr Walker, the old dentist, practised – so I didn't have far to go.

Dr Penn was on duty and injected me, cool as ever, talking away, when suddenly I jumped:

'Ouch,' I called out.

'It's alright David,' he said, 'we're finished now.'

Then he took a closer look at his needle.

'Oh, I'm sorry,' he said, 'I must have dropped this one; it does look a little bent, too!'

Dr Penn often visited my parents and he used to have a chat with Mum first, and then Dad. Mum made tea and always brought out her homemade cakes for him. Then Dr Penn saw my father. 'I must have a word with Charlie now.'

So he wandered into the front room. On one of his visits, the phone rang: 'Hello, Mrs Kuhl, it's Peggy here. Is my husband there, please?'

The next moment Dr Penn came to the phone.

'Oh, alright Peggy, I'll be up to fetch you in two minutes.'

'I've got an urgent call to Pendine, now. Peggy's going to drive me, so I'd better be on my way.'

Sharing the Sand and Sea
with Pendine Patients

IT IS INTERESTING to note that in the 'horse and cart' days
of Dolycwrt's first physician, Dr John Thomas Creswick
Williams, the geographical area of the practice was almost
as far-reaching as in later years. This meant that Dr Creswick
Williams directed his horse and cart along the winding
country lanes into the parish of Marros, where Pendine's
golden sands and sea are only two miles away.

A century later, Dr Penn was doing just the same – and
perhaps not a lot quicker in his old cars and unflurried
fashion – passing the ancient and charming little church of
Eglwys Cummin on the same twisting, but not so bumpy,
roads. Now, nearing the end of his long medical career, Dr
Penn enjoyed being recognised as the official doctor for
Pendine's caravan village. Meeting new people had always
been his joy and, with only a relatively small patient list, he
revelled at the thought of fresh encounters with visitors to this
seaside setting. Likewise, the patients enjoyed the wholesome
experience of knowing Dr Penn and visiting his surgery:

> I think I was right in saying that Dolycwrt had a special
> homely atmosphere and everybody seems to appreciate
> it. Loads of holidaymakers, in particular, said that it was
> very special. In fact, I enjoyed being the official doctor to
> Pendine holiday camp by the sea, run by Bourne Leisure. I
> consider the people in charge wonderful – and the caravans,
> the layout, and the leisure arrangements, first class. There,

I enjoyed meeting the happy people on holiday. And I often think about a nice gentleman who said that being taken ill on holiday had made his holiday! He was from Wolverhampton, I believe.

In stark contrast to the slower modes of transport that both Doctors Creswick Williams and George Penn had in common, Pendine is remembered for fast cars and land speed records. But for Dr Penn, Pendine provided a little of the 'play' that he needed during hectic days of general practice when, oftentimes, the sand and sea air were all he wanted:

> Thursday February 4th 1971
> I am terribly tired and struggled this morning to surface. I asked Mr Harold Williams to drive me to Tavernspite and Pendine on calls. I've never seen Pendine so gorgeous. The sun was out. It was clear and mild. Brook farm was really marvellous and I thought I would like to go for a walk there one day. I had an enjoyable stroll on the beach and a quick drink in the Spring Well Inn before returning to meet Dr Eirian Williams to go on a patient visit outside Whitland.

Bryant Rees, of Red Roses, knew Dr Penn and often saw him passing in one of his old cars. Affectionately known as 'Bryant the Roses', one day he gave Dr Penn a helping hand:

> I remember seeing Dr Penn standing outside his car on the road from Red Roses to Pendine, just beyond Three Gates. His car had broken down, and he was wondering what to do next.
> 'Are you out of petrol, Dr Penn?' I asked.
> 'No, I don't think so,' he replied. 'The gauge indicates it's half-full.'
> In no time, we were under the bonnet having a look, and there didn't seem to be much wrong. When I pushed

the car, I couldn't hear petrol moving around in the tank – so I went back to Red Roses for half a gallon. Then we dropped it in and the car started. I'll never forget that day. Dr Penn was such a busy man, and a wonderful doctor, that he didn't have time to understand cars. Good old Dr Penn was over the moon; he couldn't thank me enough.

As a family, we have many memories of Dr Penn bathing near the rock pools in the shade of Pendine's cliffs. In the early 1960s, we had a caravan holiday amongst the dunes behind the main beach, before venturing to Amroth Castle, and then Tenby's Atlantic Hotel in later years. This was before the 'Pendragon' in Southsea caught Dr Penn's eye as the perfect place to stay, in easy reach of Portsmouth's full and fascinating naval history. Clearly, Dr Penn was very fond of the sea – although a rather cold outdoor swimming pool once did the trick during an overnight stay in a mid-Wales hotel. For Dr Penn, every beach and cove was a dispensary for his chosen salt-sea medicine; none more so than the secluded bay of Morfa Bychan, just outside Pendine. Up the road is the Green Bridge Inn, another favourite halt where Dr Penn made his mark as David Davies and his wife, Nelda recall:

> We were in bed one night in the Green Bridge. It was summertime and it must have been approaching 2 o'clock. My mother came into the room urgently.
>
> 'Quick, get up!' she said. 'There's somebody trying to break in. He's hammering away at something outside!'
>
> I went up to the window and looked outside. Across the road, there is a telegraph pole, and somebody was climbing it – about half-way-up, on a small aluminium ladder. There was someone else with him, laughing away. I wound the window down and a voice came out of the dark:
>
> 'Don't worry, David, it's only me, George Penn.'

He was putting up poster-boards for Whitland Week, and with him was Denzil Davies.

That's Dr George Penn for you, what a character.

Nelda remembers Dr Penn arriving in Whitland in the mid-1950s, when he came out to treat her family. She was struck by his gentle and caring nature; even then, nothing was too much trouble for him. Soon, Dr Penn became friendly with her father, Cyrus, and often called to buy freshly caught mackerel from him:

> For years the local fishermen used to bring their catch to the Green Bridge. My father used to fillet them before they were sold to whoever wanted fish. Dr Penn was one of these, and either he or Peggy often called. In those days pubs such as ours were good meeting places. At lunchtime all the old characters congregated there, and when someone as popular as George Penn walked in, it was bound to lead to a bit of a session.
>
> For about thirty years, I collected money for poppies on behalf of the British Legion. In Pendine we had a strong branch, especially as one of the country's defence establishments was based nearby in Llanmiloe. Whenever I could, I accepted a lift to the furthest place where I was going, and then I'd walk back.
>
> 'Can I have a lift with you doctor, to Red Roses,' I asked one day.
>
> 'Yes, yes, no problem, Nelda,' he said, 'jump in.'
>
> I remember my knees were up to my chin, because of all the paperwork in his passenger seat. He was so comical, busily shifting a few papers here and there:
>
> 'Is that better for you now, Nelda?' he asked. What a marvellous man.

There is no doubt that the endless extent of sand and sea at Pendine played a part in feeding the spiritual side of Dr Penn's life. Strolling along Pendine's seemingly endless sands is like a walk into eternity – and this is where he allowed his deeper concerns to filter into the forefront of his mind. By the mid-1990s he was considering what had concerned his earlier colleague, Dr Creswick Williams in 1913: the passing of his medical baton to another doctor. But in this modern age of group practices, finding a fresh pair of legs to take up the running was easier said than done. Already, Dr Penn's forthcoming retirement was a cause of concern to many of his loyal patients, including Catherine Griffiths of Blaenwaun:

> No one will ever replace Dr Penn. He came up to see me late one evening when I was feeling really unwell. It was about eleven o'clock and Dr Penn phoned me from Laugharne.
>
> 'I'm on the way,' he said. 'I just need to phone the surgery and then I'll be there.'
>
> 'How's Mrs Griffiths?' he asked my husband at the door, before coming inside to see me. Later he wanted to ring home.
>
> 'Can I use your phone?' he asked. 'Peggy, I'm on my way home from Blaenwaun for supper.'
>
> But I knew as soon as he had finished his supper, he had more calls to make. 'Please don't retire, Dr Penn,' I said to him on another occasion.
>
> 'Well, I've got until I am seventy,' he smiled. He was very funny; and he had an answer every time.

Confessions of Dr Penn's Chauffeurs

D R PENN COULD not possibly have survived the heavy demands of general practice and public engagements without the support of some reliable chauffeurs. Peggy was just one of a number of willing helpers who took Dr Penn on his rounds so that he could steal a little sleep along the way. Here we have the unedited confessions of three Whitland men who have first-hand experience of adventures whilst chauffeuring Dr Penn. They are Denzil Davies, Les Evans and Charles Dunford (known as John). We start with Denzil, who will never forget the night of high drama when Dr Penn was summoned to blow into the bag:

> A few days after the breathalyser event in 1978, Dr Penn and I went along to a local solicitor to explain what had happened and to ask for some advice.
>
> 'How close was the policeman's car to Dr Penn's A35?' I was asked.
>
> 'Well I don't really know,' I said to him.
>
> 'Was it 50 yards away?'
>
> 'It's hard to tell.'
>
> 'Well, was it 20 yards away?
>
> 'I'm not sure,' I answered, 'although you could say we were being pushed up the hill!'
>
> Later, as we left the solicitor, Dr Penn turned to me: 'When you were asked if the car was 20 yards away, I thought, Come on Denzil. You can do better than this!'

This story relates to the chicken that disappeared:

One night, Dr Penn turned up on my doorstep. 'Do you fancy a little spin?' He had some business to do, he always had something on the go, and we'd usually manage a little drink. 'I'm feeling a bit peckish tonight Denzil,' said Dr Penn later on. 'Let's call for something to eat.' As soon as we walked through the door of the local pub, a few of the locals converged on Dr Penn to talk to him, and I was introduced to everyone and made welcome.

That night we met one of Dr Penn's colleagues from a previous committee.

'Will you join us for something to eat,' Dr Penn asked.

'No, I've just had supper thank you,' was his response. At the time chicken-in-the-basket was a big thing: convenient to eat on the go. When our two baskets arrived – Dr Penn invited this gentleman to help himself. Of course, he expected him to take a chip or two – but instead he took the chicken!

Dr Penn didn't want to hurt his feelings, because he had known him for years. He was too much of a gentleman to challenge him or to make a scene – but I will never forget his words when we left the pub.

'What a cheek, Denzil' he said. 'He didn't want to join us because he'd have to pay, and then he took my chicken!' But as kind as Dr Penn was, he had all the will in the world. What a man he was.

This describes a Saturday night spin in Dr Penn's A35:

On another occasion, a Saturday night, Dr Penn called with me. He was feeling a little down and had some calls to make. 'Do you want to keep me company, Denzil?' Certainly I did; I never refused Dr Penn. We were heading towards Pendine, but he had a call to make along the way: someone had taken a knock playing rugby that day. After quite some time, Dr Penn returned to the car. As he jumped in he was smiling to himself:

'That boy should be playing table tennis – not rugby. He's not hard enough.'

After a follow-up call in Pendine, we stopped in a pub in Laugharne for a 'quick one'. Then we headed to Llangynin to see Colonel Buckley for a chat. We were enjoying ourselves when the phone rang. It was Peggy; there was a new call to make. 'Sorry about this, Colonel Buckley, we have to go,' said Dr Penn. Now we were on our way to Cwm Miles, ten-minute's drive away.

We had only gone a short distance when we had a puncture. 'No trouble, I'll sort it out, Dr Penn,' I said – finding the spare wheel, but with there being no sign of a jack we needed help. It was now about 11.30 and most people had gone to bed. But, not to worry, one of Dr Penn's patients lived nearby, so we gave them a knock. As soon as they saw who it was, they were perfectly alright. They couldn't help Dr Penn enough.

Here Dr Penn helps Llanboidy onto the world map:

I was talking to Dr Penn one day about Whitland Week. The German Panzers had a summer training camp at Castlemartin, and they kept coming to our tug-o-war competition on carnival day, and winning it. 'Denzil, can we do something about the Panzers?' he asked. 'Do they have to keep winning our tug-o-war?'

On his suggestion, I got some of the boys together in Llanboidy, and started to train them with the rope. I would fetch half of them, and we'd pull against a lorry, then a tractor, until we got better. This was the start of Llanboidy's tug-o-war team, which soon became successful. When it came to the carnival, we were fully prepared, ready for action – but the Panzers didn't arrive, and we didn't see them again. Meanwhile, Llanboidy went on to become world champions – all because of Dr Penn and the Panzers!

Les Evans was a close colleague of Dr Penn during the busy years of Whitland Week and, whenever he had the chance, he drove Dr Penn on calls. Les told me that Dr Penn often used to say to him, 'Les, you can call me George; it's less formal.' But each time, his reply was the same, 'Oh, alright . . . Dr Penn.' Here Les explains more:

I used to hear people talking to Dr Penn and calling him 'George'. This used to annoy me. He was Dr Penn. He was someone special: very different. He deserved that respect.

I have a number of stories about him. In a Whitland Week meeting before the wrestling competition, Dr Penn wanted the committee to pay for the wrestlers to have a supper. We all thought that we were paying them enough, but Dr Penn, knowing they had a long journey home, believed it was the right thing to do. When he was overruled, he took it upon himself to treat them. Everyone had enjoyed the event, so he took them down to *Mary-Bob's Chip Shop*. As a committee, we often disagreed. Most members wanted to make money – but Dr Penn wanted to entertain *and* make money. He was generous to a fault.

One Christmas Eve he called with me to say that he was going up to Hebron and Glandŵr. 'Did I want to go with him?' Yes, it was nice to get out of the house and these trips were always eventful. So we set off down the road past the old school in Glandŵr. This was an urgent call and the ambulance was involved. We were there for quite some time – before we called with Sally Lewis and her husband,

David, at the Post Office nearby, now way past midnight, early on Christmas morning.

'Look, there's a light on at Sally's,' said Dr Penn. 'She'd be offended if we didn't call.' So, in we went and got talking; then the whisky bottle came out.

'Will you have one doctor?' Of course, he would have one. He wouldn't say no at Christmas, of all times. I can see Dr Penn now, standing in the doorway. He had a whisky in one hand and a cup of tea in the other. Of course, we were late getting back; Margaret was in bed.

The following morning, I was in trouble.

'You wait until I see Dr Penn. I'll give him!' said Margaret. And she didn't have long to wait; Dr Penn was soon at the door. But before the door was properly opened, she had a box of chocolates in her hands. He was too quick for Margaret. He'd hijacked her plans.

Dr Penn survived on little sleep, but he was one of the best for catnapping. I'd pick him up at the surgery, and he would be fast asleep before Black Bridge. If I brought him back from Clynderwen, his eyes had closed before we left the village. He fell asleep and woke up like a light switch. I'm sure this is how he kept going.

'John' Dunford smiles about the fun he had with Dr Penn. He, too, experienced Dr Penn's generous nature described earlier. John told me that Dr Penn's bleeper went off one day as they were passing a pub near Blaenwaun. After calling there to make a phone call to the surgery, Dr Penn returned minutes later, saying: 'The phone call cost me five-pence, John, but the visit £20.' He had bought everyone a drink, and this happened often. John also experienced Dr Penn's catnapping, and has other tales, too:

Reverend Faulkner phoned me up one morning. 'John, do you know that George was out during the night at one o'clock, then at three o'clock, and again at six o'clock? Go up and help him, John. Tell him, he's not to drive today.' When I got to Hillside, Peggy was on the point of ringing me anyway. 'You've had a busy night Dr Penn?' I said to him.

'Yes,' he replied, 'I was called out three times.'

He asked me then to take him to Bridell, about 30 minutes away. As soon as we got in the car, he was fast asleep. When we arrived, I gave him a tap. 'We're here now, Doc.'

'Bridell John, please.'

'But we're in Bridell, Dr Penn,' I replied.

One day we did 137 miles. We went up to Cardigan; then down to Saundersfoot; back up to Maenclochog; home to Whitland; over to Carmarthen – before Dr Penn was called back urgently to Whitland. There was a vehicle hold-up near Carmarthen with traffic lights and Dr Penn asked a policeman if we could go through. Then he escorted us back to St Clears; this is where he waved us goodbye. I had my foot down all the way, trying to keep up. That same day we called the ambulance out on three occasions, all emergencies. At the end of the evening the ambulance driver turned to me, jokingly, saying that we should have hired the ambulance for the day – and he wasn't wrong!

'Why don't you give up those cigarettes, Dr Penn?' I asked one day.

'Now that's a good idea, John, because I'm not really enjoying them,' he replied.

Then he gave them up just like that. I helped him to end his drinking, too.

We were in a patient's house and the woman mentioned that people were talking about Dr Penn and his whisky.

'But you're not helping the situation yourself,' I said to her. 'You're filling his glass with whisky now.'

'John . . . did she really say that?' asked Dr Penn, quite troubled by this.

'Yes,' I said – and it really shocked him; this is what drove him to give it up.

The next day we passed the Pantyblaidd Inn the other side of Blaenwaun. Dr Penn bought me my usual pint – we were allowed the one pint in those days – and a round of drinks for everybody. Then he had his last whisky.

'Come on Dr Penn, have another one,' the boys said.

'No, that's my last,' was his reply, and he meant it.

Not long after this, we had a visit to make to another pub, where Dr Penn met a person with whom he once drank.

'Have a drink, doctor,' he said.

Dr Penn refused the double whisky.

'If you're not going to have a drink with me Dr Penn, then you're no longer my friend,' is what he said.

'Well, I'm sorry about that,' replied Dr Penn. 'That's the way it is now; I've got my patients to think about.'

PART XI

FIGHTING TO KEEP DOLYCWRT ALIVE

A Starring Role in 'The Doctor's Story'

D R PENN HAD never liked the word 'retirement'. Despite a lifetime of dedication to medicine, it was always going to arrive too early for him. But, inevitably, this landmark grew nearer, prompting Dr Penn to prepare Dolycwrt for life beyond the realm of its longest serving G.P.

Saying 'goodbye' to his patients would never be easy. They were effectively bound to Dr Penn now – some by the thread of his famous stitches, worn with a sense of great attachment and immense pride. How strange for those who waited patiently for Dr Penn in his surgery, or in their homes, to imagine his retirement – and how bewildering, even unacceptable, to think of his work ending. But time, as always, has the last word.

Dr Penn's seventieth birthday, on May 17th 1997, meant his immediate retirement on the previous day. It was a case of 'here today and gone tomorrow'. However, the ever cheerful Dr Penn preferred to see it differently: perhaps a game of musical chairs where, amidst on-going happiness, his seat was quietly taken away. But, in reality, events were totally different. Dr Penn was to leave in a blaze of glory, whilst keeping Dolycwrt 'alive' was not achieved without another hard-fought struggle.

By now, nobody could teach Whitland's legendary G.P.

how to win campaigns. In fighting for the continuance of his surgery, he firstly had to secure the services of a like-minded doctor – not easy in an age of group health centres – who saw his, or her, future in a country practice and who was sufficiently independent to run the 'shooting match' alone. Next, he would turn to his faithful patients – friends who had jumped aboard his trains in earlier years – in the hope of more support, especially as most, genuinely, wanted to see Dolycwrt surgery continuing. This meant encouraging them to convey their feelings about the surgery's future, in writing, to the local medical authorities – and, whilst a favourable outcome was not guaranteed, it was felt that strong representation could win the day.

All of this was completed by September 26th 1996. Dr Ian Hood, a highly qualified and popular doctor, already an assistant working for Dr Penn, was staking a strong claim for the soon-to-be-vacant position. In a whirlwind of activity, public meetings followed, letters appeared in local newspapers, and media publicity broke forth: Dr Penn being a champion in this department, too. Now this medical conundrum in Whitland's small community was catching everybody's eye.

In the midst of a storm of emotion and public outcry, the BBC radio team visited Dolycwrt – and, in turn, this led to a BBC television crew, led by Samantha Rosie, filming the story as it unfolded for a documentary marking the fiftieth anniversary of the National Health Service. This was known as *The Doctor's Story*, part of a series entitled *Tales of the National Health Service*. It was all pretty exhausting for Dr Penn, who seriously needed a rest now, but, likewise, it was all exciting for him, too. Brian Brown, a patient, was amused how 'keen' Dr Penn was during these final few weeks in practice:

I remember going down to Dolycwrt for a medical examination.

'You don't mind if the lady sits in,' asked Dr Penn, 'because she's doing some filming for a documentary.'

At the end of the medical, I asked Dr Penn how much I owed him.

'Twenty five pounds, please, Brian,' was his reply.

It was the first time for Dr Penn to charge me. He didn't usually charge anyone. Later that evening he called round at the house. He was returning my twenty five pounds.

'Here's your cheque back, Brian,' he said. 'I didn't want to take it, but I thought I had better as we were being filmed.'

For everyone who had Dolycwrt's genuine interests at heart, good news followed. The practice was given a chance to live on and, to everyone's satisfaction, Dr Hood was officially appointed to the medical post. His wife, Margaret, has a secret to share about Dr Penn's earlier days:

When I was living in Carmarthen, Dr Penn used to look after my parents. He'd often be coming back and fore, so they got to know him well and liked him immensely. On one occasion, he was upstairs seeing my father and, when my mother followed him back down, she found him in the kitchen eating bread and butter.

Poor Dr Penn was starving. He'd been out all day, so my mother made him something to eat. This amused my parents, also proving that Dr Penn felt at home with us, and Mum and Dad were proud of this.

Dr Penn's appetite for medicine continued right up to the last day. Here is his diary note:

May 16th 1997
Although I thought I'd actually be on time today for my

last day in practice, I still didn't get to surgery until 8.40 a.m. There was a lot to do, even without seeing anyone. I took down 48 unopened retirement cards. However the T.V. people arrived and wanted me to go round Whitland with them, whilst they took shots of me in different parts of the town.

Samantha Rosie and her team had prepared painstakingly for the filming, and returned to the BBC headquarters in Cardiff with hours of quality footage. In many respects, they added immeasurably to Dr Penn's final days, taking real interest in his work ethos and personal application to medicine.

'Why do you like stitching so much, Dr Penn?' Samantha asked one day as he was filmed carrying out a complicated surgical operation – with the ease and control of an expert seamstress darning a pair of socks.

'Oh, I don't know really,' replied Dr Penn innocently for the camera – far too busy to explain about Dr Foster in Llandough, and his squeaky surgical boots!

Now the music had stopped, Dr Penn's seat had been taken away, and the game of musical chairs would, most definitely, be continuing. And Whitland's much loved Champion of the Railways was going out in style. Across the road, the entire primary school prepared to present Dr Penn with a choral rendition of 'Happy Birthday' in Welsh. And this fanfare of attention continued for weeks, before easing, but never really going away. Here are just a few of Dr Penn's many retirement messages:

Words of appreciation from a patient:

> Dr Penn, it is not often that one is so privileged to meet someone with such humanity; you restore my faith in mankind.

Words of kindness from Samantha Rosie, of the BBC film crew:

> We have had such fun being with you, Dr Penn. You are such a caring, sharing doctor. I just wish you had been mine.

And words of gratitude and respect from Mr Geraint Roberts a senior hospital consultant:

> George, you have been a great credit to the medical profession and certainly one of the most respected and caring of family doctors. Your devotion to your patients has been legendary and without exception; all your patients have spoken very highly of you at all times. In some ways, it seems unbelievable that you are about to retire . . .
>
> On a personal note, I wish to thank you for your support to me at all times and I always enjoyed having a medical dialogue with you, and your letters of referral always showed your great concern for patients. Yet again, I do wish you a most successful retirement . . .

Meanwhile, Jean Jenkins had not forgotten what Dr Penn did for Whitland Town Hall in the 1970s; now her committee was going to repay him:

> Peter Wills was chairman at the time, and we knew that George had to retire that year. One night, at the end of a monthly meeting, Peter and I were talking to one or two others. We wanted to do something special. Others had received testimonials, so George certainly deserved one. I wrote to the *Western Mail* explaining the situation, inviting people to donate, whilst also opening a bank account in the town. Then, the money just poured in – from everywhere!
>
> We wanted to give George a nice surprise. Peter came

up with a good idea and Peggy liaised closely with us, although she didn't let on. I lived on the opposite side of the road to them both, and George started to tease Peggy: 'You seem to be going across the road often now' – as if guessing something was afoot.

Dr Penn's intrigue grew over the coming weeks until the night of, what he thought was to be, a concert. Here he describes the occasion:

Saturday June 7th 1997
I couldn't decide which suit to wear, and eventually went for one of the summer weight ones, which I bought whilst on holiday in Tenby some seven years ago.

When we walked in everybody (a full house) stood up and clapped. It was very moving. Whitland Choir and their wonderful new conductor gave an enjoyable first half of the evening.

Then Peter Wills asked me onto the stage and presented me with a Red Book, *This is Your Life*. It was very exciting. People there included Gordon Hanford, of Port Talbot, who knew me in Enugu, Nigeria. Glan Phillips, Bill Clow and Pembrokeshire's Sir Eric Howells were also present.

It was all memorable in that they said wonderful things about me. I was presented with a video camera, and I gave a little speech. It was a wonderful evening and afterwards, we had a terrific feed and get-together.

That night Sarah, Dr Penn's daughter, had travelled with her family from Hampshire:

'Seeing so many friends and people from the medical world wanting to come to pay their tributes made me proud,' said Sarah.

Over the years Dad was always busy and I can remember people calling to see him at Hillside and the phone would be ringing and there were urgent messages – but everybody was appreciative and spoke well of him: 'Your father saved my life; you're lucky to have such a kind father' – this sort of thing. Of course, we didn't need to go to the surgery often – not with Dad in the house.

On one occasion Elizabeth and Roger hadn't been well and were upstairs in their rooms. When they couldn't finish their dinner they decided to throw what-was-left out of the window. Directly beneath, my parents were at the kitchen table, looking out onto the lawn. They were quite amused by this – at least knowing that they were getting better!

Dad did the family things, but likewise he was usually on the go. He liked old movies and admired the older actors and he was full of kindnesses, sometimes arranging holidays, trips or even family visits to friends. London was a favourite for us and calling at Hamleys, the toy shop was a big treat when we were young.

Seeing my parents at the *This is Your Life* evening made me think, my word, how well they had done; this is something special and, of course, it was. And, although Dad was everywhere when we were growing up, he wasn't far away.

Russell Davies, a farmer from Efailwen, was another who attended the big event, thanking Dr Penn for braving the snow to reach him in the cold winter of 1982, an incident mentioned earlier. No doubt, Russell and family were at home watching television on Tuesday evening, September 23rd, three months after the *This is Your Life* event. Indeed, who wasn't: Whitland's country lanes had never been so quiet, everyone waiting for something special to appear on their T.V. sets. This included Dr Penn and Peggy in Hillside:

> After supper we watched and taped the programme about Dolycwrt surgery and about Dr Hood applying for it.

The result was an outstanding award-winning production, soon to be beamed across the entire nation. This is when the postman's bag got heavy: beginning with a warm message from a Morris Minor enthusiast, before the letters started to flow.

From a former student friend, David Morris, living in Surrey:

> Dear George,
> Neither Barbara nor I realised when we were students that nearly fifty years later you would star in a T.V. Programme.

From a gentleman who visited Dolycwrt on official duty in 1956:

> I always looked forward to, and enjoyed, my visits to you over the years. It was a pleasure to meet you.

From a doctor's son, writing from Surrey:

> Forgive me for writing, but after seeing the beautiful film about your practice, I just felt I had to. To watch the film brought back many memories of my Dad – and he was good at stitching, too.
> The shots of you going around the countryside brought on no small amount of 'hiraeth', which is difficult to put into words. Thank you for your part in a beautiful programme . . . and please have a long and happy retirement . . .

And, from Michael Davies, in Tavistock, a classmate in Bushey School, also mentioned earlier in the story . . .

Dear George,

I am sure you will have a large fan mail following BBC's *Home Ground* programme, but I can't let another day go by without adding my own congratulations . . .

Honestly, George, you have not changed a bit since H-House! Your face is just as kindly, contented and benevolent now as I remember you all those years ago. My thoughts have inevitably gone back to those days, when we lived in trepidation of Geogger's bad moods – and elation for his good moods, too! ['Geogger' being a school house master.]

It must be gratifying to know that you are so loved in the community. As the reviewer put it: 'Not a dry eye in the house . . .'

This reviewer may have been Matthew Bond of the *Daily Telegraph*, writing on May 20th 1998:

Elderly, Welsh, Morris Minor-driving G.P. retires after 42 years in the same practice in West Wales – I'd have watched that, especially once I'd discovered that Dr Penn looked and sounded like a cross between John Betjeman and Cliff Morgan . . . Wonderful.

Likewise, Joe Joseph, reporting in *The Times* of May 20th 1998, wrote:

. . . Dr Penn has been doing more to help mankind – at least that bit of it which lives in the 200 square miles of West Wales he has been serving for the past 42 years – than all the world's well-intentioned doom-sayers.

Meanwhile, Nigel Billen of the *Daily Express*, also on May 20th 1998 added another wonderful message:

If we had all lived lives as satisfactory as Dr George Penn, local G.P. for 42 years for the people of Whitland in Carmarthenshire, then we wouldn't worry that the end was nigh.

It had been a long, lonely and brave voyage for Dr Penn, the sole practitioner, since 'setting sail' in 1983. And he could not possibly have imagined the reception, adulation, and overwhelming celebrations as his ship came safely home.

The 'Legion' Years and the Royal Albert Hall

EVER SINCE signing up with Wil Evans in the 1960s, Dr Penn had enjoyed his involvement with the Whitland & Llanboidy Branch of the now Royal British Legion. He spent many happy hours attending meetings in the low-ceilinged bar of the local headquarters, the Lamb Inn – where, in 1939, at the outset of World War II, Dr Gibbin, Dr Hugh Philipps and Dr Rowley Thomas – also a Whitland General Practitioner – attended the 'Legion' annual dinner. Dr Penn identified himself totally with the solemnity of Remembrance Sunday, the formality of laying wreaths, and the pride of honouring the country's war heroes.

Although he was Vice Chairman in the 1970s, it was not until the early 1990s that Dr Penn played a greater part in the running of the local branch, taking delight in bringing members together, perhaps for a lunch following the Remembrance Service, or an informal meal or social gathering. Often he invited an honoured guest to these occasions, such as Sir David Mansel Lewis in the later 1990s. Dr Penn's 'Legion' duties were admittedly lighter than most of his other community work, giving him time to contact guest speakers and to welcome colleagues from other branches. The following extract is from Dr Penn's letter to members and friends about a forthcoming speaker – Dr Penn's former second-row rugby partner in medical school:

> Following our meeting, there will be an informal talk by Dr David Boyns, a retired Kidwelly general practitioner

who was a medical student with me a long time ago. In his National Service, David served as a medical officer with the S.A.S. on active service in the Malayan Jungle and I believe he was regularly parachuted into the jungle with other soldiers.

Terry Griffiths, a senior member of Llandysul branch, was another person to be invited:

> I first met Dr Penn in Newcastle Emlyn in the late 1970s. At the time I used to come down from Cardiff, where I was employed as an agent for seven or eight clothing traders. I used to go as far as Pembrokeshire and I often stayed at the Cawdor Hotel in Newcastle Emlyn, because it was a central venue for my travelling. When I walked across the road to the Ivy Bush, I sometimes bumped into Dr Penn, attending railway business.
>
> In later years, he invited me to a Whitland & Llanboidy branch meeting. We gathered in the little pub in Llanboidy, and I remember Dr Penn introducing me to his colleagues. That day, I knew exactly what I was going to talk about – wanting to explain what the Chief Clerk of Works for the Commonwealth Graves Commission of Northern Europe had said only a few months earlier, at our own branch meeting in Llandysul.
>
> That particular night was the first time I said the 'Exhortation' and the 'Kohima Epitaph' in Welsh. I remember Dr Penn being interested in my address, wanting to know more.

Terry referred to words that Dr Penn memorised and held dear to his heart. Let us remind ourselves of the 'Kohima Epitaph':

When you go home, tell them of us and say –
'For Their tomorrow we gave Our Today.'

And of the 'Exhortation':

They shall grow not old, as we that are left grow old
Age shall not weary them, nor the years condemn.
At the going down of the sun and in the morning,
We will remember them.

Response: We will remember them.

On another occasion, Dr Penn reported back to members about a meeting that he had with Alfred Benjamin Finnigan, then aged 102, a survivor of the Great War, following a visit to this gentleman's home in 1998. Mr Finnigan spoke at length about the outbreak of combat, explaining that there was severe unemployment at the time, and men were encouraged to enlist for a shilling.

Dr Penn was anxious to capture and share the memories of this notable man, a veteran who served the Royal Field Artillery. There follows an extract of Dr Penn's notes; sad words of reflection on a senseless war:

We joined up in our thousands. There are photos of us in Trafalgar Square – choked with us, a crowd of silly young men.

I was a long time training – at Bishop's Stortford, Hertfordshire; then Stanstead, Essex; before moving on to Codford St Mary and Codford St Peter, in Wiltshire. The King inspected us all before we went to France.

In March 1917, we went to La Bassée and then Vimy Ridge, and the weather was appalling – it was the worst time of the whole war. It is quite impossible to explain to anyone the severity of the weather – absolutely dreadful:

snow, rain, wind, and perishing cold in March-April 1917.

The Infantry with the help of the Artillery 'took' the Ridge, but with a great number of casualties. We stayed on the Ridge for a while in May, June and July.

Getting the Ridge was a nasty affair and we had our casualties, but the Infantry were hit badly – as they always were. This was a most dreadful War. It was absolutely marvellous that the men stuck it out – not only because of the terrible danger, but the terrible conditions in which they fought.

One of the things that also upset me was the suffering of the horses. The whole war was too stupid for words. The Kaiser and all the top men of the countries involved – so called 'leaders' – were miseducated men. And when we joined up, we didn't know anything better . . .

During these 'Legion Years', Dr Penn's heart was growing steadily worse and he was admitted to hospital. Here he explains in outline the extent of his complaint:

I was railroaded by Peggy and the family to Dr Hood, who quickly got me into Carmarthen Hospital under the care of Dr Nicholas Taylor, Consultant Physician and Cardiologist; and he quickly got me to the University Hospital of Wales, Cardiff, with a view to having surgery on the two leaking valves of my heart; but, after extensive investigations, they said that I wasn't suitable for the operation because, for one reason, the heart was too enlarged!

I was sent home with lots of tablets, but then Dr Taylor readmitted me and sent me to Cardiff again – this time for a permanent 'pacemaker' which is in me 'for keeps' now – because part of my trouble was a wildly and dangerously irregular heartbeat.

Dr Penn was most grateful to all medical personnel concerned and went to hospital with the well wishes and good advice of Beryl Campbell, still a nurse at Dolycwrt:

> Keep smiling, Dr Penn . . . and, as I have said before, be nice to the nurses and they'll be nice to you!

Upon returning home Dr Penn conceded to adjusting to an even slower pace, although this did not stop his busy life or cause him to remove too many irons from the fire. Soon he and Peggy were catching a train to Cardiff, for an overnight break, looking forward to visiting the Royal Yacht berthed at the city docks.

Just as Dr Penn was a lover of all things traditional, so also was he a lover of all things 'Royal'. He had admired the Royal Family from the days of his childhood, recognising that coronations, weddings, royal visits – and the fabulous premises of Buckingham Palace, Windsor Castle, Highgrove, Balmoral – brought tourism, revenue, pomp, ceremony, happiness and much more to the country. He recognised that 'The Changing of the Guard' and other ceremonies of this nature meant so much to the country's great heritage, and seeing the Royal Yacht made him proud:

> We stayed in the Park Hotel for a night and had food there and it was really lovely. In the afternoon we saw *South Pacific* at the New Theatre and, in the evening, we went to the Docks to see the Royal Yacht. It was flood lit and looked superb and there was a lovely display of music and marching alongside the ship.
>
> In the morning we went back to see the Royal Yacht departing – to the accompaniment of more music and the Royal Marines, who were on board. And, ever since, I have felt sad about the Royal Yacht being taken out of service.

Dr Penn returned to Whitland to write a letter, which was professionally printed, before being dispatched by the dozens. This is the gist of his message:

> The Royal Yacht performs valuable services to our country – such as holding conferences, business meetings, public relations exercises, as well as carrying our monarch. 'She' could also call in the ports of our country for visitors and tourists to see and to marvel at her. At a time when the status of being British has declined, I think we should hang on to what we have got.
>
> Cost wise, keeping the present Royal Yacht would be cheap when compared with other things, such as roads and the planned Millennium construction. Surely, we should keep a possession of such majesty, elegance and beauty – at least until the year 2000 – at least until things seem more settled abroad?

Whilst recuperating at Glangwili Hospital Dr Penn was busy making arrangements to post these letters to leading names in Westminster. He also sent letters to T.V. personalities and other influential celebrities, adding an extra sentence, gently prompting them to contact their local M.Ps. He may have been the Champion of West Wales' Railways, but he was the country's King Campaigner. The Reverend Jeffrey Gainer, of St Brynach's Church, Llanboidy, was visiting Dr Penn at this time:

> When I saw Dr Penn in hospital, he was sitting up in bed writing letters to everybody about keeping the Royal Yacht. 'What do you think about it, Reverend Gainer,' he said to me, but I hadn't given it much thought. It certainly hasn't been destroyed, so I think Dr Penn has done some good.
>
> I can remember receiving tightly written letters from

him inviting me to attend the British Legion meetings in Llanboidy. They would always arrive just before the event but, nevertheless, he had taken the trouble to write, always working hard for this and other organisations in the locality.

Dr Penn was an immense character: lovable and dedicated to his profession. He couldn't do enough for his patients, sometimes staying most of the night when they were ill, also stitching people at home and in their farmhouses. It's good to hear these things.

Dr Penn took a thrill from receiving acknowledgements and positive comments from so many distinguished people and was delighted when he picked up the phone to hear the Captain of the Royal Yacht saying a personal 'Hello' to him one day. This, certainly, made his efforts worthwhile. Also, amongst the morning mail were letters sent on behalf of the Prime Minister and the Duke of Edinburgh, whilst Richard Branson and other celebrities replied. Wales' John Humphrys, from BBC Radio 4's *Today* programme, was one of these. He also added a short message, 'Give my love to Carmarthenshire – a wonderful county!'

During the following year, Dr Penn continued to take life quieter while making time to visit Tre-saith, Llangrannog and Aberporth with Peggy, places they had enjoyed during their working days at Newcastle Emlyn in 1955. Dr Penn kept busy with light public engagements, such as talking to senior citizens about the changes he had encountered in forty years at Whitland. He and Peggy also ventured down to the coast, taking lunch in seafront cafés, such as The Pirate Restaurant in Amroth. All the while, they enjoyed Hillside's offerings, and the company of Carol, the house-help, and David, the gardener:

Tuesday June 23rd
After breakfast, I went out to the garden to see David. Everything looked good, with the orchard completely transformed from what it used to be. It has changed from being a dense tropical rain forest – into a lawn containing apple trees . . .

Welsh lessons were also high on the agenda now, although Dr Penn could be a disruptive influence in class. Derrick Burnell explains:

> We had some great times learning Welsh in the Hywel Dda Centre. I remember Dr Penn arriving for the first time:
> 'For how long have you been learning Welsh, Dr Penn?' I asked.
> 'Oh, about forty-five years,' he replied, laughing.
> He and the Reverend Kingsley Taylor were hard work for the poor teacher; she had no chance. It was hilarious at times, being stuck on the first page for most of the lesson!

As the summer of 1998 gave way to autumn, Dr Penn and Peggy were looking forward to the highlight of the year. This was a visit to the Royal Albert Hall: a not-so-little 'thank you' from the local 'Legion' members:

> Saturday November 7th
> This was quite an eventful day. We got up at 7 a.m., but I still wasn't ready on time to get to the Town Hall by 8 o'clock. Carol and Denny [the house-helper and her husband] were there and had paid for our breakfast. We had a lovely meal which had been organised by the Toddler's Group in aid of the new Children's Corner.
> David arrived at 9.15 and we left soon afterwards, going up the 'Heads of the Valleys' road and then into Blackwood, calling with Thelma Watkins [a relative] who had prepared

a genealogical tree for us. I borrowed her Bible because I had been asked to read in the Service of Remembrance in the Memorial Hall [the following morning] – so I was able to read it, on and off, during the day.

After a pleasant hour or so we carried on with our journey and went to the Coach and Horses in Chepstow and had a nice meal. David had steak, Peggy had gammon and I had chicken tikka, with apple and ice cream afterwards.

Thence, on the M4 to London. We didn't stop, but we, at least, saw Windsor and the outside of the castle.

David dropped us in the Royal Albert Hall at approximately 6 p.m. and I had a glass of red wine before we took our seats for the Festival of Remembrance Service – which was really touching and enjoyable. The Queen and Duke of Edinburgh joined the gathering, too.

David was waiting for us when we came out. We started back at 9.30. We stopped at a service station and we saw Mr and Mrs Patel from Whitland. They were on their way back from Heathrow after being in India on holiday for a fortnight. We arrived home safely at 2.05 a.m.

The End of an Era for Dolycwrt Surgery

ONLY A FEW DAYS before Dr Penn and Peggy occupied their seats at the prestigious and most 'Royal' Remembrance Service at Hyde Park, London, the future of Dolycwrt surgery had been cast into a shadow of uncertainty. Single-handed practices were difficult to manage in the modern era of medicine and, sadly, Dr Hood had resigned from his post.

Another campaign, of a sort, now lay ahead of Dr Penn – although he knew in his heart that it was a lost cause. Nevertheless, he went through the motions, which included going all the way to the Medical Practices Committee, Newington Causeway, in the South East of London.

> Thursday February 4th
> I was shown into a room near to the entrance and, at 12.30 p.m., in walked Dr Griffiths. He was a nice man and looked pleasant and distinguished with grey hair, and a nice smile and a healthy looking complexion. He was obviously genuinely sympathetic towards us, but he sadly explained that neither he nor the Medical Practices Committee could help us. He said that the decision was in the hands of the Health Authorities in Carmarthen, and that they would 'rubber stamp' the decision made.

Dr Penn was not alone in his efforts. Many people came to his assistance, including Sir Eric Howells, who worked tirelessly for Dolycwrt's continuance. Sir Eric had known earlier that, as Dr Penn approached retirement, he was worried about the surgery's door closing behind him.

Dr Penn wanted, more than anything, to see Dolycwrt continue as a medical centre, never imagining its proud record ending. Now, however, its future was looking bleak as control slipped from his grasp.

It was only a question of time before the sad ending took place: arriving just weeks later on Friday February 26th 1999, Peggy's birthday:

> I wrote a letter to Beryl, Elizabeth and Linda. I went down to the surgery and presented the 'on leaving' cards to each of them and to the temporary doctor in charge. All appreciated my gifts greatly. I also took with me a bottle of Liebfraumilch white wine and we all had a glass. I tried not to make it a miserable occasion and I thanked them all. Dr Russell, of the Health Authority, was busy in the lovely room upstairs. I went up to see him and he shook my hand.
>
> The surgery was almost empty, but the middle room was full of recently acquired equipment ready to be taken to Meddygfa Taf Health Centre. I was so sad, but we all kept up a happy mood. I took a photo of the staff outside Dolycwrt.

Beryl will never forget the occasion;

> I just felt so sorry for Dr Penn; he had given so much of his life to the place – and now it was closing.

Adding to this emptiness was the fact that Myrddin and Yvonne John and their family, the former surgery caretakers, had moved on; without them Dolycwrt was simply not the same. Yvonne shared a few thoughts about the good old days:

> We had a lot of fun with Dr Penn. He did so many things for everybody. I can remember a woman coming to the surgery during the snow; she was freezing-cold. Dr Penn

asked for a blanket to keep her body warm, a pan of warm water for her feet and a bowl of hot soup.

We often used to see him at the end of the day; he'd wander down after the last patient had gone home, sometimes staying for a coffee, usually black – and he enjoyed playing with our children. Now and again Dr Penn waited with us for a patient, and when he sat next to the Rayburn, he usually fell asleep.

Understandably, the experience of Dolycwrt surgery closing its doors for the last time shattered Dr Penn who lay down and shut his eyes for forty minutes upon returning to Hillside. But, that night, he and Peggy were attending a Welsh supper and sing-along at the Lamb Inn, Llanboidy with British Legion members. They had a bus to catch – and 'thank goodness', too, this event taking Dr Penn's mind off the whole affair . . . but not for long!

Wednesday March 3rd
I nearly forgot the main event of the day. As arranged, I met Neil Jenkins with his van and members of his staff at Dolycwrt, and he took all the items of equipment, (which had been donated to us, or bought from donations) over to the other surgery. We went round the back. Dr Chris Anthony was pleased and thanked me for the equipment, and I then thanked him for taking it! Being in the almost empty Dolycwrt was a sad experience.

I felt sad on getting home and Carol spoke some comforting words – such as it would be good for me to pop into Dolycwrt, perhaps daily, or two or three times a week, and perhaps be miserable there on my own, and, in time, I would feel better.

In the meantime, Dr Penn and Peggy were determined to

enjoy a few summer outings in the warmer weather – one being to Tregaron, beyond Lampeter. There, they visited the Talbot Inn, a delightful country pub and restaurant, with a proud history. This attractive stone-faced building, which dates back hundreds of years to when drovers gathered in Tregaron before journeying across the Cambrian Mountains, appealed to Dr Penn. These trips kept him and Peggy busy, whilst also taking Dr Penn's mind away from a task he had been postponing for some time:

Monday August 16th
After breakfast, we both went into the garden. Peggy picked kidney beans, and they were really marvellous, and I let the poultry out.

Then I did something that I had been dreading. I went down to Dolycwrt. There was a lot of, mostly inconsequential, correspondence there. But there was a final notice for electricity for over £100 due since April.

I just sat numb for a while downstairs, and then upstairs in the nice long room, which had been a lovely office and sitting room when Dr Malcolm Holding and Dr Roy Allen and I had been in partnership there – and which Dr Hood had again made into a useful room, and which I should have done, too.

Dolycwrt seemed to be a lovely house and I could hardly believe that it was over six months since I had been inside it. I explored the always empty, unused room above the caretaker's kitchen. It was eerie, but also stimulating. I realised what a fine building it was, and what a pity it was not being used and what a pity I had failed to keep it going as a General Practice. I felt quite dispirited.

The occasion of Dr Penn's previous visit to Dolycwrt had been to give presents and letters to the departing staff on that final day, February 26th 1999, when the surgery door closed. Elizabeth White, a recipient, also remembers the occasion: everybody preparing to go home when Dr Penn arrived unannounced. He was full of little surprises and his offerings that day were more touching than most. Elizabeth has kept safe the letter she received which, in just a few sentences, so perfectly sums up Dr Penn – the doctor, the friend, the man:

> Dear Elizabeth,
> Well, it's a sad day today; but never mind – you have added a lot to Dolycwrt over the past few years . . .
> Best wishes for the future; anyway, we'll be seeing you. Efallai y tro nesaf fe fydda i'n siarad Cymraeg! [Perhaps next time I will be speaking Welsh.]
> Yours sincerely Peggy and George
> P. S. I hope that you like the picture.

Dr Penn's gift, a painting by Adrian Taunton, portrayed beautifully in shades of mainly light-blue, the scene of a low tide at the sea shore. It was an image of activity: two men gathering shellfish, or 'Working the Mussels' as the painting was described. Equally, there was a hint of desolation: an empty little boat that had, seemingly, run aground, and a distant sea, well out of reach.

PART XII

THE CHOIRBOY YEARS

Vicar of St Mary's Discovers
Dr Penn's Singing Voice

THERE IS A UNIQUE atmosphere within the walls of our churches and chapels and St Mary's in Whitland, where Dr Penn and Peggy attended Sunday services, is no different. When one enters the church through its main porch, where tens of thousands of people over decades have passed at one or another of their life stages, it is hard not to be humbled by a sense of overwhelming orderliness and splendour. For Dr Penn, who once harboured thoughts of joining the ministry, attending church provided a sense of real occasion. And, just as stepping inside this sacred building brings magnificent, almost magical, colour to the externally dull stained-glass windows, so also did this same experience inject life and nourishment into the spiritual nature of Dr Penn's being.

To see these mini-cathedrals closing saddened Dr Penn, who was now doing his best to bolster local church congregations. One of his first acts in this regard was to accept an invitation from the Vicar of St Mary's to join the church choir. The Reverend Kingsley Taylor reveals how he discovered Dr Penn's singing voice:

> This happened on a Maundy Thursday when I invited the congregation to stay behind after church for some

meditation and singing. We were a nice little group, all ladies except for Dr Penn. As we sang, I couldn't help hearing a nice-sounding male voice. Of course, I knew whom this belonged to – so, after the service, I invited Dr Penn to join the choir.

He was quite shocked. He didn't think he could sing. He had been told in school that he either couldn't sing or not to sing. Anyway, he agreed to take his place in the church choir when we had a special musical service. Eric Harries-Brown was another, and they both enjoyed themselves. Once or twice, I asked them to dress-up in their black cassocks and white surplices for weddings. Dr Penn was always prepared to try something different: always keen to have a go.

Today the little church in nearby Henllan Amgoed, which falls within the diocesan parish of St Mary's, has sadly been closed. Situated in peaceful farming countryside, its location, and small, but rather quaint, building appealed to Dr Penn. Of course, it had survived some amazing times, including the dropping of German bombs into a nearby field during World War II. This is when a member of Hermann Goering's Luftwaffe saw a light one dark winter night as the congregation dispersed. But bomb proof or not, Dr Penn had hoped to see the little church continue:

Sunday October 11ᵗʰ 1998
Peggy, Roger and I went to Henllan Church. We really liked it, and we are so pleased about our Vicar having no thoughts of closing it.

The Reverend Kingsley Taylor explained Dr Penn's involvement in keeping this church open in its later days:

I can remember we had a meeting concerning the closure of St David's, in Henllan Amgoed, and Dr Penn really wasn't happy about this. He made his thoughts quite clear and certainly stood up to the Archdeacon.

'Who was that man who did all the talking?' he asked me on the way out.

'Oh, that was our Dr Penn,' I replied.

'Oh, I understand,' he said, 'I've heard about Dr Penn.'

As a result, we managed to stave off the closure for a number of years. And that was put down to Dr Penn's strong stance that day.

One of Dr Penn's favourite Sunday services was evensong, which started at 6.15 p.m., usually a quieter time of the day for him, even during days of general practice. Whether it was the dark and wet nights of winter, or the fresh warm evenings of summer, he enjoyed hearing the church bells chiming from far and wide, an innocent but warm, welcoming invitation to attend:

Sunday May 23rd 1999
In the evening we went to Church and were thrilled that there were 18 people there – apart from Mrs Powell at the organ, the Vicar and Reverend Powell.

Meanwhile, 'choirboy' duties were bringing rewards for an ambitious chorister:

Sunday September 19th 1999
We left to visit the Nun's at the Holy Cross Abbey. It was the United Service of the churches and chapels of Whitland and the choir sang 'Go Forth' – which I believe sounded OK. It was a lovely service.

Wednesday December 15th 1999

There was no Welsh lesson this morning, so I went up to Waungron Residential Home with the Vicar and a few of the Church Choir to sing carols, which seemed to have been well received. Then we had coffee and tea with mince pies.

As ever, the sum total of Dr Penn's parts added up to far more than the whole; and, if anyone could defy scientific theory, it was he. Here is a story about The Good Samaritan, going back to the summer of 1979, when attending to railway business:

> I had a most interesting experience on the way to Newcastle Emlyn. I decided to call with a patient on the way – and, as I neared her home, I passed a lone walker who I thought I knew. Following my visit, which I enjoyed – sitting outside on a wooden seat having a drink of whisky – I saw this elderly gentleman again on my way back. He was obviously confused and in a bad way. He didn't know me, or where he was, and was distressed. I told him to jump in and I took him home – and I found heaps of people there, all worried about his disappearance for hours.

Understandably, everyone at St Mary's Church, Whitland was proud of Dr Penn, many having treasured memories of him today. Here Joanne Seeley pays tribute to her former neighbour:

> My late husband, Alan, had been unwell, and we were in the house when Dr Penn called.
>
> 'Alan needs to get out in the fresh air,' said Dr Penn. 'It will do him good. I've got to go into the country later. I'll call for you both.'
>
> So we waited and waited, well into the evening. Then he arrived, and we set off. He had someone to visit, so again

we waited for him, in the car. He came back, apologising; it had been a difficult case.

'Anyway, let's go for a drink,' he said.

Soon we were turning up at the 'Bont' in Llanglydwen.

Everyone was thrilled when they saw Dr Penn walking in. They all wanted to talk to him.

'I want you to meet some friends of mine,' he said.

He was bringing Alan and me into it all, making us feel welcome.

One Sunday, shortly after Alan died, I'd gone to church, having left one of the windows at home slightly open. When I came back, inside this room was a beautiful Easter egg. And I didn't know who it was from until sometime later I met Dr Penn. I couldn't believe how he had taken the time and trouble, not only to think of me, but also to place the egg onto the [inside] windowsill. It was the sort of gesture that I cannot forget; he was just so kind to everyone.

On another occasion, when I had been unwell, there was a knock on the front door late at night.

'Joanne, it's Dr Penn, George Penn. I'm calling to see that you're all right.'

Then, after phoning Peggy, he spent an hour and a half talking to me. With all his demands, he still found the time. Where can you get a person like that – let alone a doctor?

Joan Manning remembers working in Ridgeway Home and needing a doctor to come out late at night to see a resident:

I can still see Dr Penn coming through the door wearing his warm tweed hat; he never went anywhere without a hat.

'Will you want a pair of medical gloves, Dr Penn,' I asked.

'Oh no, I won't be needing gloves,' he replied. Of course, Dr Penn was a traditional doctor; he'd only use gloves if he really had to.

'Are you staying for a cup of tea Dr Penn?' I asked as he finished his work.

Of course he was staying. He loved a cup of tea. Then we had a nice chat, despite this being in the early hours of the morning.

John and Ogwen Davies in the north of the Dolycwrt practice named their son after Dr Penn – well they had to!

Our youngest was a bit slow arriving. He kept Dr Penn very busy one weekend.

'Well you'll have to slip my name in here,' he said.

So we called our son Alan George Davies.

But when we had the medical card later, our Alan was described as George Alan Davies. This was Dr Penn; he had rearranged the order – what a character!

I also remember the time he was Chairman in a concert in Whitland and Dr Hugh Philipps was standing in for him for the evening. Ogwen wanted to know something – so we spoke to this gentleman who was very helpful and he promised to update Dr Penn later.

It was now about twelve o'clock and the little boy was better. Next thing, we heard someone talking outside. Dr Penn and Peggy had both come up together.

'When I knew there was a young child involved, I couldn't go to bed until I called,' he said.

Then we had coffee and cakes until the early hours.

Janet and Ernest Jones have a 'Kempton' in their family, Mark Kempton Jones, whose own son, aged eight, is Harri Kempton Jones:

'Dr Penn was wonderful,' said Earnest, 'and the one regret of Janet's father was that he didn't give Dr Penn a load of hay during his farming days at Hillside.'

Meanwhile, Brian Brown, mentioned earlier when the Triumph Herald caught fire, gives two examples of the Rolls Royce service that Dr Penn gave to his patients:

> I can remember the time I had an eye problem and I went along to Dolycwrt. Dr Penn thought it might be a good idea to see a specialist, so he rang Moorfields Eye Hospital in London to arrange this. But it was quite out of the question, because there was such a long waiting list – so Dr Penn sent me in as an emergency! He wrote a letter of introduction and I travelled up with Reverend David Faulkner.
>
> When we arrived we were seen at the Accident and Emergency unit and the doctor in the clinic couldn't believe it. He knew that I shouldn't have been there – but, as I had travelled such a long way, I was able to see a specialist there and then.
>
> On another occasion Dr Penn asked me to paint the windows in Hillside. When I started to work on the upstairs rooms, he was taking a break from medical work because he was suffering with nosebleeds. And as he lay in bed taking rest, we chatted through the window, me being at the top of the ladder. I remember mentioning that I wasn't sleeping too well: 'When you go home for lunch, I'll give it some thought,' he said to me.
>
> When I returned later, Peggy handed me a letter: 'George has written something for you, Brian,' she told me – and when I went back up the ladder, he explained what he had written – again from his bed! And I've kept the letter ever since . . .
>
> 'Brian, I've given a prescription for two lots-of-help for sleeping and you could try them for a while, at least until you catch up . . .

'The yellow tablets are very good . . . but it's essential to keep them out of sight of Dylan, or a young person, as they look attractive, like sweets!'

Dr Penn sometimes referred to a biblical sounding quotation, which may have emanated from his days of study at Bushey School:

He who steals my purse steals trash, but he who steals my name, steals my everything.

This can be related to another incident that saw Dr Penn supporting an elderly couple who found themselves in the middle of a dispute. This had disturbed Dr Penn who, having established the facts, and having known these patients for many years, felt that they really were not at fault.

For Dr Penn, this was a matter of 'right and wrong'; it was also a matter of principle and 'honour'. And he was so convinced by the protestations of innocence from them both that he was adamant that they should defend their name when events led to a court case. When they were found guilty, Dr Penn, also in attendance that day giving his moral support, was devastated.

'Don't worry Dr Penn,' said the gentleman. 'You gave me the strength to defend my name. I may have lost the case, but I know in my heart that I was right, and I will always be thankful to you for this.

In or out of his choirboy's cassock, he was an extraordinary man. Eifion James sums him up in a few words:

I have heard many people talking about Dr Penn over the years, but I have never, ever, heard one bad word. Do you know, I think he was a saint; he was a saint of a man.

A Farewell to Bushey School for a Fun-loving Grandfather

WHO WOULD HAVE guessed that choirboy duties entitled Dr Penn to attend the annual Sunday school outing? Next up was an excursion to Oakwood Leisure Park, Dr Penn and Peggy boosting the small number of travellers on the day of an eclipse of the sun:

> We arrived and sat on a seat near the restaurant waiting for the eclipse. Most people had special dark spectacles but, in the event, they were not needed and it was easy and exciting to make out the sun being almost completely covered. For a few minutes, the light faded and it was darker and colder, but everything soon reverted to normal . . . so we had, more or less, seen the eclipse of the sun by the moon! Apparently, it last happened in 1927, the year I was born, and it will next happen in 2000-and-something, about 70 years hence! It's all very amazing.
>
> We went into the restaurant and treated ourselves to breakfast. From there we could see the frightening 'Vertigo', not far away; it was incredible. Three people were strapped onto something face-downwards and then taken up an unbelievable height. Then they just came hurtling down.
>
> We indulged in candyfloss, doughnuts and a new pellet-form of ice cream plus a delightful sorbet type of coloured drink. We met some of the Sunday school party who took us to Jake's Theatre, where we saw a puppet show on a huge scale – before boarding the bus for home.

Uplifted by this venture, it was again time for Dr Penn to turn back the clock. Many years had passed since the closure of both the Junior and Senior sections of the Royal Masonic School for Boys in Bushey, whose combined influences had a major bearing on the young George Penn. Plans had now been put in place for the luxurious apartments of today's Royal Connaught Park, which would soon give the clock tower and its adjoining buildings a wonderful new lease of life. But, before the builders moved in and made permanent changes to its proud interior features, Dr Penn and former schoolboys were invited to take one last look around the premises. This proved to be a whistle-stop excursion in the company of Arthur Brown, an old friend. It was also a memorable day, as Dr Penn stepped back in time:

> It was a glorious, warm summer's day and Bushey looked lovely; indeed, the school – both schools – seemed fine. We went up London Road and passed the Junior School and it looked from the road as it always had looked. It was lovely to see the Avenue again and to turn into the school front gates. All the lovely playing areas were still there as far as I could see.

> The front hall was remarkably unaltered. We signed a register there and went over to the classrooms. The 'Geography School' had changed somewhat with different seating. We saw the plans for the school; a property owner had seemingly, bought it and was going to restructure and build. Old Masonians were pleased that the place was tasteful but, of course, we were all also sad.

> There was a good buffet lunch in the dining hall. The 'Big School' looked lovely – also the chapel, soon to be turned into offices. I met Bill Wright, a farmer and a nice chap, and his wife but as far as I could make out, there weren't many others from my time there.

The Quadrangle looked remarkably the same. In fact it was all a most wonderful experience. But I suppose the experience was tinged with sadness and mixed feelings, too.

Bob Fountaine, who today lives at Rickmansworth in the vicinity of the old school, can remember Dr Penn returning to Bushey for the annual school open day:

> 'I also believe that George was outspoken at the time when the closure of the school was still under discussion,' explained Bob. 'I think all of us had the best intentions, but were slow to fully understand the costs necessary in raising the school to modern day standards. But we all took heart in knowing that the spirit of the craft continued, with excellent schooling for both boys and girls still being provided by the Royal Masonic Movement.'

Dr Penn continued to pack into the remainder of his life all that he could. Well, his vessel had always overflowed; why should he change now? He and Peggy were planning an outing to Aberystwyth where, not many years earlier, they had met a lady from Whitland who was enjoying a short break on an organised bus tour. Excited to see Dr Penn and Peggy, she could not help mentioning that her friend from this same travelling party was unwell: restricted to her hotel room, feeling sorry for herself and missing Dr Penn.

'And where exactly is she?' asked Dr Penn, before he and Peggy picked up a bunch of flowers and knocked on the bedroom door. What an encounter that must have been; what a lift for the lady concerned!

They were now in the company of Beryl Campbell, former practice nurse at Dolycwrt, and her husband, Bill. Dr Penn and Peggy often enjoyed outings with Beryl, Bill and their three sons, Mark, Darren and Steven. Now, as they made their way past the pier to the seafront, Dr Penn wanted to paddle in the sea. Beryl recalls:

Dr Penn was determined to go into the water. He took his shoes and socks off, and walked in, otherwise fully clothed. Mind you, he nearly fell over; someone steadied him – before Bill went down to help him back. He was determined not to give up – but he knew in his heart that this was his last dip in Aberystwyth.

We enjoyed some fantastic times with Dr Penn and Peggy, and our three boys looked to them as grandparents. And wherever we went, Dr Penn was busy sending postcards. We have quite a collection ourselves, all written in his familiar way. When he ran out of space, he continued writing up the sides, and then along the top – until the card was covered all the way around with his writing.

Dr Penn's retirement years had given him time to spend with his own family, too. He had always enjoyed visiting Southampton to see Sarah, Marek and their children, Anna and Stefan, and here he describes one such visit:

We all set off in the car for Portsmouth and Southsea. We stopped at H.M.S. *Warrior* and enquired about going aboard. We were told that it would take about an hour, so we decided to have something to eat first of all, and, lo and behold, we arrived at the Pendragon Hotel, Southsea [the scene of past family holidays]. It was wonderful to see this hotel again and we had a lovely full lunch before going back to H.M.S. *Warrior*. It really was fascinating – the first ironclad British warship, commissioned in 1860, and apparently kept going until being dumped in Pembroke Dock in 1929. Then it was brought back to Portsmouth and refurbished to what it once was.

When Sarah and her family returned home to Whitland, they enjoyed taking Dr Penn and Peggy around the local countryside. This note is from Dr Penn's diary during his last summer, in 2001:

> Sarah and her family wanted to treat us to an afternoon tea somewhere, and we went to a lovely café just past Templeton. I had scones, butter, jam and cream and tea, and a bottle of water, and ice cream. I thought this was great.

Living close to hand, it was always easier for Elizabeth and Ken and their children Hywel, Iwan and Nia to see more of Dr Penn. Now, he was following the progress of Hywel and Iwan as two new cricketers in the family, and he enjoyed seeing them in action at Whitland's Cricket Club.

In this same year, Dr Penn spent his last birthday with Elizabeth and her family:

> In the afternoon we went to Elizabeth's home with my birthday cake, with the idea of sharing it with the family. But Elizabeth went one better, and fetched a lovely Indian Takeaway for us. It was Vindaloo for me and I really enjoyed it.

But the real treat came about a week later when they were chauffeured by Elizabeth and Ken to the annual book festival at Hay-on-Wye. This year, none other than Bill Clinton, former American President, was talking to a large crowd about his newly published book. Elizabeth described the scene:

> My father genuinely liked Bill Clinton so he made an effort to buy tickets to hear him speak. I remember there were a lot of security guards around and no one could get too close to him in the marquee. When Mr Clinton finished

his address, my parents waited until the hall was almost empty before leaving. Then all of a sudden about twenty people came from nowhere. This was Mr Clinton and his entourage, passing just a few feet away.

At home in Hillside, Dr Penn and Roger found time to go through Dr Penn's mountains of old papers, whilst also sharing their mutual love of the sea:

> Roger kindly took me down to Pendine in his car to have another dip. When we got there, it was swarming with people and the tide was as far out as it was possible to be. We then set off for the 'point' nearest to Morfa Bychan. When we got to the 'point', where there were hardly any people at all, I went in the sea. After the dip, I walked around the corner to Morfa Bychan, where Roger waited with his car.

As for an occasional break with Peggy, Weston-Super-Mare had been a popular choice for the past few years. It is there that Dr Penn, ever the traditional G.P., liked to breathe in the fresh air that blew across the sandy beaches and mud-stretches of the sea front. Of course, Dr Penn was doing what he could to help himself and, not far away working in this same town, was Whitland's Brian Cook, mentioned earlier when Dr Penn borrowed his car:

> George and Peggy and I used to meet at the Royal Hotel, Weston-Super-Mare. This is where they stayed and where I picked them up to go down to the beach. Of course, George went in the sea for a swim whenever he could. We had a lovely time together: a typical reunion, happily reminiscing about the old days.

In the pleasant surroundings of this beautiful hotel, Dr Penn could sit and watch the sun going down, at a time when his days, too, were beginning to ebb away. And in these twilight hours, he would take solace from more of the beautiful words of 'Desiderata' that had uplifted him throughout his life. This is a piece of prose written by Max Ehrmann, an American, around the time that Dr Penn was born, and a copy of it had, for many years, adorned his waiting room at Dolycwrt Surgery. Its offerings of wisdom are many but the following passage may have seemed particularly apt to Dr Penn at this time:

> Take kindly the counsel of the years, gracefully surrendering the things of youth . . . whether or not it is clear to you, no doubt the Universe is unfolding as it should. Therefore be at peace with God, whatever you conceive him to be . . .

A Last Luncheon for the Probus President

IN THIS SAME YEAR, 2001, Dr Penn had one last surprise to pull out from his amazing bag of tricks. After years of undivided loyalty to old cars, he walked into Jeff Courts's Station Garage in Whitland and drove away with a cherry-red Mini Metro. Here was a turn-up for the books, signifying that it was not too late to 'go modern' once again, but, more importantly, that there was more mileage left in Dr Penn – despite regular hospital check-ups and everybody's advice to let the world come to him at Hillside. But he could never sit at home counting the daisies – as this diary note reveals:

> Saturday June 30th
> I was trying to put together a speech for tonight because I had been asked to be President of Whitland Choir's open-air concert at Lampeter House. I thought I'd mention a few things which give me pride and delight to think about, such as, the transmission of the first over-water 'Morse Code' and the start of the wonderful communications of today. Then I intended mentioning personal face-to-face communications, as when Hywel Dda gathered all the rulers of Wales together in Whitland around about the year 940, as I understand, to put over his code of conduct and laws.

Returning home with thoughts of uplifting choir-singing fresh in his mind, Dr Penn began working for the annual chapel concert which marked the official start of Whitland Week, usually held at Tabernacle. Ever since retiring from the

'Week' committee, he liked to contribute towards the concert's success, a formal event at which the incoming president receives his, or her, chain of office. Of course, selling tickets was his forte, and he sometimes enlisted the support of Carol at Hillside who kindly called on his behalf at people's homes. But this year, he was spreading the word further afield in the north of Pembrokeshire:

> I drove into Newport and put several posters up, and left a note for Roger in Lloyds Bank; and I had a cup of coffee in the Beehive café – where there was a nice lady, who not only put up a poster, but also bought two tickets! She knew the Royal Masonic School; she had taught Russian there after the Boy's School closed.

Dr Penn knew that the people of Whitland were proud of their talented musicians and singers who had entertained over the years. They were booked well in advance for Whitland Week concerts, alongside artists from further afield who added their own refreshing mix to the proceedings. Gethin and Jenny Lewis often saw Dr Penn and Peggy at these and other events, as Gethin recalls:

> We had an unforgettable evening in the company of Dr Penn and Peggy during the early-nineties. A friend of ours was headmaster of the senior school at the time, and, because he travelled into Whitland from outside the area, he wanted to meet some of the local characters. So we invited the vicar and the vet, and the doctor and one or two other dignitaries – perhaps a dozen of us in all – round for supper and we set things up with a drink or two before the meal.
>
> That night Dr Penn absolutely enthralled everybody with stories about his days in Africa; if I had paid a lot of money for an entertainer he'd have been no better. We

sipped our drinks and sat back for about an hour listening, while Peggy beamed quietly throughout, knowing what was coming next. Our guest told me later that he'd never before been captivated in such manner at a supper party; he felt privileged to have met Dr Penn.

Jenny, Gethin's wife, a former director at Glangwili Hospital, Carmarthen, has a few words to say about Dr Penn, the professional practitioner:

> He was held in such high regard. He was a doctor who had earned the greatest of respect.

Gwyn Lewis, brother-in-law, has his own story:

> I loved Dr Penn, and whatever life threw at him he took it in his stride. I remember sometime in the early 1980s we had ordered a load of straw, which was delivered to the farm by a large lorry, the bales stacked perhaps eight layers high. We had a gate at the top of the field with a track running down to the shed and the lorry driver turned right through this opening instead of continuing down the lane. Effectively, he cut across the steep slope and, of course, the whole lorry and load toppled over.
>
> When the driver climbed out, he put his foot on the front-wheel which spun around, causing him to fall heavily to the ground, where he lay motionless. In one mad panic we phoned for Dr Penn, who arrived a few minutes later, driving into the field. Understandably, we were all extremely worried, but Dr Penn totally defused the situation – in fact, paying greater initial attention to the straw that was scattered all around, than the man on the ground!
>
> But Dr Penn was smart. He knew from our initial telephone message and a quick glance at the man's colour and body language that this was no emergency. In no time,

he helped the gentleman to a full recovery, and soon he was walking around again.

Ann, Gwyn's wife, remembers sharing good news with Dr Penn about winning a tourism award for the farmhouse accommodation she provided in earlier years:

> The next day he called with a little keepsake. It was a small crown, with lovely detail, and it's in our china cabinet today. It is these caring gestures, the smaller things, which set Dr Penn apart.

We all know that Dr Penn was known for generosity and, throughout his retirement years, he gave his full commitment to the local Probus Club. There he enjoyed close companionship with members who met regularly for pleasant social luncheons, when a speaker joined the party to give an address. Now, in early December 2001, Dr Penn, as president, was planning to go along to recite an amusing poem, 'The Green Eye of the Little Yellow God', written by J. Milton Hayes in 1911. Dr Penn certainly had not lost his sense of fun, although he was noticeably a lot weaker now – and, despite his family's suggestion that he stay at home to rest, he was determined not to miss the luncheon.

On Wednesday December 12th, Bill Allen – the local vet, former mayor and a leading man in the community – called to see Dr Penn as he was reciting the poem out aloud. Next day, came the big event, a 'Christmas spread' with all its tasty trimmings and a recital from Dr Penn, ready, willing and able – and raring to go!

> We had a lovely meal and, afterwards, I spoke my monologue and I'm pleased that it went down well. We also had some carol singing; altogether, it was a lovely occasion, and we arrived back home at about 4.30 p.m.

Here are the first and second verses of this long poem:

> There's a one-eyed yellow idol to the north of Kathmandu;
> There's a little marble cross below the town;
> There's a broken-hearted woman tends the grave of Mad Carew,
> And the Yellow God forever gazes down.
>
> He was known as 'Mad Carew' by the Subs at Kathmandu.
> He was hotter than they felt inclined to tell;
> But for all his foolish pranks, he was worshipped in the ranks,
> And the Colonel's daughter smiled on him as well.

'Mad' Carew had made a big impression – but so had Dr Penn, whose many followers were smiling on him from every direction! Indeed the world was now coming to Hillside as the following testifies:

> Friday December 14th
> Before I got back to bed, we had exciting visitors from Australia! – no less than Elwyn's brother, Colin, and his partner.

No doubt Colin – whose brother Elwyn was once a gardener at Hillside – has his own stories about Dr Penn – as do others. Here is a selection, starting with John and Caroline Williams, who remember the time Dr Penn was on his rounds one Christmas morning:

> I had made arrangements to meet Dr Penn in Efailwen where he was attending to a patient. I had to collect a tonic from him for one of our boys who was unwell and, as I stood alongside his A35 car, I couldn't help glancing through the window. What an amazing sight; I saw a nest of Teacher's Whisky bottles! I'd imagine these were presents for Dr Penn, all spread across the back seat.

Not far from here, Hedydd Lewis preferred to give Dr Penn a cup of tea:

> He often stayed for a sandwich, too, and he always made us laugh. One day the television was on in the background as he examined my husband.
>
> 'Do you mind turning the channel over, Hedydd?' he asked. 'I was watching a good film next door and it was getting exciting. I'd like to know how it ends.'
>
> He was a character and a half. You couldn't find anyone like him in a million years. And Peggy, she was lovely, too.

One day, Bertie John went along to Dolycwrt for a medical:

> Dr Penn was a great friend of mine. I had moved from Whitland and had registered with another doctor near my new home. I needed a medical and I mentioned that Dr Penn would be able to do this for me, and I would like to go along to him. Then, when I visited him in Dolycwrt for a preliminary discussion, he said to me:
>
> 'Now promise me this, Bertie, stay off beer and cigarettes for at least two weeks before you come to see me.'
>
> When the day arrived, he made me feel special as he always did. Then he reminded me about a past Whitland Week event.
>
> 'Do you remember the donkey derby, Bertie?' he asked.
>
> Of course, I could never forget it, even though it happened years earlier. At the time Dr Penn saw me as I was walking in; he needed an experienced jockey to ride a spare pony. 'Would I help out?' But when we took our place at the starting line, the donkey would not budge.
>
> But having ridden horses all my life, and knowing exactly what to do, I got the animal to move – and we ended up winning the race! Dr Penn witnessed all of this

as he did the official commentary on the microphone. I can still remember him laughing: 'Well done Bertie,' he called out, 'keep it going.'

Bertie's brother Huw had the sad experience of seeing his father collapsing at his home:

I immediately knew that it was serious. I telephoned Dr Penn and he arrived within minutes.

But what I will always remember is that after doing all he could for my father, he went along to see my mother a few miles away. He sat down with her and spent time explaining what had happened.

And what I learnt afterwards, was that he had left his surgery full of patients to be with us. They were all sat down waiting their turn, but without realising that Dr Penn had left; he wasn't even there! I was quite amused when I heard this, but this was Dr Penn down to a 'T'.

Bryant Rees, mentioned earlier, could sympathise with those waiting:

I went down to Dolycwrt one morning. It was during surgery hours, and I was met by a receptionist.

'I want to see Dr Penn, please,' I said to her.

'Dr Penn is not here now; he's out on a visit, but he'll be back later,' I was told.

So I was taken inside to sit in the waiting room. The fire was put on for me, and I remember thinking how strange it was that there was no other patient there. But never mind, I sat and watched the television.

After some time, the receptionist came back.

'I should imagine that Dr Penn's been called to see someone seriously ill,' I said to her, 'probably life and death, I should think.'

'Oh, Dr Penn will not be too long now,' she replied.

A little later, a gentleman receptionist came into the room.

'Dr Penn's on his way back. He's expected any minute,' he said.

'Good, I'm glad about that,' I replied – well, I had been there nearly two hours.

Then Dr Penn came through the front door: 'Dr Penn, you've been saving someone's life,' I said to him.

'Well, to tell you the truth, Bryant,' he said, 'I went along to the funeral of an old friend of mine – and, on the way out, I was delayed.'

That's Dr Penn – a marvellous doctor and a marvellous man. I have wonderful memories of him; and may his soul rest in peace.

Dorian Phillips gives another example of the relaxed Dr Penn in his surgery:

I remember going along to Dolycwrt one day because I had a cauliflower ear after playing a lot of rugby. It was starting to irritate me, but I wanted to be fit for the following Saturday's match. When Dr Penn started to examine me, he stopped and said:

'Excuse me a minute Dorian; I think I saw Bill Allen in the waiting room. Let's ask for Bill's opinion.'

When he returned to the room with Bill Allen, the local vet, Dr Penn said,

'Bill, what do you think about Dorian's ear? He wants to play rugby on Saturday. Do you reckon he should?'

Of course, Dr Penn was never short of a stitching job or two with the rugby boys. Former Whitland player David (Dai) Hughes has a funny story:

I had taken a bump to the head in a rugby match, so I went along to Dolycwrt to see 'Doc Penn', as I liked to call him. He was a big friend of my family, and he and my father were in the British Legion together. We were making some good progress with the stitching – just the two of us present in the surgery – when Mrs Penn arrived at the front door with a message. But when she left to go home in the Baby Austin, it wouldn't start.

'I wonder what that is, Peggy,' said Dr Penn, but not in the least disturbed. 'Would you have any ideas, David?'

'It sounds like it could be the electrics, Dr Penn,' I replied – before we all went to have a look.

I remember I had the thread hanging from the cut above my eye as I peeped under the bonnet and gave the plugs a quick wipe.

'Have a go now, Mrs Penn,' I suggested – and it started.

'Well, how did you know that, David,' he said laughing.

Then Mrs Penn drove away and we went back to finish the stitching.

Dr Penn certainly left his mark at the Masonic Lodge in Cardigan. Bennice Williams has this to say:

What a character! The best story, according to my husband, Cecil, relates to George bringing a bucket full of coal to the Lodge committee meetings. It seems that the room got rather cold as the night went on, so the coal came in handy. He always said the 'Cardis' were mean! As you can imagine, this caused great hilarity.

The social side of Freemasonry was also important to George and Peggy, who were usually last to leave a function. The ladies used to prepare a meal after Lodge. Everything – and I mean everything – was brought to the Lodge kitchen to be cooked. Where on earth George and Peggy put all the food in the A35 is beyond comprehension. There were vegetables, tins of soup, cheese, biscuits, pudding – all packed in – miraculous! Those were happy, often hilarious times. We can honestly say it was a pleasure and an experience to have known George and Peggy.

Throughout his life, Dr Penn and Peggy kept in contact with Fred Gillett and his family from Bushey. Here Susan, Fred's daughter, mentioned earlier, has a few stories to share:

As a family we so much enjoyed seeing George and Peggy and the children, either in Hertfordshire or at Hillside – always finding time to keep in touch. And, I will never forget George travelling to Bushey for the funeral of my mother. We were just leaving the family home at Bourne Hall Road, when George came running up the road. He made it just in time – having jumped off the High Street bus, his raincoat folded over his arm. It was so wonderful to see him, and what a huge effort he had made. After the service he stayed with us for a short while, before asking to be excused. Then he travelled back to Whitland that same night!

On another occasion, David and I were staying for a few days in Hillside and we offered to take George around his practice in our Range Rover. I don't know how many patients we saw dotted around the countryside but, wherever we went, George came away with half a dozen eggs, or a bag of tomatoes, or some vegetables. Everybody was so kind to him. Later that same day a woman in the milk factory caught her hand in a machine. Instead of sending her to the hospital, George spent hours stitching her wounds. At one stage he invited us to take a look and I was just amazed at how meticulous he was with those tiny stitches – being ever so careful so that she wouldn't later be scarred.

And finally a word from Joanne Seeley, a neighbour, whose grandson, Andrew, went to Hillside to thank Dr Penn for his birthday present, during Dr Penn's last few days:

> When Kingsley called at Hillside on his way back to Andrew's birthday party, Dr Penn and Peggy dropped a five pound note into his card. Andrew, only aged seven at the time, went down to thank them.
> 'And was Mrs Penn there?' I asked.
> 'No,' he replied, 'she wasn't. But *Peggy* was.'

A Bracelet for Peggy – as the Christmas Lights go out

THERE COULD ONLY be one Peggy Penn. She, too, was 'one in a million' and everybody loved her kind, friendly face. But, for Dr Penn, she was a huge steadying influence before generally letting him do what he thought was best. This was enough for Peggy; she respected the good intentions of a unique man, never stepping in his way. Nancy Davies of Cwmfelin Boeth put this into her own words:

> Without Peggy behind him, Dr Penn wouldn't have been the same man. She was so very patient, kind, gentle – and charming. Oftentimes, when he was out all hours, she wouldn't know when to prepare a meal for him. Bless her, she was a wonderful lady.

'George, where have you been?' Peggy often asked at home in Hillside. But by the time she had prepared him a cup of tea, any earlier disappointment or frustrations had evaporated into the kitchen air like the steam of her kettle. She was just happy to be with him. They shared a lifetime of good deeds, a sackful of letters from Nigeria, and an ocean of memories.

Interestingly, Peggy arrived on the scene when the title 'Doctor' completed the name George Kempton Penn. Likewise, her presence was the making of this same man. She was a receptionist then at Neath General Hospital – just as she was his receptionist and secretary throughout their time together. Occasionally she manned the fort at Dolycwrt, answering the phones and the front door with the same pleasant manner and youthful, cheerful voice that stayed with her throughout her life. At Dolycwrt she shared Dr Penn's last day in medicine, Friday May 16th 1997, in his surgery, at his side.

Understandably, this was an emotional occasion for them both, and Peggy was seen on the BBC documentary wiping her eyes. But she was ready and prepared for the grand finale when she followed Dr Penn into the front garden, where the primary school pupils and teachers waited to make a presentation. Under the full glare of the cameras, Peggy was part of the touching, poignant moment when young Craig Storer thanked Dr Penn for saving his life.

This act, along with the singing of 'Penblwydd Hapus' (Happy Birthday) and the presentation of flowers – was to bring the curtain down on an amazing forty-five year medical career that they had shared together. And, as Dr Penn collected his thoughts, Peggy was privately willing him on. Of course, he would not let her down. Out poured the perfect choice of words for the occasion, wrapped up in the eloquence of a masterful orator who had wooed many a crowd in his day:

> Thank you Craig. Thank you very much . . . I'm really overwhelmed. It's most terrific, most beautiful, most wonderful, most memorable, most unforgettable.

Now, as far as Peggy was concerned, the curtain could come down – so let it drop! They had discharged their duties to the full; it was game, set, and match to a unique doubles partnership.

It is true that medicine took up a mighty big part of their lives, and so did railway activities and all Dr Penn's other commitments, but they also found time for adventures of their own. One was never far from the other:

Friday July 21st 1989

We caught a boat to Caldey Island at 10.30 a.m. and had a choppy and rough crossing. When we arrived, we started a cross-country, or cross-island, walk to a beach the other side. But we met someone who advised us to bathe at Priory Bay, where we had landed. We therefore went back and it was quite idyllic and gorgeous and we spent the next five hours there. We couldn't get over how pleasant it was on that Priory Beach at Caldey – facing Tenby and Penally. We had the added attraction of seeing boats coming and going all the time.

Around 3 p.m., I went off for another swim. I went about 300 yards to the east in order to get away from the stony part of the beach, and it was very pleasant when I eventually settled for a swim. By now, the water was much warmer and I was enjoying splashing, floating, swimming, and just lying in the water at the water's edge. I was away from Peggy for about an hour – *whilst she watched me through the binoculars.*

Dr Penn and Peggy were on this occasion enjoying a few days' holiday at Tenby's Atlantic Hotel on the Esplanade, where they could head directly through the cliff gardens of the hotel down to the sea. Peggy also kept notes, and these tell us what happened next:

We went back to Tenby and had a meal in the Beach Café. We had a big salad roll and curry and chips between us. It was very nice too. We then went back to the hotel where George had another dip.

This is Dr Penn's diary entry for Wednesday April 1st 1998, at a time when he was already struggling with his breathing:

It was the day of Mr James' funeral and I went to Rhiwbwys chapel, Llanrhystud, nine miles this side of Aberystwyth. I went on my own in the Morris-Minor and quite enjoyed the trip. The only trouble was that the chapel was on a steep hill, and there were a lot of cars parked outside by the time I arrived about 1.40 p.m. I pushed on up the hill past the chapel – which meant that I had a pleasant walk down, but not such a good walk back. However, I returned when people were not about, so I was able to stop and rest frequently.

I didn't go to the graveside, because that was another steep hill, but I went into the vestry where we had refreshments. After the service, I travelled to Aberystwyth for the sea air, and I sent a postcard to Peggy. Peggy had given me a thermos flask of tea and some sandwiches. I had half of these near Synod Inn on the way, so now I had the remainder sitting on a public seat.

Many years earlier at a 'Mr and Mrs Contest' during Whitland Week – when questions were asked of one partner about the other (winners demonstrating the greatest knowledge and understanding) – Peggy was asked what it was about Dr Penn that attracted her in the first place. Was it A, or B or C. Peggy ignored all three: 'George had everything!' she said.

Theirs was a unique bond, cemented in these final days by a mutual appreciation of a popular song called 'No Matter What', sung by the Irish pop band, Boyzone. Although they had acquired this recording a few years earlier, it was now heard more often in Hillside. Light and cheerful, its 'catchy' tune rises to a pleasing crescendo. Above all, Dr Penn and Peggy knew that its words best summarised their unity in these advancing years. Here are a few of the closing lines:

No matter if the sun don't shine or if the skies are blue
No matter what the end is, my life began with you.

December 2001 was their last Christmas together. As usual, a big six-foot Christmas tree stood on the wooden block floor of the spacious hall at Hillside and, underneath, brightly coloured packages of different shapes and sizes were arranged in a friendly heap. The Christmas tree lights added the final ingredient to an inviting festive scene for visitors who called – including Dr Malcolm Holding, Reverend Kingsley Taylor, Les Evans and Doreen Adams. Doreen remembers the time:

> Dr Penn was in bed, but he insisted on coming down in his dressing gown and warm hat. We laughed about the time he sent me to see a specialist in Haverfordwest because my right foot kept swelling up. My mother accompanied me to the appointment that day and she asked the surgeon if the trouble was due to me wearing high heels.
>
> 'But you wear high heels on both feet,' was his sharp response – as if to say, 'Don't be ridiculous.' Dr Penn often used to laugh about that, and we did so on this occasion.

This year Dr Penn, still full of surprises, did something different. For the first time, he Sellotaped Christmas cards to the sitting room walls. No doubt, he and Peggy had received a deluge of greetings to fill the usual spaces, but here was, perhaps, one final act of individualism. Certainly, the lovely room looked a picture of warmth and cosiness as they sat happily together enjoying the delightful open fire. But, shortly after the chimes of Big Ben heralded a New Year, and the strains of 'Auld Lang Syne' wafted away into the dark night chill, the Christmas lights that Dr Penn and Peggy had shared together went out for the last time.

'And in God's house for evermore
my dwelling place shall be'

THE SAD NEWS dreaded by all arrived on Friday January 11th 2002. In the early hours of that morning, Dr Penn departed this world, peacefully in his sleep. Whitland and district had lost a dear friend and, as many said, it was the end of an era.

Immediately Hillside became a scene of major activity as people descended upon the doctor's residence, paying their respects. The porch front-door entrance saw new faces arriving throughout the following days, bringing cards, letters and messages – all kind, thoughtful, tearful words for Peggy and her family. The community had lost a wonderful character, too, and, overnight, a lot of the town's colour had disappeared.

As the tributes flowed from far and wide this message from Mervyn Matthews, who lived in Cowbridge but was previously of North Wales, said much about the man that so many mourned. It was taken from an article that appeared in a later edition of the *Journal of the Teifi Valley Railway Society* and it accompanied his personal letter. Here is an extract:

> I became a life member of the Teifi Valley Railway Society in the early 1970s through my contact with Dr George Penn. At the time, George was Chairman of the West Wales Railway Action Committee, and had led a hard-fought campaign to retain railways in West Wales.
>
> We had formed the *Welsh* Railways Action Group in

December 1971 and George became my Vice Chairman. Our brief was to bring together interacting organisations and people prepared to campaign for better railways in Wales.

I should like to pay tribute to George as a great friend and campaigner . . . [from] the early adrenaline-flowing days of our group trying to save the Cambrian Coastline [Railway]. George became a powerful ally; victory for the line came in 1974.

I can never forget George's timeless energy, enthusiasm, railway knowledge *etc*. He travelled up from Whitland to meetings in North Wales in his A30 car. Campaigning can be tough, but George never flagged.

In a variety of ways, George had devoted most of his life to making this small country of ours a better place. The welfare of the people, and the railways, have been his principal interests.

Deana Seeley, who had known Dr Penn since childhood explained what he meant to her in an earlier 'get-well' message:

My mother has been keeping me informed about you Dr Penn, and everyone thinks such a lot of you, that I wanted to tell you just that!

Nancy Davies, a mile up the road from Hillside and mentioned earlier, summed up Dr Penn in a handful of beautiful words:

He was such a gentleman. There was nothing too good to call him; there was never anyone like him. He was uniquely different from anyone else; he was a gem of a man.

At this sad time, it was heartening to share a few lighter tales about Dr Penn when visitors called at the house. One of these, from a gentleman in Carmarthen, whose name has sadly escaped me, described the time Dr Penn was visiting his mother – calling briefly one afternoon to check on her progress before moving on. That day, Dr Penn was thrilled to be given some freshly baked pies to eat on his journey, and, as he went down the drive, an audience was watching him:

> We saw Dr Penn leaning over and pulling one of the pies out of the bag. Next thing, he was eating it. It was so amusing. Good for Dr Penn.

In the early afternoon of the following Tuesday, January 15th, a huge gathering of people converged upon St Mary's Church in Whitland. In readiness, a loudspeaker had been assembled for the many who could not be accommodated inside the church that day. Everyone was a friend of Dr Penn – none more so than Gwilym, a close pal in early days at Brynmenyn School. Gwilym and his wife, Anne, had travelled from Penarth that morning. Gwilym explained when he last saw Dr Penn:

> It was in Bridgend about 10 years earlier. He came up for the memorial service in honour of Rudolph Winn. He was a schoolteacher in Brynmenyn when George was a pupil – before he left for Bushey.
>
> 'Come over here, Gwilym,' he smiled, 'sit with me; I don't know these people.'

Anne spoke about Dr Penn's funeral:

> We thought that we had better play it safe – so we set off early. We had a long journey, and we didn't really know where we were going. Certainly we had never been to the church before. So we arrived with hours to spare and sat in the car to wait. But soon crowds of people started to turn

up. We thought that there must be another funeral taking place, so we went over to the church to check.

'Is there another funeral?' we asked.

'No, it's Dr Penn's funeral today,' was the reply.

'But the church is filling up already.'

'Oh yes,' the gentleman said, 'there'll be a huge crowd today. Everyone will be saying "goodbye" to Dr Penn. I know because I am the grave digger.'

Gwilym and I had never seen anything like this before. There must have been thousands at the funeral. We count ourselves lucky to have got inside the church. As far as we could see, there was little room even in the churchyard that day.

In Hillside, the Reverend Kingsley Taylor – a regular visitor to the house during the past few weeks – conducted a private service before the hearse made its way slowly down the drive. Soon it crossed the bridge over Whitland's new bypass. Despite his objections to 'by-pass mania', mentioned earlier, Dr Penn understood the need for this new road. Furthermore, he preferred it to cut across his own small field rather than follow an alternative route that would have meant destroying traditional stone-built houses on Intermediate Terrace nearer the town. He was generous, as Les Evans said, to a fault.

Half way down North Road was the old grammar school, now Dyffryn Taf School – the scene of great frenzy during the railway meetings in the late 1960s. 'Are the Railway Boards going Crazy,' he wrote on his advertisements. 'Do you want a Rail Service? Then your place is Whitland Grammar School on . . . ' This was a high-profile slog, and victory left a long-term legacy.

At the bottom of the road was a glimpse of Whitland Town Hall. This is where the late Peter Wills remembers another side to Dr Penn when he was secretary of the Whitland Town Hall committee:

> You could never underestimate George Penn. In the days of the Town Hall dances in the 1970s, one character stepped way out of line. George realised that he was spoiling the fun for everybody else, so he asked him if anything was the matter.
>
> 'And who are you? he replied in a rude and disrespectful manner.
>
> George marched that man down the steps and out of the front door – by the scruff of his neck and the seat of his pants.

As the hearse turned into Market Street, Dolycwrt stood in solemn silence at the end of the road . . . but not even a shadow now of its former glory.

That day many people were delayed because of the railway crossing, right alongside the Yelverton courtyard where Dr Penn once paraded his prize bullock. Suffice to say that this delay was due greatly to him – once upon a time the champion of railways in West Wales.

At the church, a sea of sad faces waited patiently. Dr Penn had enjoyed some happy and sad moments there; it was hard to believe that today's burial would be his own. But, as he had told Roger late in the evening before he died, 'There comes a time when a nurse needs a nurse, and a doctor a doctor.'

Few will have noticed Trevaughan bridge that sad day, whose solid stone uprights date back to 1767; its continued survival was another of Dr Penn's legacies. We must not forget that by fighting to keep something alive, we preserve the good work and intentions of its creation.

Dr Penn had always favoured the hymn that considers 'those in peril on the sea'. It was the first hymn this sad day, as it had been at his brother's funeral also – dedicated to their late father, Captain Stanley Penn, lost at sea, and Beatrice, their mother.

The service was conducted by the Reverend Kingsley Taylor who faced the difficult task of doing justice to a life so full of events. He started by reciting Rudyard Kipling's famous 'If'.

'This poem is about Dr Penn,' said the vicar, as he read aloud all thirty-two of its memorable lines. There was room for just two of these on the funeral service booklet that day – Dr Penn's love of people determining a difficult choice:

> If you can talk with crowds and keep your virtue,
> Or walk with kings – nor lose the common touch.

Two of St Mary's former clergy assisted in the service, both close family friends, the Reverend David Faulkner and the Reverend Nigel Griffin. It fell upon the Reverend Nigel Griffin to summarise Dr Penn's lifetime of efforts with a well-known biblical quotation, 'Well done good and faithful servant.'

It was soon time for the last hymn, 'The Lord is My Shepherd, I shall not want', harmonious voices being carried loudly into the higher levels of the church and out into the crowded churchyard. These are the soothing and reassuring words of Psalm 23, the embodiment of hope and humility as we are encouraged to follow the good shepherd in our journey through life. They are, likewise, the words of a choirboy who couldn't sing, of a young man with naked ambition, of a doctor who went beyond the call of duty, and of a gentleman with an indomitable spirit.

They are also the words of a traditionalist who challenged change, of a servant of the community who never tired, of a giver of kindnesses and good deeds whose generosity knew no bounds. And they are the words of 'a gem of a man' who, with Peggy at his side, touched many hearts along the way. Here is the final verse:

> Goodness and mercy all my life
> Shall surely follow me;
> And in God's house for evermore
> My dwelling place shall be.

But the last words about Dr Penn belong to Peggy – written in her own hand on a piece of paper inside another old diary. They describe her extraordinary husband, and the way he lived his life:

> My candle burns at both ends; it will not last the night;
> But oh my foes, and oh my friends, it gives a lovely light!

finis

ABOUT THE AUTHOR

ROGER PENN is the son of the late Dr George Penn and his wife, Peggy. He is a native of Whitland in west Wales and attended the local primary and grammar schools before joining Lloyds Bank Limited in 1976.

After a 34-year career Roger retired in January 2010, still a believer in the traditional bank values of old. He served in many branches across South Wales between Newport (Pembrokeshire) and Chepstow, whilst also venturing into the Forest of Dean at Lydney, Gloucestershire, in 1982. His last post was in his father's homeland, Bridgend, at Wyndham Street Branch.

Since retiring, Roger has enjoyed dedicating more time to writing. His first major work, *Dolycwrt – the Days of a Country Doctor's Surgery*, was published in November 2011, a popular book describing one hundred years of life, traditional medicine and community events as seen by Dolycwrt surgery, in Whitland.